ISOCRATES I

THE ORATORY OF CLASSICAL GREECE

Translated with Notes • Michael Gagarin, Series Editor

VOLUME 4

ISOCRATES I

Translated by David Mirhady & Yun Lee Too

UNIVERSITY OF TEXAS PRESS, AUSTIN

First edition, 2000

Requests for permission to reproduce material from
this work should be sent to Permissions, University
of Texas Press, Box 7819, Austin, TX 78713-7819.

⊗ The paper used in this book meets the minimum
requirements of ANSI/NISO Z39.48-1992 (R1997)
(Permanence of Paper).

Library of Congress Cataloging-in-Publication Data

Isocrates
    [Works. English. 2000]
    Isocrates I / translated by David Mirhady & Yun
Lee Too. — 1st ed.
        p. cm. — (The oratory of classical Greece ;
v. 4)
    Includes bibliographical references and index.
    ISBN: 0-292-75238-5

    1. Isocrates — Translations into English.
2. Speeches, addresses, etc., Greek — Translations
into English.   I. Title: Isocrates 1.   II. Title:
Isocrates one.   III. Mirhady, David C.,
date. IV. Too, Yun Lee. V. Title.   VI. Series.
    PA4217.E5   M57   2000
    885'.01 — dc21

                                        99-050863

CONTENTS

The Works of Isocrates   vii
Acknowledgments   ix
Series Introduction   xi
   Oratory in Classical Athens   xi
   The Orators   xiv
   The Works of the Orators   xvii
   Government and Law in Classical Athens   xix
   The Translation of Greek Oratory   xxvi
   Abbreviations   xxvii
   Note on Currency   xxvii
   Bibliography of Works Cited   xxviii

Introduction to Isocrates   1
   Life and Career   1
   Philosophia, Education, and Politics   3
   Style   6
   A Note on Terminology   8
   Text   9
   The Works of Isocrates   9

PART ONE (David Mirhady)   13
   Introduction   15
     1. To Demonicus   19
    10. Encomium of Helen   31
    11. Busiris   49
    13. Against the Sophists   61
    16. On the Team of Horses   67
    17. Trapeziticus   80
    18. Special Plea against Callimachus   96

19. Aegineticus   112
20. Against Lochites   123
21. Against Euthynus, without Witnesses   128

PART TWO (Yun Lee Too)   135
    Introduction   137
    9. Evagoras   139
    2. To Nicocles   157
    3. Nicocles   169
    7. Areopagiticus   182
    15. Antidosis   201

Glossary   265
Bibliography   269
Index   273

THE WORKS OF ISOCRATES

VOLUME ONE

  1. To Demonicus
  2. To Nicocles
  3. Nicocles
  7. Areopagiticus
  9. Evagoras
10. Encomium of Helen
11. Busiris
13. Against the Sophists
15. Antidosis
16. On the Team of Horses
17. Trapeziticus
18. Special Plea against Callimachus
19. Aegineticus
20. Against Lochites
21. Against Euthynus, without Witnesses

VOLUME TWO

  4. Panegyricus
  5. To Philip
  6. Archidamus
  8. On the Peace
12. Panathenaicus
14. Plataicus
Epistle 1. To Dionysius
Epistle 2. To Philip 1
Epistle 3. To Philip 2
Epistle 4. To Antipater
Epistle 5. To Alexander

Epistle 6. To the Children of Jason
Epistle 7. To Timotheus
Epistle 8. To the Rulers of the Mytileneans
Epistle 9. To Archidamus

ACKNOWLEDGMENTS

This is the fourth volume in a series of translations of *The Oratory of Classical Greece*. The aim of the series is to make available primarily for those who do not read Greek up-to-date, accurate, and readable translations with introductions and explanatory notes of all the surviving works and major fragments of the Attic orators of the classical period (ca. 420–320 BC): Aeschines, Andocides, Antiphon, Demosthenes, Dinarchus, Hyperides, Isaeus, Isocrates, Lycurgus, and Lysias.

This volume is the first of two devoted to Isocrates. Volume One has two parts, the first with translations by David Mirhady, the second by Yun Lee Too; Volume Two will be translated by Terry Papillon. The "Introduction to Isocrates" represents the combined effort of three translators and the Series Editor; the "Glossary" in Volume One combines the work of the two translators.

On behalf of the translators and myself, I would like to acknowledge the many valuable suggestions made by the press reviewer, Edward Schiappa. I am again grateful for the full support of the University of Texas Press, especially from Director Joanna Hitchcock, Humanities Editor Jim Burr, Copyeditor Nancy Moore, and Designer Ellen McKie.

—M.G.

My thanks are due to the Department of History at the University of Lethbridge and the Faculty of Humanities at the University of Calgary for providing office space during the preparation of this volume and to David Cheney, Martin Cropp, Bill Fortenbaugh, John Humphreys, Terry Papillon, Yun Lee Too, and especially Michael Gagarin for help of other kinds no less important.

—D.C.M.

I would like to thank warmly Michael Gagarin for his patience, assistance, and advice in preparing this set of translations. Work on this project was made possible in part by a Junior Fellowship held at the Center for Hellenic Studies, Washington, D.C., 1997–1998.

—Y.L.T.

SERIES INTRODUCTION
Greek Oratory

By Michael Gagarin

ORATORY IN CLASSICAL ATHENS

From as early as Homer (and undoubtedly much earlier) the Greeks placed a high value on effective speaking. Even Achilles, whose greatness was primarily established on the battlefield, was brought up to be "a speaker of words and a doer of deeds" (*Iliad* 9.443); and Athenian leaders of the sixth and fifth centuries,[1] such as Solon, Themistocles, and Pericles, were all accomplished orators. Most Greek literary genres—notably epic, tragedy, and history—underscore the importance of oratory by their inclusion of set speeches. The formal pleadings of the envoys to Achilles in the *Iliad,* the messenger speeches in tragedy reporting events like the battle of Salamis in Aeschylus' *Persians* or the gruesome death of Pentheus in Euripides' *Bacchae,* and the powerful political oratory of Pericles' funeral oration in Thucydides are but a few of the most notable examples of the Greeks' never-ending fascination with formal public speaking, which was to reach its height in the public oratory of the fourth century.

In early times, oratory was not a specialized subject of study but was learned by practice and example. The formal study of rhetoric as an "art" (*technē*) began, we are told, in the middle of the fifth century in Sicily with the work of Corax and his pupil Tisias.[2] These two are

---

[1] All dates in this volume are BC unless the contrary is either indicated or obvious.

[2] See Kennedy 1963: 26–51. Cole 1991 has challenged this traditional picture, arguing that the term "rhetoric" was coined by Plato to designate and denigrate an activity he strongly opposed. Cole's own reconstruction is not without prob-

scarcely more than names to us, but another famous Sicilian, Gorgias of Leontini (ca. 490–390), developed a new style of argument and is reported to have dazzled the Athenians with a speech delivered when he visited Athens in 427. Gorgias initiated the practice, which continued into the early fourth century, of composing speeches for mythical or imaginary occasions. The surviving examples reveal a lively intellectual climate in the late fifth and early fourth centuries, in which oratory served to display new ideas, new forms of expression, and new methods of argument.[3] This tradition of "intellectual" oratory was continued by the fourth-century educator Isocrates and played a large role in later Greek and Roman education.

In addition to this intellectual oratory, at about the same time the practice also began of writing speeches for real occasions in public life, which we may designate "practical" oratory. For centuries Athenians had been delivering speeches in public settings (primarily the courts and the Assembly), but these had always been composed and delivered impromptu, without being written down and thus without being preserved. The practice of writing speeches began in the courts and then expanded to include the Assembly and other settings. Athens was one of the leading cities of Greece in the fifth and fourth centuries, and its political and legal systems depended on direct participation by a large number of citizens; all important decisions were made by these large bodies, and the primary means of influencing these decisions was oratory.[4] Thus, it is not surprising that oratory flourished in Athens,[5] but it may not be immediately obvious why it should be written down.

The pivotal figure in this development was Antiphon, one of the fifth-century intellectuals who are often grouped together under the

---

lems, but he does well to remind us how thoroughly the traditional view of rhetoric depends on one of its most ardent opponents.

[3] Of these only Antiphon's Tetralogies are included in this series. Gorgias' *Helen* and *Palamedes*, Alcidamas' *Odysseus*, and Antisthenes' *Ajax* and *Odysseus* are translated in Gagarin and Woodruff 1995.

[4] Yunis 1996 has a good treatment of political oratory from Pericles to Demosthenes.

[5] All our evidence for practical oratory comes from Athens, with the exception of Isocrates 19, written for a trial in Aegina. Many speeches were undoubtedly delivered in courts and political forums in other Greek cities, but it may be that such speeches were written down only in Athens.

name "Sophists."[6] Like some of the other sophists he contributed to the intellectual oratory of the period, but he also had a strong practical interest in law. At the same time, Antiphon had an aversion to public speaking and did not directly involve himself in legal or political affairs (Thucydides 8.68). However, he began giving general advice to other citizens who were engaged in litigation and were thus expected to address the court themselves. As this practice grew, Antiphon went further, and around 430 he began writing out whole speeches for others to memorize and deliver. Thus began the practice of "logography," which continued through the next century and beyond.[7] Logography particularly appealed to men like Lysias, who were metics, or noncitizen residents of Athens. Since they were not Athenian citizens, they were barred from direct participation in public life, but they could contribute by writing speeches for others.

Antiphon was also the first (to our knowledge) to write down a speech he would himself deliver, writing the speech for his own defense at his trial for treason in 411. His motive was probably to publicize and preserve his views, and others continued this practice of writing down speeches they would themselves deliver in the courts and (more rarely) the Assembly.[8] Finally, one other type of practical oratory was the special tribute delivered on certain important public occasions, the best known of which is the funeral oration. It is convenient to designate these three types of oratory by the terms Aristotle later uses: forensic (for the courts), deliberative (for the Assembly), and epideictic (for display).[9]

---

[6] The term "sophist" was loosely used through the fifth and fourth centuries to designate various intellectuals and orators, but under the influence of Plato, who attacked certain figures under this name, the term is now used of a specific group of thinkers; see Kerferd 1981.

[7] For Antiphon as the first to write speeches, see Photius, *Bibliotheca* 486a7–11 and [Plut.], *Moralia* 832c–d. The latest extant speech can be dated to 320, but we know that at least one orator, Dinarchus, continued the practice after that date.

[8] Unlike forensic speeches, speeches for delivery in the Assembly were usually not composed beforehand in writing, since the speaker could not know exactly when or in what context he would be speaking; see further Trevett 1996.

[9] *Rhetoric* 1.3. Intellectual orations, like Gorgias' *Helen*, do not easily fit into Aristotle's classification. For a fuller (but still brief) introduction to Attic oratory and the orators, see Edwards 1994.

THE ORATORS

In the century from about 420 to 320, dozens—perhaps even hundreds—of now unknown orators and logographers must have composed speeches that are now lost, but only ten of these men were selected for preservation and study by ancient scholars, and only works collected under the names of these ten have been preserved. Some of these works are undoubtedly spurious, though in most cases they are fourth-century works by a different author rather than later "forgeries." Indeed, modern scholars suspect that as many as seven of the speeches attributed to Demosthenes may have been written by Apollodorus, son of Pasion, who is sometimes called "the eleventh orator." [10] Including these speeches among the works of Demosthenes may have been an honest mistake, or perhaps a bookseller felt he could sell more copies of these speeches if they were attributed to a more famous orator.

In alphabetical order the Ten Orators are as follows: [11]

• AESCHINES (ca. 395–ca. 322) rose from obscure origins to become an important Athenian political figure, first an ally, then a bitter enemy of Demosthenes. His three speeches all concern major public issues. The best known of these (Aes. 3) was delivered at the trial in 330, when Demosthenes responded with *On the Crown* (Dem. 18). Aeschines lost the case and was forced to leave Athens and live the rest of his life in exile.

• ANDOCIDES (ca. 440–ca. 390) is best known for his role in the scandal of 415, when just before the departure of the fateful Athenian expedition to Sicily during the Peloponnesian War (431–404), a band of young men mutilated statues of Hermes, and at the same time information was revealed about the secret rites of Demeter.

---

[10] See Trevett 1992.

[11] The Loeb volumes of *Minor Attic Orators* also include the prominent Athenian political figure Demades (ca. 385–319), who was not one of the Ten; but the only speech that has come down to us under his name is a later forgery. It is possible that Demades and other fourth-century politicians who had a high reputation for public speaking did not put any speeches in writing, especially if they rarely spoke in the courts (see above n. 8).

Andocides was exiled but later returned. Two of the four speeches in his name give us a contemporary view of the scandal: one pleads for his return, the other argues against a second period of exile.

- ANTIPHON (ca. 480–411), as already noted, wrote forensic speeches for others and only once spoke himself. In 411 he participated in an oligarchic coup by a group of 400, and when the democrats regained power he was tried for treason and executed. His six surviving speeches include three for delivery in court and the three Tetralogies—imaginary intellectual exercises for display or teaching that consist of four speeches each, two on each side. All six of Antiphon's speeches concern homicide, probably because these stood at the beginning of the collection of his works. Fragments of some thirty other speeches cover many different topics.

- DEMOSTHENES (384–322) is generally considered the best of the Attic orators. Although his nationalistic message is less highly regarded today, his powerful mastery of and ability to combine many different rhetorical styles continues to impress readers. Demosthenes was still a child when his wealthy father died. The trustees of the estate apparently misappropriated much of it, and when he came of age, he sued them in a series of cases (27–31), regaining some of his fortune and making a name as a powerful speaker. He then wrote speeches for others in a variety of cases, public and private, and for his own use in court (where many cases involved major public issues), and in the Assembly, where he opposed the growing power of Philip of Macedon. The triumph of Philip and his son Alexander the Great eventually put an end to Demosthenes' career. Some sixty speeches have come down under his name, about a third of them of questionable authenticity.

- DINARCHUS (ca. 360–ca. 290) was born in Corinth but spent much of his life in Athens as a metic (a noncitizen resident). His public fame came primarily from writing speeches for the prosecutions surrounding the Harpalus affair in 324, when several prominent figures (including Demosthenes) were accused of bribery. After 322 he had a profitable career as a logographer.

- HYPERIDES (390–322) was a political leader and logographer of so many different talents that he was called the pentathlete of orators.

He was a leader of the Athenian resistance to Philip and Alexander and (like Demosthenes) was condemned to death after Athens' final surrender. One speech and substantial fragments of five others have been recovered from papyrus remains; otherwise, only fragments survive.

- ISAEUS (ca. 415–ca. 340) wrote speeches on a wide range of topics, but the eleven complete speeches that survive, dating from ca. 390 to ca. 344, all concern inheritance. As with Antiphon, the survival of these particular speeches may have been the result of the later ordering of his speeches by subject; we have part of a twelfth speech and fragments and titles of some forty other works. Isaeus is said to have been a pupil of Isocrates and the teacher of Demosthenes.

- ISOCRATES (436–338) considered himself a philosopher and educator, not an orator or rhetorician. He came from a wealthy Athenian family but lost most of his property in the Peloponnesian War, and in 403 he took up logography. About 390 he abandoned this practice and turned to writing and teaching, setting forth his educational, philosophical, and political views in essays that took the form of speeches but were not meant for oral delivery. He favored accommodation with the growing power of Philip of Macedon and panhellenic unity. His school was based on a broad concept of rhetoric and applied philosophy; it attracted pupils from the entire Greek world (including Isaeus, Lycurgus, and Hyperides) and became the main rival of Plato's Academy. Isocrates greatly influenced education and rhetoric in the Hellenistic, Roman, and modern periods until the eighteenth century.

- LYCURGUS (ca. 390–ca. 324) was a leading public official who restored the financial condition of Athens after 338 and played a large role in the city for the next dozen years. He brought charges of corruption or treason against many other officials, usually with success. Only one speech survives.

- LYSIAS (ca. 445–ca. 380) was a metic—an official resident of Athens but not a citizen. Much of his property was seized by the Thirty during their short-lived oligarchic coup in 404–403. Perhaps as a result he turned to logography. More than thirty speeches survive in whole or in part, though the authenticity of some is doubted.

We also have fragments or know the titles of more than a hundred others. The speeches cover a wide range of cases, and he may have delivered one himself (Lys. 12), on the death of his brother at the hands of the Thirty. Lysias is particularly known for his vivid narratives, his *ēthopoiïa,* or "creation of character," and his prose style, which became a model of clarity and vividness.

THE WORKS OF THE ORATORS

As soon as speeches began to be written down, they could be preserved. We know little about the conditions of book "publication" (i.e., making copies for distribution) in the fourth century, but there was an active market for books in Athens, and some of the speeches may have achieved wide circulation.[12] An orator (or his family) may have preserved his own speeches, perhaps to advertise his ability or demonstrate his success, or booksellers may have collected and copied them in order to make money.

We do not know how closely the preserved text of these speeches corresponded to the version actually delivered in court or in the Assembly. Speakers undoubtedly extemporized or varied from their text on occasion, but there is no good evidence that deliberative speeches were substantially revised for publication.[13] In forensic oratory a logographer's reputation would derive first and foremost from his success with jurors. If a forensic speech was victorious, there would be no reason to alter it for publication, and if it lost, alteration would probably not deceive potential clients. Thus, the published texts of forensic speeches were probably quite faithful to the texts that were provided to clients, and we have little reason to suspect substantial alteration in the century or so before they were collected by scholars in Alexandria (see below).

In addition to the speaker's text, most forensic speeches have breaks for the inclusion of documents. The logographer inserted a notation

---

[12] Dover's discussion (1968) of the preservation and transmission of the works of Lysias (and perhaps others under his name) is useful not just for Lysias but for the other orators too. His theory of shared authorship between logographer and litigant, however, is unconvincing (see Usher 1976).

[13] See further Trevett 1996: 437–439.

in his text—such as *nomos* ("law") or *martyria* ("testimony")—and the speaker would pause while the clerk read out the text of a law or the testimony of witnesses. Many speeches survive with only a notation that a *nomos* or *martyria* was read at that point, but in some cases the text of the document is included. It used to be thought that these documents were all creations of later scholars, but many (though not all) are now accepted as genuine.[14]

With the foundation of the famous library in Alexandria early in the third century, scholars began to collect and catalogue texts of the orators, along with many other classical authors. Only the best orators were preserved in the library, many of them represented by over 100 speeches each (some undoubtedly spurious). Only some of these works survived in manuscript form to the modern era; more recently a few others have been discovered on ancient sheets of papyrus, so that today the corpus of Attic Oratory consists of about 150 speeches, together with a few letters and other works. The subject matter ranges from important public issues and serious crimes to business affairs, lovers' quarrels, inheritance disputes, and other personal or family matters.

In the centuries after these works were collected, ancient scholars gathered biographical facts about their authors, produced grammatical and lexicographic notes, and used some of the speeches as evidence for Athenian political history. But the ancient scholars who were most interested in the orators were those who studied prose style, the most notable of these being Dionysius of Halicarnassus (first century BC), who wrote treatises on several of the orators,[15] and Hermogenes of Tarsus (second century AD), who wrote several literary studies, including *On Types of Style*.[16] But relative to epic or tragedy, oratory was little studied; and even scholars of rhetoric whose interests were broader than style, like Cicero and Quintilian, paid little attention to the orators, except for the acknowledged master, Demosthenes.

Most modern scholars until the second half of the twentieth century continued to treat the orators primarily as prose stylists.[17] The

---

[14] See MacDowell 1990: 43–47; Todd 1993: 44–45.

[15] Dionysius' literary studies are collected and translated in Usher 1974–1985.

[16] Wooten 1987. Stylistic considerations probably also influenced the selection of the "canon" of ten orators; see Worthington 1994.

[17] For example, the most popular and influential book ever written on the orators, Jebb's *The Attic Orators* (1875) was presented as an "attempt to aid in giving

reevaluation of Athenian democracy by George Grote and others in the nineteenth century stimulated renewed interest in Greek oratory among historians; and increasing interest in Athenian law during that century led a few legal scholars to read the orators. But in comparison with the interest shown in the other literary genres—epic, lyric, tragedy, comedy, and even history—Attic oratory has been relatively neglected until the last third of the twentieth century. More recently, however, scholars have discovered the value of the orators for the broader study of Athenian culture and society. Since Dover's groundbreaking works on popular morality and homosexuality,[18] interest in the orators has been increasing rapidly, and they are now seen as primary representatives of Athenian moral and social values, and as evidence for social and economic conditions, political and social ideology, and in general those aspects of Athenian culture that in the past were commonly ignored by historians of ancient Greece but are of increasing interest and importance today, including women and the family, slavery, and the economy.

GOVERNMENT AND LAW IN CLASSICAL ATHENS

The hallmark of the Athenian political and legal systems was its amateurism. Most public officials, including those who supervised the courts, were selected by lot and held office for a limited period, typically a year. Thus a great many citizens held public office at some point in their lives, but almost none served for an extended period of time or developed the experience or expertise that would make them professionals. All significant policy decisions were debated and voted on in the Assembly, where the quorum was 6,000 citizens, and all significant legal cases were judged by bodies of 200 to 500 jurors or more. Public prominence was not achieved by election (or selection) to public office but depended rather on a man's ability to sway the

---

Attic Oratory its due place in the history of Attic Prose" (I.xiii). This modern focus on prose style can plausibly be connected to the large role played by prose composition (the translation of English prose into Greek, usually in imitation of specific authors or styles) in the Classics curriculum, especially in Britain.

[18] Dover (1974, 1978). Dover recently commented (1994: 157), "When I began to mine the riches of Attic forensic oratory I was astonished to discover that the mine had never been exploited."

majority of citizens in the Assembly or jurors in court to vote in favor of a proposed course of action or for one of the litigants in a trial. Success was never permanent, and a victory on one policy issue or a verdict in one case could be quickly reversed in another.[19] In such a system the value of public oratory is obvious, and in the fourth century, oratory became the most important cultural institution in Athens, replacing drama as the forum where major ideological concerns were displayed and debated.

Several recent books give good detailed accounts of Athenian government and law,[20] and so a brief sketch can suffice here. The main policy-making body was the Assembly, open to all adult male citizens; a small payment for attendance enabled at least some of the poor to attend along with the leisured rich. In addition, a Council of 500 citizens, selected each year by lot with no one allowed to serve more than two years, prepared material for and made recommendations to the Assembly; a rotating subgroup of this Council served as an executive committee, the Prytany. Finally, numerous officials, most of them selected by lot for one-year terms, supervised different areas of administration and finance. The most important of these were the nine Archons (lit. "rulers"): the eponymous Archon after whom the year was named, the Basileus ("king"),[21] the Polemarch, and the six Thesmothetae. Councilors and almost all these officials underwent a preliminary examination (*dokimasia*) before taking office, and officials submitted to a final accounting (*euthynai*) upon leaving; at these times any citi-

---

[19] In the Assembly this could be accomplished by a reconsideration of the question, as in the famous Mytilenean debate (Thuc. 3.36–50); in court a verdict was final, but its practical effects could be thwarted or reversed by later litigation on a related issue.

[20] For government, see Sinclair 1988, Hansen 1991; for law, MacDowell 1978, Todd 1993, and Boegehold 1995 (Bonner 1927 is still helpful). Much of our information about the legal and political systems comes from a work attributed to Aristotle but perhaps written by a pupil of his, *The Athenian Constitution* (*Ath. Pol.*—conveniently translated with notes by Rhodes 1984). The discovery of this work on a papyrus in Egypt in 1890 caused a major resurgence of interest in Athenian government.

[21] Modern scholars often use the term *archōn basileus* or "king archon," but Athenian sources (e.g., *Ath. Pol.* 57) simply call him the *basileus*.

zen who wished could challenge a person's fitness for his new position or his performance in his recent position.

There was no general taxation of Athenian citizens. Sources of public funding included the annual tax levied on metics, various fees and import duties, and (in the fifth century) tribute from allied cities; but the source that figures most prominently in the orators is the Athenian system of liturgies (*leitourgiai*), by which in a regular rotation the rich provided funding for certain special public needs. The main liturgies were the *chorēgia*, in which a sponsor (*chorēgos*) supervised and paid for the training and performance of a chorus which sang and danced at a public festival,[22] and the trierarchy, in which a sponsor (trierarch) paid to equip and usually commanded a trireme, or warship, for a year. Some of these liturgies required substantial expenditures, but even so, some men spent far more than required in order to promote themselves and their public careers, and litigants often try to impress the jurors by referring to liturgies they have undertaken (see, e.g., Lys. 21.1–5). A further twist on this system was that if a man thought he had been assigned a liturgy that should have gone to someone else who was richer than he, he could propose an exchange of property (*antidosis*), giving the other man a choice of either taking over the liturgy or exchanging property with him. Finally, the rich were also subject to special taxes (*eisphorai*) levied as a percentage of their property in times of need.

The Athenian legal system remained similarly resistant to professionalization. Trials and the procedures leading up to them were supervised by officials, primarily the nine Archons, but their role was purely administrative, and they were in no way equivalent to modern judges. All significant questions about what we would call points of law were presented to the jurors, who considered them together with all other issues when they delivered their verdict at the end of the trial.[23] Trials were "contests" (*agōnes*) between two litigants, each of whom presented his own case to the jurors in a speech, plaintiff first,

---

[22] These included the productions of tragedy and comedy, for which the main expense was for the chorus.

[23] Certain religious "interpreters" (*exēgētai*) were occasionally asked to give their opinion on a legal matter that had a religious dimension (such as the prosecution of a homicide), but although these opinions could be reported in court

then defendant; in some cases each party then spoke again, probably in rebuttal. Since a litigant had only one or two speeches in which to present his entire case, and no issue was decided separately by a judge, all the necessary factual information and every important argument on substance or procedure, fact or law, had to be presented together. A single speech might thus combine narrative, argument, emotional appeal, and various digressions, all with the goal of obtaining a favorable verdict. Even more than today, a litigant's primary task was to control the issue—to determine which issues the jurors would consider most important and which questions they would have in their minds as they cast their votes. We only rarely have both speeches from a trial,[24] and we usually have little or no external evidence for the facts of a case or the verdict. We must thus infer both the facts and the opponent's strategy from the speech we have, and any assessment of the overall effectiveness of a speech and of the logographer's strategy is to some extent speculative.

Before a trial there were usually several preliminary hearings for presenting evidence; arbitration, public and private, was available and sometimes required. These hearings and arbitration sessions allowed each side to become familiar with the other side's case, so that discussions of "what my opponent will say" could be included in one's speech. Normally a litigant presented his own case, but he was often assisted by family or friends. If he wished (and could afford it), he could enlist the services of a logographer, who presumably gave strategic advice in addition to writing a speech. The speeches were timed to ensure an equal hearing for both sides,[25] and all trials were completed within a day. Two hundred or more jurors decided each case in the popular courts, which met in the Agora.[26] Homicide cases and

---

(e.g., Dem. 47.68–73), they had no official legal standing. The most significant administrative decision we hear of is the refusal of the Basileus to accept the case in Antiphon 6 (see 6.37–46).

[24] The exceptions are Demosthenes 19 and Aeschines 2, Aeschines 3 and Demosthenes 18, and Lysias 6 (one of several prosecution speeches) and Andocides 1; all were written for major public cases.

[25] Timing was done by means of a water-clock, which in most cases was stopped during the reading of documents.

[26] See Boegehold 1995.

certain other religious trials (e.g., Lys. 7) were heard by the Council of the Areopagus or an associated group of fifty-one Ephetae. The Areopagus was composed of all former Archons—perhaps 150–200 members at most times. It met on a hill called the Areopagus ("rock of Ares") near the Acropolis.

Jurors for the regular courts were selected by lot from those citizens who registered each year and who appeared for duty that day; as with the Assembly, a small payment allowed the poor to serve. After the speakers had finished, the jurors voted immediately without any formal discussion. The side with the majority won; a tie vote decided the case for the defendant. In some cases where the penalty was not fixed, after a conviction the jurors voted again on the penalty, choosing between penalties proposed by each side. Even when we know the verdict, we cannot know which of the speaker's arguments contributed most to his success or failure. However, a logographer could probably learn from jurors which points had or had not been successful, so that arguments that are found repeatedly in speeches probably were known to be effective in most cases.

The first written laws in Athens were enacted by Draco (ca. 620) and Solon (ca. 590), and new laws were regularly added. At the end of the fifth century the existing laws were reorganized, and a new procedure for enacting laws was instituted; thereafter a group of Law-Givers (*nomothetai*) had to certify that a proposed law did not conflict with any existing laws. There was no attempt, however, to organize legislation systematically, and although Plato, Aristotle, and other philosophers wrote various works on law and law-giving, these were either theoretical or descriptive and had no apparent influence on legislation. Written statutes generally used ordinary language rather than precise legal definitions in designating offenses, and questions concerning precisely what constituted a specific offense or what was the correct interpretation of a written statute were decided (together with other issues) by the jurors in each case. A litigant might, of course, assert a certain definition or interpretation as "something you all know" or "what the lawgiver intended," but such remarks are evidently tendentious and cannot be taken as authoritative.

The result of these procedural and substantive features was that the verdict depended largely on each litigant's speech (or speeches). As one speaker puts it (Ant. 6.18), "When there are no witnesses, you (jurors) are forced to reach a verdict about the case on the basis of the prose-cutor's and defendant's words alone; you must be suspicious and ex-amine their accounts in detail, and your vote will necessarily be cast on the basis of likelihood rather than clear knowledge." Even the tes-timony of witnesses (usually on both sides) is rarely decisive. On the other hand, most speakers make a considerable effort to establish facts and provide legitimate arguments in conformity with established law. Plato's view of rhetoric as a clever technique for persuading an igno-rant crowd that the false is true is not borne out by the speeches, and the legal system does not appear to have produced many arbitrary or clearly unjust results.

The main form of legal procedure was a *dikē* ("suit") in which the injured party (or his relatives in a case of homicide) brought suit against the offender. Suits for injuries to slaves would be brought by the slave's master, and injuries to women would be prosecuted by a male relative. Strictly speaking, a *dikē* was a private matter between individuals, though like all cases, *dikai* often had public dimensions. The other major form of procedure was a *graphē* ("writing" or "indict-ment") in which "anyone who wished" (i.e., any citizen) could bring a prosecution for wrongdoing. *Graphai* were instituted by Solon, prob-ably in order to allow prosecution of offenses where the victim was unable or unlikely to bring suit himself, such as selling a dependent into slavery; but the number of areas covered by *graphai* increased to cover many types of public offenses as well as some apparently private crimes, such as *hybris*.

The system of prosecution by "anyone who wished" also extended to several other more specialized forms of prosecution, like *eisangelia* ("impeachment"), used in cases of treason. Another specialized prose-cution was *apagōgē* ("summary arrest"), in which someone could arrest a common criminal (*kakourgos*, lit. "evil-doer"), or have him arrested, on the spot. The reliance on private initiative meant that Athenians never developed a system of public prosecution; rather, they presumed that everyone would keep an eye on the behavior of his political ene-mies and bring suit as soon as he suspected a crime, both to harm his opponents and to advance his own career. In this way all public offi-cials would be watched by someone. There was no disgrace in admit-ting that a prosecution was motivated by private enmity.

By the end of the fifth century the system of prosecution by "any one who wished" was apparently being abused by so-called sykophants (*sykophantai*), who allegedly brought or threatened to bring false suits against rich men, either to gain part of the fine that would be levied or to induce an out-of-court settlement in which the accused would pay to have the matter dropped. We cannot gauge the true extent of this problem, since speakers usually provide little evidence to support their claims that their opponents are sykophants, but the Athenians did make sykophancy a crime. They also specified that in many public procedures a plaintiff who either dropped the case or failed to obtain one-fifth of the votes would have to pay a heavy fine of 1,000 drachmas. Despite this, it appears that litigation was common in Athens and was seen by some as excessive.

Over the course of time, the Athenian legal and political systems have more often been judged negatively than positively. Philosophers and political theorists have generally followed the lead of Plato (427–347), who lived and worked in Athens his entire life while severely criticizing its system of government as well as many other aspects of its culture. For Plato, democracy amounted to the tyranny of the masses over the educated elite and was destined to collapse from its own instability. The legal system was capricious and depended entirely on the rhetorical ability of litigants with no regard for truth or justice. These criticisms have often been echoed by modern scholars, who particularly complain that law was much too closely interwoven with politics and did not have the autonomous status it achieved in Roman law and continues to have, at least in theory, in modern legal systems.

Plato's judgments are valid if one accepts the underlying presuppositions, that the aim of law is absolute truth and abstract justice and that achieving the highest good of the state requires thorough and systematic organization. Most Athenians do not seem to have subscribed to either the criticisms or the presuppositions, and most scholars now accept the long-ignored fact that despite major external disruptions in the form of wars and two short-lived coups brought about by one of these wars, the Athenian legal and political systems remained remarkably stable for almost two hundred years (508–320). Moreover, like all other Greek cities at the time, whatever their form of government, Athenian democracy was brought to an end not by internal forces but by the external power of Philip of Macedon and his son Alexander. The legal system never became autonomous, and the rich sometimes complained that they were victims of unscrupulous litigants, but there is no indication that the people wanted to yield control of the legal process to a professional class, as Plato recommended. For most Athenians—Plato being an exception in this and many other matters—one purpose of the legal system was to give everyone the opportunity to have his case heard by other citizens and have it heard quickly and cheaply; and in this it clearly succeeded.

Indeed, the Athenian legal system also served the interests of the rich, even the very rich, as well as the common people, in that it provided a forum for the competition that since Homer had been an important part of aristocratic life. In this competition, the rich used the courts as battlegrounds, though their main weapon was the rhetoric of popular ideology, which hailed the rule of law and promoted the ideal of moderation and restraint.[27] But those who aspired to political leadership and the honor and status that accompanied it repeatedly entered the legal arena, bringing suit against their political enemies whenever possible and defending themselves against suits brought by others whenever necessary. The ultimate judges of these public competitions were the common people, who seem to have relished the dramatic clash of individuals and ideologies. In this respect fourth-century oratory was the cultural heir of fifth-century drama and was similarly appreciated by the citizens. Despite the disapproval of intellectuals like Plato, most Athenians legitimately considered their legal system a hallmark of their democracy and a vital presence in their culture.

THE TRANSLATION OF GREEK ORATORY

The purpose of this series is to provide students and scholars in all fields with accurate, readable translations of all surviving classical Attic oratory, including speeches whose authenticity is disputed, as well as the substantial surviving fragments. In keeping with the originals, the language is for the most part nontechnical. Names of persons and places are given in the (generally more familiar) Latinized forms, and names of officials or legal procedures have been translated into English equivalents, where possible. Notes are intended to provide the nec-

---

[27] Ober 1989 is fundamental; see also Cohen 1995.

essary historical and cultural background; scholarly controversies are generally not discussed. The notes and introductions refer to scholarly treatments in addition to those listed below, which the reader may consult for further information.

Cross-references to other speeches follow the standard numbering system, which is now well established except in the case of Hyperides (for whom the numbering of the Oxford Classical Text is used).[28] References are by work and section (e.g., Dem. 24.73); spurious works are not specially marked; when no author is named (e.g., 24.73), the reference is to the same author as the annotated passage.

ABBREVIATIONS:

Aes.	=	Aeschines
And.	=	Andocides
Ant.	=	Antiphon
Arist.	=	Aristotle
Aristoph.	=	Aristophanes
Ath. Pol.	=	*The Athenian Constitution*
Dem.	=	Demosthenes
Din.	=	Dinarchus
Herod.	=	Herodotus
Hyp.	=	Hyperides
Is.	=	Isaeus
Isoc.	=	Isocrates
Lyc.	=	Lycurgus
Lys.	=	Lysias
Plut.	=	Plutarch
Thuc.	=	Thucydides
Xen.	=	Xenophon

NOTE: The main unit of Athenian currency was the drachma; this was divided into obols and larger amounts were designated minas and talents.

1 drachma	=	6 obols
1 mina	=	100 drachmas
1 talent	=	60 minas (6,000 drachmas)

---

[28] For a listing of all the orators and their works, with classifications (forensic, deliberative, epideictic) and rough dates, see Edwards 1994: 74–79.

It is impossible to give an accurate equivalence in terms of modern currency, but it may be helpful to remember that the daily wage of some skilled workers was a drachma in the mid-fifth century and 2–2½ drachmas in the later fourth century. Thus it may not be too misleading to think of a drachma as worth about $50 or £33 and a talent as about $300,000 or £200,000 in 1997 currency.

BIBLIOGRAPHY OF WORKS CITED

Boegehold, Alan L., 1995: *The Lawcourts at Athens: Sites, Buildings, Equipment, Procedure, and Testimonia.* Princeton.
Bonner, Robert J., 1927: *Lawyers and Litigants in Ancient Athens.* Chicago.
Cohen, David, 1995: *Law, Violence and Community in Classical Athens.* Cambridge.
Cole, Thomas, 1991: *The Origins of Rhetoric in Ancient Greece.* Baltimore.
Dover, Kenneth J., 1968: *Lysias and the Corpus Lysiacum.* Berkeley.
———, 1974: *Greek Popular Morality in the Time of Plato and Aristotle.* Oxford.
———, 1978: *Greek Homosexuality.* London.
———, 1994: *Marginal Comment.* London.
Edwards, Michael, 1994: *The Attic Orators.* London.
Gagarin, Michael, and Paul Woodruff, 1995: *Early Greek Political Thought from Homer to the Sophists.* Cambridge.
Hansen, Mogens Herman, 1991: *The Athenian Democracy in the Age of Demosthenes.* Oxford.
Jebb, Richard, 1875: *The Attic Orators*, 2 vols. London.
Kennedy, George A., 1963: *The Art of Persuasion in Greece.* Princeton.
Kerferd, G. B., 1981: *The Sophistic Movement.* Cambridge.
MacDowell, Douglas M., 1978: *The Law in Classical Athens.* London.
———, ed. 1990: *Demosthenes, Against Meidias.* Oxford.
Ober, Josiah, 1989: *Mass and Elite in Democratic Athens.* Princeton.
Rhodes, P. J., trans., 1984: *Aristotle, The Athenian Constitution.* Penguin Books.
Sinclair, R. K., 1988: *Democracy and Participation in Athens.* Cambridge.
Todd, Stephen, 1993: *The Shape of Athenian Law.* Oxford.

Trevett, Jeremy, 1992: *Apollodoros the Son of Pasion.* Oxford.

———, 1996: "Did Demosthenes Publish His Deliberative Speeches?" *Hermes* 124: 425–441.

Usher, Stephen, 1976: "Lysias and His Clients," *Greek, Roman and Byzantine Studies* 17: 31–40.

———, trans., 1974–1985: *Dionysius of Halicarnassus, Critical Essays.* 2 vols. Loeb Classical Library. Cambridge, MA.

Wooten, Cecil W., trans., 1987: *Hermogenes' On Types of Style.* Chapel Hill, NC.

Worthington, Ian, 1994: "The Canon of the Ten Attic Orators," in *Persuasion: Greek Rhetoric in Action,* ed. Ian Worthington. London: 244–263.

Yunis, Harvey, 1996: *Taming Democracy: Models of Political Rhetoric in Classical Athens.* Ithaca, NY.

ADDENDA

Carey, Christopher, 1997: *Trials from Classical Athens.* London.

Usher, Stephen, 1999: *Greek Oratory: Tradition and Originality.* Oxford.

ISOCRATES I

INTRODUCTION TO ISOCRATES[1]

LIFE AND CAREER

Isocrates (436–338) differs from the other Attic Orators in that his reputation was not based on speeches that he delivered in the courts or the Assembly, or wrote for others to deliver, but rather on "speeches" (*logoi*) that were intended to be circulated in writing and read by others. This is important for his representation of himself and his career (and his dissociation of himself from those he called "sophists") and for understanding the important role he played in the intellectual life of fourth-century Athens.

Early in his career Isocrates did write speeches for others to deliver in the lawcourts, but he soon gave up this practice and opened a school where he taught about education and rhetoric, that is, politics. His views on these subjects put him at odds with Plato (and later Aristotle), who had a rival school, and his generally aristocratic political views brought him into conflict with politicians like Demosthenes. But among his pupils were many prominent Greeks of the time, and in antiquity and the Renaissance he enjoyed a reputation as a political writer, a stylist, and the foremost teacher of rhetoric in his day (e.g., Cicero, *De Oratore* 2.94–95).

Details of Isocrates' life are provided by his own works and by several later biographies, notably those of Dionysius of Halicarnassus and Pseudo-Plutarch (*Moralia* 836–839). But Isocrates was a controversial figure, and so all our sources may be influenced by political agendas,

---

[1] This Introduction to Isocrates is a joint effort of the three translators of Isocrates (David Mirhady, Terry Papillon, and Yun Lee Too) and the Series Editor.

by literary and biographical conventions, and sometimes by misunderstanding. He was born into a wealthy Athenian family during the height of Athens' power before the Peloponnesian War. According to tradition, his father Theodorus owned a workshop that manufactured flutes; his mother's name was Heduto, and he had three brothers and a sister. He is reported to have studied with several prominent teachers, including Tisias (one of the traditional founders of rhetoric), the sophists Prodicus and Gorgias, and the moderate oligarch Theramenes, and to have associated with Socrates, but such reports may reflect later views of his intellectual roots more than historical fact.[2] Late in his life he married a woman named Plathane, daughter of the sophist Hippias, and adopted Aphareus, one of her sons by a previous marriage.

Isocrates apparently avoided public life during the turbulent years of the Peloponnesian War (431–404). After the war he had a brief career as a logographer, writing forensic speeches for others (speeches 16–21), but he apparently gave this up around 390 and turned to teaching, in part to recover his fortunes after suffering financial losses in the Peloponnesian War (15.161). He was so successful at this that he was later enrolled among the wealthiest 1,200 Athenian citizens, who were responsible for public liturgies, such as the financing of warships (trierarchies) and choruses (see Series Introduction: xix). He says that he and his son voluntarily undertook three trierarchies during his lifetime (15.145).

Isocrates distinguishes himself from those who treat public speaking largely as a means of amassing personal fortunes and instead represents himself as a principled and responsible teacher of what he calls "philosophy," but later ages down to the present have more often interpreted as "rhetoric." Tradition has it that he taught as many as a hundred students, including many who became prominent orators (Isaeus, Hyperides), writers (Theopompus, Ephorus, Androtion), and military and political leaders (Timotheus, Nicocles). Many of his letters dramatize the teacher offering political instruction and advice to various potentates of the Greek-speaking world, including the tyrant Dionysius of Syracuse (*Epistle* 1), Philip of Macedon (*Epistles* 2 and 3),

---

[2] See Too 1995: 235–239.

Timotheus, ruler of Heracleia (*Epistle* 7), and Archidamus III, king of Sparta (*Epistle* 9).

In 378 Athens established a new naval confederation, the so-called Second Athenian League, and regained much of its former prominence. During the next two decades Isocrates enjoyed the friendship of the leading Athenian general Timotheus, and it was probably during this period that he developed his relationship with Evagoras, king of Cyprus, and his son Nicocles (see speeches 2, 3, 9). The power of Athens and Timotheus' standing in the city both diminished sharply in the 350s, and Isocrates retired from teaching in 351 at the age of 85. He continued to write, however, and became increasingly interested in engaging the leadership of Philip in the cause of panhellenism— the ideal of a unified Greek political and cultural world that the individual Greek cities had thus far been unable or unwilling to achieve. He is reported to have died at the age of 98 by starving himself after hearing the news of Athens' defeat by Philip in the battle of Chaeronea in 338. In any case he did not live to see the actual unification of the Greek world that was achieved rather differently from what he had imagined by Philip's son Alexander the Great (reigned 336–323).

PHILOSOPHIA, EDUCATION, AND POLITICS

Isocrates devoted many of his writings to proclaiming his views (and criticizing those of his opponents) on a broad range of educational and political issues. At the core of his teaching was an aristocratic notion of *aretē* ("virtue, excellence"), which could be attained by pursuing *philosophia*—not so much the dialectical study of abstract subjects like epistemology and metaphysics that Plato marked as "philosophy" as the study and practical application of ethics, politics, and public speaking. His views are most fully expounded in two works, one early in his career, the other near the end of it.

Against the Sophists (13) is a polemic against his rival professional teachers. As he characterizes them, these sophists are primarily interested in disputation ("eristic") as a tool for victory in debates, particularly debates between litigants in court. Although the text breaks off just as Isocrates announces that he will give a more comprehensive account of his teaching, this work can be read as a partial account of his pedagogical methods: his essential point is that in order to become a skilled practitioner of public speech, a student requires both the appropriate natural ability, including a capacity for hard work and a good memory, and also the guidance of a good teacher.

Antidosis (15), in which Isocrates seeks to justify his life as a professional teacher in Athens, offers a fuller account of his own pedagogical views.[3] He stresses that his teaching (*paideia*) is practical and is aimed at preparing young men broadly as gentlemen. It includes more than what later ages called rhetoric—instruction in the art of public speech and persuasion—and is essentially an education in political leadership, a mechanism for the construction of authority among the traditional elite groups that comprise Isocrates' ideal pupils (15.304). He demonstrates that Athens was founded and made great through the oratorical skills of men like Solon, Themistocles, and Pericles, and he argues that because public speaking is the basis of the ideal democratic community, it should continue to be a structuring principle of Athens. Despite the six forensic speeches that are preserved in his name, Isocrates denies having had anything to do with the lawcourts, and he repudiates any possible identification with the culture of forensic oratory (15.36). Only the sophists concern themselves with private lawsuits (15.45–46); by contrast, Isocrates asserts that he has devoted himself only to the interests of the Greek people.

Isocrates' political agenda is thus conservative, verging on oligarchy, though he is always careful to designate it democracy. As an advocate of public speaking, he promotes an earlier culture of public discourse, reminding his audience that although the contemporary culture of oratory has caused wealthy, respectable citizens like himself to be involved in trials motivated by personal grudges and jealousy, public discourse originally and ideally constitutes the basis of the community. He returns frequently to the historical role of discourse (as he sees it) in the establishment of Athenian military and cultural supremacy, which has allowed the people (the *dēmos*) to wield the power

[3] In *Antidosis* Isocrates devises the elaborate scenario of a trial in which he was accused of being an unscrupulous teacher who corrupted his pupils and failed to disclose his true earnings. This trial is the pretext for writing the *Antidosis,* in which Isocrates assumes the role of the philosopher wrongly attacked by his community, explicitly modeling himself after the Socrates of Plato's *Apology* (see Papillon 1997).

it does. Through speech (*logos*) men persuaded one another, associated with one another, created cities, established customs and laws (*nomoi*), educated others, disputed with one another, and invented the arts (3.5–9, 15.253–257). For Isocrates *logos* (discourse) and *philosophia* (the study of and training in discourse) are at the core of any orderly, civilized community and have been essential to the success of Athens, the classical democratic city *par excellence*. Discourse institutionalizes morality and makes possible debate, persuasion, and the instruction of others; and an individual who provides a true education in this subject demonstrates his own civic virtue (*aretē*) and deserves the gratitude of the city for helping to maintain its ideals and power.

Isocrates' political views also found expression on contemporary issues, primarily in his advocacy of panhellenism—the promotion of a united Greek opposition to Persia. He sees Athens as the natural leader of Greece and urges cooperation among the leading cities in the fourth century, Athens, Sparta, and Thebes, with Athens assuming a leading role. These views are first set forth in *Panegyricus* (4), composed for the panhellenic Olympic festival in 380. In this work he argues that freedom and other common values divide Greeks from non-Greeks, so that Greek cities should put aside their differences and unite against the common enemy. Isocrates returns to these themes often, but as time revealed the inability of Athens and the other Greek cities to give up their long-standing independence from and distrust of one another, he increasingly saw Macedonia—on the fringe of the Greek world and ambiguously straddling Greek and "barbarian" elements—as the best hope for unifying the Greek states in common cause against Persia. To this end, in speeches such as *To Philip* (5) and *Panathenaicus* (12), in particular, he lobbied for a panhellenic military expedition against Persia led by Philip. He still hoped for a leading role for Athens, a hope that was dashed at Chaeronea, just before his death.

Another feature of Isocrates' rhetorical teaching, which may be partly responsible for both ancient and modern devaluing of him,[4] is

---

[4] Marrou (1956: 131), for instance, judges that despite his preeminent position as a teacher of rhetoric in antiquity, Isocrates is to be regarded as standing in second place to his contemporary Plato where personality, temperament, depth of intellect, and art are concerned.

that he challenges the common perception of discourse as predominantly oral. Indeed, he explicitly rejects the spoken word as a political medium, claiming that a "small voice" and lack of courage prevent him from speaking in public (cf. 5.81, 15.190–191, *Epistle* 8.7). This account may best be understood as the product of a paradoxical self-fashioning, since in claiming to be unable to speak in public, Isocrates conveniently excuses himself from his contemporary culture of public oratory, which he characterizes as petty, litigious, and promoted by self-interested and unscrupulous sophists.[5] By preserving his distance from contemporary oratory and its limited concerns, Isocrates could explore larger political issues, in particular those concerning Athens' leadership of the Greek states. For him, the written word was the basis of interactions with the larger Hellenic community. His works were thus a testimony to his political interactions with individuals and states outside Athens.

STYLE

Like several other Athenian orators, Isocrates was and continues to be known for his distinctive literary style. Although he was influenced by the stylistic innovations of Gorgias, verbal assonance is not nearly as prominent in his work as in Gorgias' writings, and he generally employs parallelism and antithesis at the level of whole clauses and sentences rather than individual words and short phrases. The result may not rival the forcefulness of Demosthenes, but Isocrates' prose has generally been admired for its smoothness and charm.

Isocrates seems to offer an account of his literary method in *Against the Sophists* (13.16–17), where he speaks of the hard work and superior natural ability required in order to choose from the various forms of discourse

> the necessary forms for each subject, to mix them with each other and arrange them suitably, and then, not to mistake the circumstances (*kairoi*) but to embellish the entire speech properly with considerations (*enthymēmata*) and to speak the words rhythmically and musically.

---

[5] For discussion of this aspect of the rhetorician's self-representation, see Too 1995: 74–112.

In following this method Isocrates developed a style characterized by long, artfully constructed, "periodic" sentences, which by their architectural structure of balanced clauses convey a strong sense of order and reason. For example, in a translation that tries to follow as closely as possible the Greek word order, a single sentence from *Antidosis* (15.48–49)[6] might read as follows (Isocrates is distinguishing between those who write for the courts and those like himself who do not):

[48] [Many men] recognize that the one group (*tois men*)[7] through political meddling have become experienced in legal contests, but the others (*tous de*) through philosophy have developed their skill in the speeches I have just described, and that those (*tous men*) who appear to be skilled in forensic speeches, on that day only are tolerated on which they happen to be pleading, whereas the others (*tous de*) are honored in all gatherings all the time and have acquired a high reputation; [49] and furthermore, that the former (*tous men*), if they are seen two or three times in the courts, are hated and derided but the latter (*tous de*), the more people they associate with and the more often, the more they are admired; and in addition to this, those (*tous men*) who are skilled in legal pleadings are far from the eloquence of the others, but the others (*tous de*), if they wished, could quickly master that kind of speaking.

The structure of this sentence (which needless to say is impossible to reproduce consistently in a readable English translation) reinforces the polarization Isocrates seeks to convey and supports his assertion of the superiority of his own endeavor, while at the same time giving the reader no specific information about the exact nature of that endeavor.[8]

---

[6] It should be noted that in Isocrates' day punctuation marks such as the period did not exist, so that the determination of sentence end is the work of modern editors. In places a period could arguably be substituted for a semicolon or comma and vice versa.

[7] The particles *men* and *de* are used in Greek as early as Homer to designate antithetical words and clauses.

[8] Isocrates' style is also characterized in Greek by the avoidance of hiatus—the collision of vowels between two successive words. In English hiatus is avoided by, e.g., inserting an "n" between the vowels ("an apple" instead of "a apple"). Greek avoids hiatus primarily by the careful placement of words. Our translations do not attempt to reproduce this effect.

A NOTE ON TERMINOLOGY

As noted above, Isocrates never uses the term "rhetoric," (*rhētorikē,* i.e., *rhētorikē technē,* "the rhetorical art") to refer to public speaking or instruction in the art of discourse, though he does occasionally use the adjective "rhetorical" (*rhētorikos*).[9] Instead, to designate his own work he uses *philosophia* and various expressions involving *logos* ("word, speech, argument, discourse," etc.) in both singular and plural (*logoi*). The use of these terms and the avoidance of *rhētorikē* must be intentional on Isocrates' part and may be linked to his rivalry with Plato, who uses *rhētorikē,* most notably in the *Gorgias,* to condemn the teaching of public speaking.[10] Isocrates instead seeks to appropriate the term *philosophia* to describe his intellectual activity and teaching, thereby implicitly challenging Plato, who was seeking to appropriate the term for his own work.[11]

In view of this, although *philosophia* and other expressions may overlap with various meanings of the English term "rhetoric," we do not use "rhetoric" in our translations (though we do use "rhetorical" for *rhētorikos*). We generally translate *philosophia* as "philosophy" (with an occasional reminder that this means something close to our "rhetoric"), and use such terms as "speaking," "speech," "discourse," "oratory," and "eloquence" as the occasion requires for various expressions with *logos.*

Finally, a note of caution to the reader. Interest in Isocrates has been growing rapidly in recent years, and scholars in different fields have been exploring new ways of reading him. As a result, a diversity of views is reflected in the three translators, and although we have coordinated our translations and discussed our differences among ourselves with a view to achieving consensus wherever possible, this di-

---

[9] He also uses *rhētoreia* ("[artful] speaking") in 5.26, 12.2, and 13.21, and *rhētoreuō* ("to speak publicly") in 5.25 and *Epistle* 8.7. *Rhētores* ("public speakers," always in the plural) is fairly common (21 instances).

[10] *Gorgias* 448–466 *passim.* As Schiappa 1990 and Cole 1991 argue, Plato may have created the term *rhētorikē* as part of his attack on this competing cultural force.

[11] See Too 1995: 180, 193; Papillon 1995; Timmerman 1998.

versity is still evident, both among the three translators and perhaps even within the translators themselves. Thus the reader should not always expect to find a single voice in these two volumes but will, we hope, enter into our discourse and create his or her own voice for Isocrates.

TEXT

A number of medieval manuscripts of Isocrates' works have survived, one dating back to the late ninth or early tenth century, and a very recent papyrus find in Egypt has given us the earliest texts of speeches 1–3 (fourth century AD). The most notable modern editions of Isocrates are the Budé edition in four volumes by Georges Mathieu and Emile Brémond, *Isocrate: Discours* (Paris, 1929–1966), and the Loeb text in three volumes by George Norlin and LaRue Van Hook, *Isocrates* (Cambridge, MA and London, 1928–1945).

The translations in this volume are based on the Budé text, except where noted.

THE WORKS OF ISOCRATES

According to Pseudo-Plutarch as many as sixty works were associated with Isocrates' name, but not all these are authentic. Today thirty works are generally ascribed to him. They are traditionally numbered as in Table 1 (the Roman numerals indicate the volume of Isocrates in this series that contains the work; most dates are approximate guesses).

There is no obvious or generally accepted arrangement of the speeches of Isocrates. In this translation we use the traditional numbering of the manuscripts but do not follow this order in our translations. Instead, Mirhady translates the earlier speeches; Too, the speeches that concern education in its various manifestations; and Papillon, the remainder.

Scholars have offered various generic descriptions and classifications of these works. To cite just one example, Richard Jebb proposed a generic scheme that divided them into the following four categories: *A.* Scholastic, which included hortatory, display, and educational works (1, 2, 3, 9, 10, 11, 12, 13, 15). *B.* Political works (4, 5, 6, 7, 8, 14).

Table 1. The Works of Isocrates

Oration	Date	Volume
1. *To Demonicus*	(374–370)	I
2. *To Nicocles*	(374)	I
3. *Nicocles*	(372–365)	I
4. *Panegyricus*	(380)	II
5. *To Philip*	(346)	II
6. *Archidamus*	(366)	II
7. *Areopagiticus*	(ca. 357)	I
8. *On the Peace*	(355)	II
9. *Evagoras*	(370–365)	I
10. *Encomium of Helen*	(370)	I
11. *Busiris*	(391–385)	I
12. *Panathenaicus*	(342–339)	II
13. *Against the Sophists*	(390)	I
14. *Plataicus*	(373–371)	II
15. *Antidosis*	(354–353)	I
16. *On the Team of Horses*	(397–396)	I
17. *Trapeziticus*	(393)	I
18. *Special Plea against Callimachus*	(402)	I
19. *Aegineticus*	(391–390)	I
20. *Against Lochites*	(394)	I
21. *Against Euthynus, without Witnesses*	(403)	I
Epistle 1. To Dionysius	(368)	II
Epistle 2. To Philip 1	(342)	II
Epistle 3. To Philip 2	(338)	II
Epistle 4. To Antipater	(340)	II
Epistle 5. To Alexander	(342)	II
Epistle 6. To the Children of Jason	(359)	II
Epistle 7. To Timotheus	(345)	II
Epistle 8. To the Rulers of the Mytileneans	(350)	II
Epistle 9. To Archidamus	(356)	II

C. Forensic speeches (16–21). *D.* Letters and fragments.[12] Such broad generic descriptions may help a modern reader understand the conventions governing the writing of a particular work, but they may also conceal the extent to which works in all categories form part of a larger whole, which Isocrates identifies as *logos politikos*.[13] Thus although Isocrates at times seems to insist on generic differentiation (e.g., 1.5), at other times he resists such classifications, and a generic taxonomy may sometimes conceal the complexity of his literary self-representation.

---

[12] See Jebb 1876: 2.82–84.
[13] See Poulakos 1997.

PART ONE

Translated by David Mirhady

INTRODUCTION TO PART ONE

〰〰

The works in Part One are from the early part of Isocrates' career (approximately 401–380), before his interest in and influence on politics had become very significant.[1] Aside from the speeches he wrote as a *logographos* (16–21) or speechwriter for those lacking the expertise to compose speeches for themselves to deliver before the lawcourts, Isocrates is concerned with staking out his claims as a practitioner and teacher of public affairs, especially public speaking. Plato refers to this practice as "rhetoric" (*rhētorikē*),[2] but Isocrates designates his activity *philosophia* and his teaching simply *paideusis* or "education" (see Introduction to Isocrates). He thus throws down a challenge to those whom we now recognize as philosophers, like Plato. The term *philosophos* means simply "lover of wisdom," and those who pursued more theoretical studies during Isocrates' time had no more an established claim to it than Isocrates had. Neither Plato nor Aristotle ever explicitly criticizes Isocrates, and he too never mentions these two rivals, even though they clearly have opposing views.

The order of the speeches here is not chronological.[3] In the open

---

[1] The exception may be *Encomium of Helen* (10). Most scholars believe that it was written about 370, although some have argued for 390. See the introduction to the speech.

[2] This term is likely to have been coined by Plato as a denigration of the crass professionalization of what had traditionally been the preserve of amateur practitioners (see Plato, *Gorgias* 462b–d and Schiappa 1990). A *rhētōr* in Athens was simply a public speaker, and all Athenian men had theoretically equal rights to speak in the Assembly or courts.

[3] Those interested in following the development of Isocrates' thinking, about public speaking for instance, might start with *Against the Sophists* (13) and then

letter *To Demonicus* (1), for instance, Isocrates characterizes himself as the established older man, completely confident in advising the son of a now deceased friend. He presents a healthy store of Greek wisdom in the form of precepts for the aristocratic young man. He makes no attempt, however, to entice him to further study, and certainly none to engage him in public speaking. (This fact is of the greatest significance for those who might want to identify Isocrates' teaching and "philosophy" exclusively with rhetoric and public speaking.) The advice is unadorned and practical, sometimes even a little cynical, and it appears without any apparent order. It is important to note, however, that such moral instruction formed a foundation for Isocrates' other teaching. It is thus an appropriate starting point for the study of his writings.

The examples of epideictic ("display") speeches here, *Encomium of Helen* (10) and *Busiris* (11), serve to distinguish Isocrates from his predecessors and contemporaries. In both speeches Isocrates takes up themes that had already become standards in the epideictic canon, but he takes pains to distance himself from, among others, Gorgias, his famous predecessor and teacher, and Polycrates, his less famous older contemporary. He rejects the apologetic form of Gorgias' *Encomium of Helen,* arguing that there is nothing about Helen to be apologetic for. In *Busiris,* he rejects the transparency and paradox that characterized Polycrates' writings. They were designed as rhetorical *tours de force* of the sort that were common among the sophists; they liked to display their virtuosity by obviously championing the "weaker" argument against the "stronger."

Isocrates' attempts at improvements over Gorgias and Polycrates have appeared less than successful to many. His praise of Helen, for instance, largely amounts to saying that many important gods and heroes found her beautiful, the emphasis being on the importance of the gods and heroes rather than on any personal qualities of Helen, other than beauty. And although his defense of Busiris is interesting for the picture it draws of Greek attitudes toward Egypt, it begs the central question set out in the speech, namely, whether Busiris was

---

move on to *Busiris* (11) and *Encomium of Helen* (10). A complete chronology of the speeches can be found in the Introduction to Isocrates.

guilty of killing and eating Greeks who found themselves in Egypt. Particularly striking in both speeches, however, is the extent to which Isocrates embraces traditional mythology and religion. He shared with Plato the view that it was incorrect to impute wrongdoing to the gods. But unlike Plato, who was led for this reason to throw out much of the Greek mythology that was handed down from Homer and Hesiod, Isocrates accepts it, claiming justification for the actions of many legendary figures, like Helen, Agamemnon, and Busiris, who are vilified by earlier writers. For Isocrates, the only reason to talk about such figures is that they may serve as an inspiration for good behavior.[4]

In *Against the Sophists* (13), Isocrates attempts to distance his own teaching from that of other sophists, principally by showing that it takes a broader focus and develops not only skill in public speaking but the entire character of the student. The category "sophist" is, however, problematic. It is applied without dispute to the professional teachers of public speaking from the fifth century, like Protagoras and Gorgias. But it is also applied to, for example, Lysias (Dem. 59.20), and there is no reason it should not apply to Isocrates himself, inasmuch as he was also a professional teacher of public speaking. Our sources about the sophists, including Isocrates, the comic playwright Aristophanes, and Plato, are all quite critical, characterizing sophists as deceivers and panderers to popular tastes. But they clearly had a great and positive influence in liberating and invigorating Athens' intellectual climate and in creating a positive atmosphere for free debate in Athens' democracy. There was much about Isocrates' form of education, on the other hand, that was clearly elitist and superior. It was practical, since it aimed at aristocratic young men bound for political careers, but it did not lend itself to open debate or to the frank discussion of competing viewpoints, a form of education that Isocrates would characterize dismissively as "eristic."[5]

The remainder of Part One consists of Isocrates' six surviving lawcourt speeches (16–21), which represent a cross-section of judicial cases: assault, inheritance, and theft. They were composed in the years following Athens' defeat in the Peloponnesian War and the subse-

---

[4] For a fuller explanation, see Papillon 1996b.
[5] See also Benoit 1991.

quent tyranny of the Thirty (404–403). Several speeches make references to those events, although it is impossible to discern from them what role Isocrates was playing in Athenian life during this time, since they were all written for delivery by others. He appears from other evidence to have been a supporter of the moderate oligarch Theramenes, and one of the speeches, *On the Team of Horses* (16), expresses effusive praise for Alcibiades, a highly controversial figure of the late fifth century (cf. Lys. 14–15). Of course, the speech may not represent Isocrates' own views, but it is hard to imagine that he would have lent his talents to composing arguments that diverged very far from his own convictions. Several of the speeches contain sharp attacks against sykophants, the "malicious prosecutors" or "vexatious litigators" who attempted to settle scores after, and in some ways despite, the settlement of 404/3. The settlement had largely succeeded in healing the wounds caused by the irrational behavior of the Athenian democratic Assembly in the final years of the Peloponnesian War and the cruelty of the oligarchic tyranny, the Thirty, in the war's aftermath. All the lawcourt speeches project support for the Athenian democracy and the rule of law. Again, these were not necessarily Isocrates' own views, but only a hardened skeptic would deny that they give some indication of Isocrates' political program.

A NOTE ON THE TRANSLATION

Beyond what has been mentioned in the Introduction to Isocrates, we may note that Greek uses many more connective particles, such as *gar* ("for"), than are common in modern, idiomatic English. Many of these are therefore untranslated here, except in 1, where *gar* plays an essential role connecting each precept to its explanation.

1. TO DEMONICUS

INTRODUCTION

Although this speech may seem to a modern reader to encompass simply a random collection of bland pieces of advice, it was widely read and quoted from antiquity through the Renaissance. Strangely enough, however, for a work so often identified with the values of Isocrates, its authenticity has been challenged, both in antiquity and in modern times. Nevertheless, the overwhelming consensus is that the work is Isocratean.

What we know about Demonicus and his father Hipponicus must be gleaned from the speech itself, although the author of a fourth-century AD introduction says that he was Cyprian. Demonicus lived under a king (36) and appears to have been prosperous (49). His father was well known as a man of high morals (11). It is supposed—and it is no better than a supposition—that the work was written about the same time as the two other "hortatory" works, *To Nicocles* (2) and *Nicocles* (3) (374–370), and so may be called one of the "Cyprian" speeches. Like those works and other "gnomic" (*gnōmē* = maxim) works of the time, it is loosely organized. It may be profitably compared with the poetry of Theognis of Megara (sixth century BC) in that it treats a succession of loosely connected topics. Such a comparison would show a remarkable continuity in Greek popular wisdom, which often betrays a conflicting mixture of practical advice and idealism.

The work has three parts: an introduction (1–12), a long list of precepts (13–43), and an epilogue (44–52).

1. TO DEMONICUS

[1] We shall find, Demonicus, that the thoughts of honorable people and the opinions of the base stand far apart in many respects. But by far the greatest way in which these people differ is in their associations with one another: the base honor their friends only when they are present, but the honorable love them even when they are far away; a short time destroys relationships among the base, but not even an entire age could wither the friendships of the honorable. [2] Since I believe it proper for those striving for renown and seeking an education to imitate the honorable, not the base, I have sent you this discourse as a gift, evidence of my goodwill for you and an indication of my intimacy with Hipponicus: it is fitting that children inherit not only the property but also the friendships of their fathers. [3] I see that luck is also with us and that the present occasion is on our side: you are eager for education, and I endeavor to educate others; the peak moment to do philosophy is upon you, and I guide those doing philosophy.[1] Those who compose words of encouragement for their friends take on a noble task, [4] but they are not devoting themselves to the most noble aspect of philosophy. Rather, those who direct the young, not in the ways of practicing cleverness (*deinotēs*) in speeches (*logoi*) but in how to become renowned as serious in the constitution of their character, do their hearers a much greater benefit to the extent that while others may exhort them only to speech, they improve their characters.

[5] Therefore, we intend to counsel you not by composing an exhortation[2] but by writing an address about what young people ought to strive for, what actions they should avoid, with what sort of people they should keep company, and how they should manage their lives. Only those who have walked this path of life have been able to reach virtue (*aretē*)[3] genuinely, which is the most valuable and secure acqui-

---

[1] On what Isocrates means by "philosophy," see Introduction to Isocrates and the Glossary (*philosophia*).

[2] Isocrates is ever mindful of distinctions in genre (*eidos*). Here he distinguishes an exhortation (*paraklēsis*) from an address (*parainesis*). The distinction flows from what he says in 1.4.

[3] *Aretē* (pl. *aretai*) is the central word in Greek ethics. It is translated here and elsewhere as "virtue," but it has a wide range of meanings, running from

sition. [6] Beauty is destroyed by time or marred by disease.⁴ Wealth supports evil rather than noble conduct: it provides a basis for laziness and exhorts the young to pleasures. Strength is a benefit when it is joined with practical wisdom (*phronēsis*), but without this, it does more harm to those who have it: it embellishes the bodies of those who exercise, but it obscures their care for the soul. [7] If virtue grows purely in our thoughts, it is the only acquisition that will age with us; it is stronger than wealth and more useful than good birth; it makes possible what is impossible for others. It endures with tenacity what is fearful to most; it believes hesitation blameworthy, toil praiseworthy. [8] It is easy to learn this from the labors of Heracles and the deeds of Theseus, whose virtue of character cast such a stamp of glory on their works that all of time cannot make us forget what they did.

[9] Even better, if you recall the principles of your father, you will have your own fine example of what I am saying. He did not scorn virtue or live an indolent life. He trained his body through toil and endured dangers with his soul. He did not love wealth unduly: he enjoyed his possessions like a mortal but took care of his estate like an immortal. [10] He did not manage his life cheaply; he was a lover of beauty and was generous and open to his friends; he admired more those who treated him honorably than those related to him by blood. He thought that in camaraderie (*hetaireia*) nature was more important than law,⁵ behavior than kinship, and principle than compulsion. [11] All of time would be inadequate to enumerate all his accomplishments. We shall elucidate their details on other occasions, but for now we have furnished an indication of Hipponicus' nature as a model by which you must live, believing his behavior a law and becoming an imitator and emulator of your father's virtue. It is a shameful thing that painters create representations of beautiful animals, but children

---

"morality" to "courage" or even "manliness." The word's origin is associated with the Greek god of war, Ares, but there is seldom any direct connotation of military courage implied in its use. Moreover, there are times when other core values, such as a sense of justice (*dikaiosynē*) or soundness of mind (*sōphrosynē*), are referred to as *aretai*. Cf. Glossary.

⁴ In 10.54–60, Isocrates gives an altogether different view of beauty.

⁵ The distinction between law (*nomos*) and nature (*physis*) was the basis of much discussion among the sophists of late-fifth-century Athens. See Gagarin and Woodruff 1995: xxii.

do not imitate their honorable ancestors. [12] Take the view that no athlete should train against his competitors as much as you must examine how to rival your father's habits.

It is impossible to mold your understanding in this way without filling it with many fine precepts. Bodies are naturally built up through measured tasks, the soul through honorable words. Therefore, I shall try briefly to set out for you habits through which you may advance most toward virtue and win a good reputation among all people.

[13] First, venerate what relates to the gods,[6] not only by performing sacrifices but also by fulfilling your oaths. Sacrifices are a sign of material affluence, but abiding by oaths is evidence of a noble character. Honor the divine always, but especially in public worship, for in this way you will gain a good reputation both for sacrificing to the gods and for abiding by the laws.

[14] Treat your parents as you would hope your children will treat you.

Practice bodily exercises that contribute to health, not to strength; you will achieve this if you stop exercising while you are still able to exercise more.

[15] Do not engage in uncontrolled laughter, and do not admit bold speech: the former lacks sense, the latter is madness.

Believe that what is shameful to do is not good even to mention.

Accustom yourself to being thoughtful, not sullen, for the latter will make you seem selfish, but the former pragmatic.

Think that a sense of shame and justice and soundness of mind are an especially fitting regimen, for all agree that the character of the young should be controlled by these things.

[16] Never expect to do something shameful and get away with it, for although you may escape the notice of others, you will be conscious of it yourself.

Fear the gods; honor your parents; respect your friends; obey the laws.

Pursue pleasures that bring a good reputation, for enjoyment ac-

---

[6] Greek had no word that corresponds to our "religion." Isocrates is essentially saying, "be religious."

companied by nobility is a very good thing, but without this it is very bad.

[17] Guard against slanders, even if they are false, for most people are ignorant of the truth and look only at reputation.

Resolve to do everything as if everyone noticed, for even if you get away with it for the moment, you will be noticed later. You will be especially well regarded if you clearly avoid doing what you would criticize others for doing.

[18] If you love learning, you will be very learned.

What you know, guard through practice; what you have not learned, add to your knowledge. For it is just as shameful to hear something useful without learning it as to be given something good by friends without taking it.

Apply your life's leisure time to a fondness for listening to discussion, for in this way you will easily learn what is discovered by others only with difficulty.

[19] Believe that many lessons are better than many possessions, for possessions disappear quickly, but lessons remain for all time. Wisdom is the only immortal acquisition.

Do not hesitate to travel a long way to find those who offer to teach something useful. It is a shame that merchants travel over such large seas in order to expand their material wealth, but the young do not even put up with trips over land in order to improve their thinking.

[20] Be affable in your manner and courteous in your speech. Affability involves speaking to those who approach you; courtesy involves conversing with them in familiar speech.

Act pleasantly toward all, but cultivate the best, for in this way you will not be offensive to anyone, but you will become a friend of the best.

Do not have frequent conversations with the same people or long conversations about the same subjects, for there is a limit to everything.

[21] Train yourself in hard work willingly so that you will be able to endure it even against your will.

Strengthen your soul against all those things by which it is shameful for it to be overcome, such as profit, anger, pleasure, and pain. You will succeed in this if you believe that profit is the means by which to win a good reputation, not to become rich, if you manage your anger toward those who make mistakes in the same way as you would have others treat you if you make mistakes, if you assume while enjoying yourself that it is shameful to rule servants and yet to be a slave to pleasures, and if, while working, you observe the misfortunes of others and recall that you are yourself human.

[22] Guard words deposited with you more than deposits of money, for good men must display a character more trustworthy than an oath.

Regard it as fitting to distrust bad people, just as it is fitting to trust the good.

Talk about secrets to no one, unless it is equally advantageous both for you in speaking and for those listening to keep the matters quiet.

[23] Consent to an oath when requested[7] for only two reasons, either to free yourself from a disgraceful charge or to rescue friends from great dangers; and do not swear by the gods for the sake of money, not even if you intend to swear faithfully, for you will appear to some to be committing perjury and to others to be greedy.

[24] Make no one a friend before you investigate how he has treated his friends before. Expect him to treat you just as he treated them.

Be slow to take on a friendship, but once you have, try to maintain it, for it is equally shameful to have no friends and to be continually changing companions.

Do not make a trial of your friends when it does harm, but do not consent to having unproven companions. You will accomplish this if you pretend to be in need although you are not. [25] Communicate about open matters as if they were secret, for you will suffer no harm if you are wrong but will learn more about their character if you are right.

Scrutinize your friends in life's misfortunes and in shared dangers, for we test gold in the fire but discern our friends in misfortunes.

You will treat friends best if you do not await their requests but come forth on your own to help them in crises (*kairoi*).

---

[7] Greeks commonly settled disputes by working out an oath to be sworn by one side or the other, or sometimes by both sides. But an over-reliance on such oath-swearing could indicate that a person took the practice lightly and was thus impious. See Sophocles, *Oedipus at Colonus* 650.

[26] Regard it a similar disgrace to be outdone by your enemies in doing harm and to be beaten by your friends in doing good.

Admit as companions those who feel distress at your bad times and no envy in your good times, for many commiserate with those in misfortune but envy those doing well.

Recall absent friends to those around you, so that they will not think that you belittle them when they are not there.

[27] Wish to be attractive in your dress, but not a dandy. Elegance is the mark of attractiveness, excess that of a dandy.

Appreciate not the excessive acquisition of material goods but their measured enjoyment.

Despise those who take wealth seriously but cannot use what they have; for their experience is like someone who acquires a fine horse although he has a poor knowledge of riding.

[28] Try to think of using wealth as well as acquiring it. Its use is for those who know how to enjoy it, its acquisition simply for those who can acquire it. Honor your property for only two purposes, to be able to pay a large fine and to help an honorable friend in misfortune, but in the rest of your life, appreciate it without any exaggeration but in a measured way.

[29] Value your present circumstances, but seek better. Reproach no one for misfortune, for luck and the future are unforeseeable.

Treat good men well, for gratitude owed by an honorable man is a fine treasure. By treating bad men well you will have the same experience as those who feed other people's dogs, for these dogs bark at people who feed them just like any passersby, and the bad injure those who assist them, just like those who harm them.

[30] Hate flatterers as much as deceivers, for if trusted both do injustice to those who trust them. If you accept into friendship those who gratify for the worst reasons, your life will lack friends who will risk animosity for the best reasons.

Be sociable toward your acquaintances, but not proud. Even slaves would scarcely endure the pretensions of the conceited, but everyone gladly puts up with the conduct of the sociable.

[31] You will be sociable if you are not argumentative or disagreeable or competitive toward everyone, if you do not harshly oppose the anger of those you are with, even if their anger is unjust, but yield to them when they are upset and rebuke them only when their anger has

stopped, if you do not take jokes seriously and do not enjoy a laugh at serious things, for what is untimely is always irritating, if you do not return favors ungraciously,[8] as most people do by helping their friends in an unpleasant manner, and finally, if you are not overly fond of finding fault, for that is burdensome, or carping, for that is annoying.

[32] Take special caution against drinking parties, but if the occasion arises, get up and leave before you are drunk. Whenever the mind is impaired by wine, it experiences the same things chariots do that have thrown their drivers. Just as they are borne along without order when their guides are missing, so the soul makes many mistakes when its thinking is impaired.

Think like an immortal by being great-hearted, and like a mortal by enjoying your property in moderation.

[33] Realize that education is so much better than lack of education that while all people profit from other dishonorable things, only a lack of education punishes even those who have it, for they often pay a penalty in actions for the pain they cause in words.

Say something good about those you wish to befriend to those who will report it, for praise is the beginning of friendship just as blame is the beginning of enmity.

[34] When deliberating, make past events models for the future, for the unseen is most quickly comprehended from the seen.

Deliberate slowly, but carry out your resolutions quickly.

Believe it best to receive good fortune from the gods and good counsel from ourselves.

If you want to consult with some of your friends about something that would cause shame to discuss openly, speak as if it were someone else's affair, for in this way you will learn their view without revealing that it concerns you.

[35] Whenever you intend to consult an adviser about your own affairs, first see how he has managed his own, for someone who has shown poor judgment about his own affairs will never plan well about another's. The best incentive you can have to plan your affairs is to observe the misfortunes that result from not planning, for we have the

---

[8] More literally, "if you do not with respect to favors do favors ungraciously." Isocrates uses three words in succession with the base *charis*, which means "grace" or "favor."

most concern for health when we recall the pains that result from sickness.

[36] Imitate the manners of kings and follow their habits, for you will be thought to approve and emulate them and will thus achieve more distinction in the eyes of the multitude and more reliable good-will from kings.

Obey also the laws set down by the kings, but consider their conduct the strongest law, for just as someone practicing politics in a democracy must serve the multitude, so it is also fitting for someone living in a monarchy to respect the king.

[37] If you are put in office, do not employ anyone base in your service, for whatever mistakes he makes will be blamed on you.

Retire from public responsibilities not wealthier but more esteemed, for the praise of the multitude is better than many possessions.

Do not support or advocate any bad cause, for people will think that you are doing the sorts of things yourself that you help others do.

[38] Equip yourself to be able to get ahead, but hold back when you have your share so that you may have a reputation for desiring justice, not because you are weak but because you are fair-minded.

Prefer a just poverty over unjust wealth, for justice is better than money inasmuch as money benefits only the living, but justice furnishes a good reputation even to the dead, and while bad men may have money, it is impossible for the wicked to have a sense of justice.

[39] Emulate no one who profits from injustice, but follow those who suffer on the side of justice, for the just surpass the unjust at least in their honorable hopes, even if they do not profit in any other respect.

[40] Take concern for everything in life, but train your practical wisdom especially, for a good mind in a human body is something very great in something very insignificant.

Try to be a lover of toil with your body and a lover of wisdom[9] with your soul, so that you can fulfill your resolutions with the former and know how to foresee what is advantageous with the latter.

[41] Whatever you are about to say, examine first in your thought, for in many the tongue outruns the intention.

Make two occasions for speaking, either when you know the sub-

[9] I.e., a philosopher.

ject clearly, or when there is compulsion to discuss it, for on these occasions alone speech is better than silence; on others, it is better to be silent than to speak.

[42] Recognize that nothing in human affairs is certain, for in this way you will not be overly happy during good times or overly grieved during misfortune.[10] Rejoice at the occurrence of good things, but grieve in moderation at the occurrence of bad things, and in either case do not be obvious to others, for it is absurd to conceal your belongings in your house but to walk about with your thoughts open for all to see.

[43] Be more careful about disapproval than about danger, for while the wicked fear the end of life, the honorable fear disrepute during their lives. Try especially to live safely. But if it ever falls to you to undergo danger, seek a safe return from war with a noble reputation, not shameful rumor, for fate has decided that everyone will die, but it has allotted a noble death only to the honorable.

[44] Do not be surprised if much of what I have said does not apply to you at your present age. This fact did not escape me. But I preferred in a single work both to offer advice for your present life and to leave you a guide for the future. You will easily see its usefulness, but you will have difficulty finding someone with goodwill to give advice. Therefore, so that you do not have to look for the rest from someone else but may obtain it here, as if from a treasury, I thought I should not omit any of the advice I have for you.

[45] I would be very thankful to the gods if I am not mistaken in the opinion that I have formed of you. We shall find many others associating with friends who join them in their mistakes rather than admonish them, just as they enjoy the most tasty food rather than the healthiest. But I believe you take the opposite view of this, and I use as evidence your industry regarding education in general. For the person who imposes on himself to do what is best is likely to heed only those who exhort him to virtue. [46] You would be most stimulated

---

[10] The Budé edition transposes this and the preceding sentence without explanation. All other editors have followed the manuscripts, which provide a smoother train of thought.

to desire noble actions if you learned that we gain pleasure most genuinely from them. For in indolence and love of excess, pains follow immediately upon pleasures, but industry in pursuit of virtue and sound management of one's life always return pure and secure enjoyment. [47] In the former case, we first feel pleasure and then pain; in the latter, we have the pleasures after the pains. In all actions, we do not recall the beginning so much as we form an impression of the end, for we do not do most things in life for the sake of the activities themselves, but we work for the results. [48] Consider the fact that base people can do whatever they may, for they have constructed this sort of basis for their lives from the beginning. But for honorable people it is impossible to disregard virtue because many people will criticize them. Everyone hates not so much those who do wrong as those who claim to be fair-minded but who are no different from average men. And that is reasonable, [49] for when we condemn those who deceive us only in speech, won't we say that those who disappoint in the entire conduct of their lives are base? We would rightly conclude that such people not only wrong themselves but also betray their good fortune. Good fortune has handed them money, a good reputation, and friends, but they have made themselves unworthy of the prosperity they possess.

[50] If a mortal must take a guess at the thought of the gods, I believe that they have made very clear with regard to their closest relations how they feel toward base and honorable humans. Zeus fathered Heracles and Tantalus, as the stories say and all believe. He made Heracles immortal because of his virtue, but he disciplined Tantalus with the most severe punishments because of his depravity.[11]

[51] You must follow these examples and aspire to nobility. Do not just follow what we have said, but learn the best advice of the poets

---

[11] Heracles was the most important of the Greek heroes. He was rewarded at the end of his life by being granted a home on Mt. Olympus. Tantalus was at first blessed by being a favorite of the gods, but he tested their omniscience by serving them his own son, Pelops, to eat at a banquet. This crime became representative of the worst sort of evil a person could commit, and Tantalus was condemned to perpetual suffering in the underworld (see Homer, *Odyssey* 11.581–590). Isocrates uses the same two figures in 5.144.

and read the other sophists, if they have said anything useful. [52] For just as we see the bee settling on all the plants, taking the best from each one, in this way those who desire an education must also leave nothing untried but must collect advice from everywhere. For through this discipline one may slowly overcome the failings of nature.

10. ENCOMIUM OF HELEN [1]

INTRODUCTION

An encomium is technically a speech of praise, but one can almost say that there are three speeches within this speech. The first is a critique of philosophers (1–15), the second is an encomium of Theseus, the Athenian national hero (16–38), and the third is the encomium of Helen herself (39–69). The beginning of the speech has much in common with *Against the Sophists* (13), but it is addressed not against the sophists, who were primarily instructors in public speaking, but at philosophers like Plato and the other followers of Socrates, who had largely abandoned public life for more purely theoretical pursuits. The work serves as an exhortation to them to embrace traditional culture (see 66). As Isocrates also reveals in the speech, it has been written ostensibly as a reaction to a misguided "encomium," which is actually an *apologia,* that is, a defense speech. Scholars today are almost unanimous in identifying that work as the extant *Encomium of Helen,* which is ascribed to Gorgias. [2]

The focus on Theseus has raised great interest. As the national hero of Athenian legend, Theseus was portrayed in varying ways, depending on the political outlook of the person doing the portrayal. Thus Isocrates' description of him, and especially of his political persona in 31–37, may reveal significant aspects of Isocrates' own political views.

---

[1] Although this is the title of the work that appears in our manuscripts, Aristotle, *Rhetoric* 3.14.1, refers to it simply as *Helen.*

[2] For English versions of this speech, see Gagarin and Woodruff 1995: 190–195, and Kennedy 1991: 283–288.

The dating of this speech has proved problematic. It is included here because we are using the Greek text of Mathieu and Brémond. They date the speech to ca. 390, about the same time as *Busiris* (11) and *Against the Sophists* (13). But the favorable light that the speech casts on the Spartans seems at odds with the fact that in 390 Athens and Sparta were at war. Compare section 63 in this speech with 11.19 – 20, where Isocrates' hostility to the Spartans is palpable. Most commentators thus date the speech to 370, after Sparta's military strength became less threatening.

Almost every generation in ancient Greek culture might be evaluated in terms of its understanding of Helen. For a recent survey, see Zagagi 1985 and Papillon 1996a; Austin 1994 is idiosyncratic but useful.

10. ENCOMIUM OF HELEN

[1] There are some who think it a great thing if they put forward an odd, paradoxical theme and can discuss it without giving offense. Some people have grown old denying that it is possible to say what is false, to contradict anything, or to compose two opposing speeches about the same subjects,[3] others maintaining that courage, wisdom, and a sense of justice[4] are all the same thing—that we have none of them by nature and that there is a single science (*epistēmē*) concerning all of them.[5] Still others spend their time in disputes that provide no benefit but can make trouble for their students.[6] [2] If I saw that this wasted effort in speeches had come about recently and that these

---

[3] This description probably refers to Antisthenes and his followers. He was a student of Socrates but became hostile to Plato. He believed in an austere form of happiness and had interests in language that are reflected here and by Aristotle, *Metaphysics* 1024b32–34. Later writers identified Antisthenes as the founder of the Cynic tradition.

[4] Greek has separate words for justice as an abstract concept (*to dikaion*) and the sense of justice (*dikaiosynē*) that a just person has.

[5] This description reflects a view of Plato; see, e.g., *Protagoras* 333b.

[6] This description fits another group of Socrates' followers, the Megarian school, which was founded by Euclides of Megara. They were well known for their "questionings," which others called eristic.

people were taking pride in the originality of their discoveries, I would
not be so amazed at them. But who is there now who is so behind in
learning that he does not know that Protagoras[7] and the sophists of
his time left us compositions such as these, as well as some that are
even more troublesome? [3] How would anyone top Gorgias,[8] who
dared to say that none of the things that are is, or Zeno,[9] who tried
to show that the same things are possible and again impossible, or
Melissus,[10] who put his hand to discovering demonstrations that the
things in nature, which are infinitely many in number, are altogether
one? [4] Nevertheless, although those people already demonstrated so
clearly that it is easy to contrive a false argument on any subject someone might put forward, these people still spend their time in this activity. They should throw away this hairsplitting, which pretends to
make refutations (*elenchoi*) in speech but which has long since been
refuted in action. They should pursue the truth, [5] educate their students about the affairs in which we act as citizens, and develop their
students' experience of these matters, with the consideration that it is
much better to conjecture reasonably about useful things than to have
precise knowledge of what is useless, and that to be a little ahead in
important matters is better than to excel in small matters that are no
help in life.

[6] But these people have no other concern than making money
from young people, and it is their philosophy,[11] which is directed to
disputation, that can do this. Without a thought for private or public

---

[7] Protagoras of Abdera (ca. 490–420) was the most celebrated of the sophists.
See Gagarin and Woodruff 1995: 173–189.

[8] Gorgias of Leontini (ca. 485–380), another influential sophist, is reputed to
have taught Isocrates. He wrote a work, *On Not Being,* the seriousness of which
has been much debated. See Gagarin and Woodruff 1995: 190–209.

[9] Zeno of Elea (fl. 475?) was a pupil of Parmenides. He raised several para-
doxes that are reported by Aristotle (*Physics* 6.9), who saw in him the founder of
dialectic.

[10] Melissus of Samos was the last of the "Eleatic" philosophers. As a general,
he defeated the Athenians in 441.

[11] Isocrates may be using the word ironically here. For him philosophy as such
should be directed to practical issues of citizenship rather than eristic argument.
Clearly, it was a contested term.

affairs, they delight most in arguments that find no use at all. [7] I certainly have great sympathy with the young people who hold this view—they tend toward excess and fantasy in everything. But those who pretend to teach them deserve criticism, because while they condemn those who deceive in private business dealings by using speeches unjustly, they themselves do something more terrible. Those people injure others, but these harm their own students most. [8] They have advanced the practice of lying so greatly that there are already some who, on seeing that these men profit from this practice, dare to write that the life of beggars and exiles is more enviable than that of other people,[12] and they offer as evidence of this that if their students have something to say about contemptible matters, they will easily be equipped to speak on admirable subjects.[13] [9] To me the most ridiculous thing of all is that they seek to persuade us through their speeches that they have knowledge of politics, when they could demonstrate this in the very field in which they claim to teach. Those who argue that they are intelligent and claim to be sophists[14] ought to surpass and be superior to private citizens not on subjects that have been ignored by others but on those over which everyone competes! [10] But as it is now they are acting like someone who pretends to be the best athlete but enters an arena where no one else cares to compete. What intelligent person would try to praise misfortune? They clearly take refuge there because of their weakness. [11] There is only one method (*hodos*)[15] for such compositions, which it is not difficult to discover, to learn, or to imitate. But speeches of general import and credibility and the like are devised and spoken through many forms (*ideai*) and

---

[12] These are the sorts of paradoxical arguments that were advanced by Polycrates, to whom *Busiris* is addressed.

[13] This is an instance of the common criticism against the sophists that they attempt to make the weaker argument the stronger.

[14] Here Isocrates refers to the original sense of the word *sophistēs* as "seer" or "expert" rather than the technical sense that became common in the fifth century, when the word was applied to the itinerant teachers whom we now refer to as sophists. See Introduction to Isocrates.

[15] Our word "method" is formed from the Greek *hodos* (lit. "road, way") combined with the prefix *meta* ("with"). See Arist., *Rhetoric* 1.1 1354a8.

circumstances (*kairoi*) that are difficult to learn.[16] Matching them[17] is more difficult—just as being solemn is more difficult than making jokes, and being serious is more demanding than play. [12] The greatest indication (*sēmeion*) of this is that no one wanting to praise bumblebees and salt[18] has ever been at a loss for words, but those who have attempted to discuss subjects that are commonly agreed to be good or noble or excelling in *aretē*[19] have all fallen short of the possibilities when they have spoken. [13] It is not characteristic of the same intelligence to speak worthily about both kinds of subjects. It is easy to exaggerate the former, insignificant subjects in speeches, but it is difficult to match the importance of the others. It is rare to discover something that no one has said before about well-known subjects, but about base and insignificant matters, whatever one happens to say is entirely his own.

[14] Therefore, among those who have desired to say something well, I praise especially the man[20] who has written about Helen because he has recalled a woman of such quality, who was greatly superior in her birth, beauty, and reputation. However, a small point escaped him. He says that he has written an encomium about her, but he has actually spoken a defense (*apologia*) for what she did.[21] [15] His argument is not drawn from the same forms (*ideai*) nor is it about the same subject matter as an encomium. It is entirely the opposite. It is fitting to make a defense for those who have been accused of injustice, but one praises those who excel in some good.

---

[16] Isocrates uses the same terms in 13.16.

[17] I.e., matching the forms to the circumstances.

[18] See Plato, *Symposium* 177b.

[19] Isocrates clearly has a conception of "epideictic" (display) speeches that anticipates that of Aristotle (cf. *Rhetoric* 1.3 1358b1–7), in which speeches of praise do not require a judgment from the listener since they are already "commonly agreed." As in Aristotle's scheme, Isocrates' speeches of praise also focus on *aretē*.

[20] Gorgias, presumably. It is odd that he has named Gorgias in 3 but fails to do so here.

[21] As in 1.5, Isocrates makes a point of defining the genre of his speech. He continues here to prefigure Aristotle's distinction between forensic and epideictic speeches. See above, 12n.

In order to avoid the appearance of doing what is easy, criticizing others while making no point of my own, I shall try to speak about the same woman, leaving aside everything that others have said. [16] I shall make the beginning of her family the beginning of my speech. Of the many demigods sired by Zeus, he was proud to be called father of this woman alone. Although he had taken special interest in the son of Alcmene (Heracles) and the sons of Leda (Castor and Pollux), he honored Helen so much more than Heracles that although he gave him strength, which can overcome others by force, he endowed her with beauty, which naturally rules even might itself. [17] Since he knew that distinction and brilliance arise not from peace but from wars and struggles, and wanted not only to raise them physically to the level of the gods [22] but to give them everlasting renown, he made Heracles' life onerous and dangerous, but he gave her a nature that was admired and fought over.

[18] First there was Theseus, who was said to be Aegeus' son but was in fact Poseidon's. [23] On seeing her, not yet at her peak but already surpassing the others, he who was accustomed to conquering others was so overwhelmed by her beauty that despite his great homeland [Athens] and secure kingship, he thought life was not worth living, even with the good things he already had, without intimacy with her. [19] Since he could not obtain her from her parents—they were awaiting the girl's adulthood and the oracle of the Pythian priestess [24]—he ignored the empire of Tyndareus (her father), scorned the might of Castor and Pollux (her brothers), and belittled all the terrors in Lacedaemon. He seized her by force and deposited her in Aphidna, in Attica. [25] [20] He had so much gratitude toward Pirithoüs for shar-

---

[22] In both myth and religion, Helen and Heracles became gods.

[23] Isocrates also discusses Theseus in 12.126–130, where he alludes to this narrative. Theseus' mother was Aethra, the daughter of Pittheus, the king of Troezen in the Argolid (see 19.22). In a version of his birth that is reported by Plutarch (*Theseus* 3), his father was Aegeus, the king of Athens, but Pausanias (2.33.1) reports the story of her seduction by Poseidon, to which Euripides, *Hippolytus* 887, also alludes.

[24] The famous oracle of Apollo at Delphi. Before making any momentous decision, Greeks of all periods tended to consult this oracle.

[25] Plut., *Theseus* 31, reports that Theseus' mother lived at Aphidna.

ing in her capture, that when Pirithoüs wanted to pursue the Maiden (*Korē*),[26] the daughter of Zeus and Demeter, and asked him to join in his descent into Hades, Theseus first advised him unsuccessfully to turn back, since their coming misfortune was clear,[27] but nevertheless he accompanied him in the belief that he owed him this gift (*eranos*),[28] not to decline any request of Pirithoüs, in return for the dangers that that man had shared with him.

[21] If the person who did these things had been average and not really distinguished, it would not yet be clear whether my speech is in praise of Helen or a prosecution of Theseus.[29] But as it is, although we shall find that other famous people lack something—the one courage, another wisdom, another some other share of virtue—this person alone was in need of nothing: he had achieved complete virtue (*aretē*).

[22] It seems appropriate to me to speak somewhat more about Theseus. For those who wish to praise Helen, I think that the strongest basis for argument (*pistis*) will be if we can demonstrate that those who loved and admired her were themselves more admirable than the rest. It is reasonable that we judge events in our own time according to our own opinions (*doxai*), but for events that are so ancient, it is fitting that we show ourselves to be like-minded with the intelligent people of that time.

[23] The finest thing I can say about Theseus is that although he was born during the same time as Heracles, he gained a reputation that rivaled that man's. Not only did they equip themselves with similar weapons, they adopted the same habits by performing actions that suited their birth. They were begotten by brothers, the one from Zeus, the other from Poseidon, and they had related ambitions.[30] Among

---

[26] Persephone, who lived in Hades.

[27] They were seized in the underworld, and Theseus had to be rescued by Heracles.

[28] An *eranos* is a gift that implies the existence of responsibilities for mutual support that are outside those inherent in, for instance, family relationships.

[29] Plut., *Theseus* 31, reports that some writers cited this incident as one of the most serious charges against Theseus.

[30] Isocrates makes a play on words here. Literally he says, "begotten from brothers . . . they also had ambitions that were sisters," the Greek word for ambition, *epithymia*, being feminine.

past generations they alone made themselves champions for human life. [24] It happened that Heracles undertook dangers that were more renowned and greater, but those of Theseus were more useful, especially for the Greeks. Eurystheus[31] ordered Heracles to fetch the cattle of Eurythea, to get the apples of the Hesperides, to bring Cerberus up from Hades, and to perform other such tasks, which would not benefit others and would be dangerous for him alone.[32] [25] Theseus was his own master, and he chose these struggles in order to become the benefactor of the Greeks as much as of his homeland. By single-handedly defeating the bull that was sent by Poseidon,[33] which was laying waste the land and which none dared to resist, Theseus freed the inhabitants of the city from great fear and distress. [26] After this he allied himself to the Lapiths and fought against the two-natured Centaurs, who excelled in speed, might, and daring and who were sacking, were about to sack, or threatened to sack city after city. He conquered them in battle and immediately put a stop to their violence. Not much later he eliminated their race from human contact. [27] At about the same time, the monster[34] was reared in Crete, born of Pasiphaë the daughter of the Sun (*Hēlios*); by the oracle's command the city was sending it twice seven youths as tribute. When Theseus saw them being led off, escorted by the entire populace to a lawless death—yet one foreseen, so that they were mourned while still living—he was so upset that he thought it would be better to die than to live and rule a city that was compelled to pay such a sorrowful tribute to its enemies. [28] He joined the sailing and conquered a nature that combined man and bull and had the strength to fit such a physical combination. He returned the youths safely to their parents and liberated the city from so lawless, terrible, and inescapable an injunction.

---

[31] Eurystheus was Heracles' cousin, for whom he had to perform labors in order to gain expiation for having killed his own wife and children.

[32] The more commonly held view is that Heracles' labors deal generally with the domestication of animals, like cattle and dogs, the word for apple, *mēlon*, having been confused with that for sheep early in the mythical tradition. This was surely a benefit for humans.

[33] The Bull of Marathon. It was the sire of the Minotaur and had been brought to Attica by Heracles. Theseus sacrificed it to Apollo.

[34] The Minotaur.

[29] I am at a loss what use to make of the rest of the story. Having embarked on the works of Theseus and begun to speak about them, I hesitate to stop now and leave aside the lawlessness of Sciron and Cercyon[35] and the other criminals Theseus challenged as he freed the Greeks from many great misfortunes. I see myself being carried beyond the circumstances (*kairoi*) of this speech and fear that some may think that I am more serious about Theseus than I am about Helen, with whom I began. [30] For these two reasons I have decided to leave aside most of it, because of those who are listening restlessly, and to recount the rest as succinctly as I can so that I may please both them and myself and not surrender to those who are regularly jealous and criticize everything that is said.

[31] Theseus displayed his courage in these actions, in which he faced dangers by himself. He also displayed military knowledge in battles that he fought with the whole city at his side. He displayed piety toward the gods when Adrastus[36] and the children of Heracles were suppliants:[37] he rescued the children of Heracles by defeating the Peloponnesians in battle, and despite the Thebans he delivered to Adrastus for burial those who had met their end under the Cadmeia.[38] He displayed the other aspects of his virtue and soundness of mind in the actions I noted before and especially in his management of the city. [32] He saw that those who seek to rule the citizens by force become slaves to others and that those who put others' lives in danger live in fear themselves. They are compelled to wage war with citizens against outside invaders, and with outsiders against fellow citi-

---

[35] Sciron was a bandit from Megara who compelled travelers to wash his feet before he kicked them over a cliff, where they were eaten by a huge turtle. Cercyon was a wrestler at Eleusis who compelled all visitors to wrestle to the death with him. Theseus beat both at their own game. These were two of Theseus' canonical six labors, which he is usually said to have performed while on his way from his birthplace in Troezen to Athens.

[36] Adrastus was the only survivor of a disastrous campaign to restore his son-in-law, Polynices, one of the sons of Oedipus, to the throne of Thebes. Isocrates treats the story in more detail in 12.168–171.

[37] After Heracles' death, his cousin Eurystheus, for whom he had performed his labors, persecuted his children, who fled to Athens for refuge. See 4.56.

[38] The Cadmeia was the citadel of Thebes; it was named for the city's founder, Cadmus, who is mentioned in 68, below.

zens. [33] They pillage the temples of the gods and kill the best of the citizens. They distrust their closest friends, living no more at ease than those sentenced to death. They are envied for their external advantages, but within themselves they suffer more than any others. [34] What is more painful than to live in constant fear that someone close by may kill you, to fear your guards as much as any conspirators?

Theseus scorned all these things in the belief that such people were not rulers but diseases over their cities. He demonstrated that it is easy at the same time both to rule (*tyrannein*) and to be no worse off than those practicing politics on the basis of equality.³⁹ [35] First, he brought together the city, which had been sporadically organized into villages, into the same political unit and made it so great that from that time to this it is the greatest in Greece.⁴⁰ After this, after he had established a common nation and liberated the citizen's lives, he established for them an equitable rivalry, based on merit (*aretē*).⁴¹ He trusted that he would surpass them whether they practiced this competition or disregarded it, but he knew that honors bestowed by high-minded people are more pleasant than those from slaves. [36] Far from doing anything against the citizens' wishes, he made the people (*dēmos*) master of the state, and they in turn decided that only he was worthy to rule. They thought that his monarchy was more trustworthy and beneficial to the common good than their democracy. He did not act like other rulers, who impose tasks on others while enjoying pleasures by themselves alone. He made the dangers his private affair and handed over the benefits to all in common. [37] Indeed, he passed his life not as a target for conspiracy but as an object of love, protecting his rule not through imported power but guarded by the spears of his citizens' goodwill.⁴² His authority was that of a king (*tyrannos*), but his good deeds made him a leader of the people (*dēmagōgos*). He man-

---

³⁹ Isocrates shows his political stripes here. He sees no conflict between having a single ruler and equality.

⁴⁰ This is the famous *synoikismos*, or unification of all of the communities in Attica under Athens, which was attributed in legend to Theseus.

⁴¹ We would call this simply an election, where the best person for office is chosen. Later, as a democracy, Athens selected most of its officials through a random lottery, which Isocrates is implicitly rejecting.

⁴² This awkwardly translated metaphor refers to the Greek commonplace that tyrants needed the protection of bodyguards, called spear-carriers (*doryphoroi*).

aged the city so lawfully and nobly that even now a trace of Theseus' mildness remains in our customs.

[38] Now the daughter of Zeus who conquered such virtue and soundness of mind—how can we not praise her, honor her, and believe her to have excelled over all who have ever lived? We cannot produce a more credible witness—or a more competent judge—of Helen's good qualities than the insight of Theseus. However, in order that I not seem to be dwelling on the same topic because of a lack of material, exploiting the opinion[43] of a single man to praise her, I wish to continue with the subsequent events.

[39] After Theseus' descent into Hades, when she had returned to Lacedaemon and reached the age of marriage, all the kings and sovereigns of the time had the same thought about her. They could have taken first-rate women in their own cities, but they scorned marriages at home and came to court her. [40] Before it was decided who would marry her and the chances were still equal, it was already clear to all that she would be the object of armed struggle. So they came together and gave each other pledges to give assistance if anyone should take her from the man found worthy of receiving her. Each thought he was providing himself with this protection. [41] It is true that in their individual hopes all but one were deceived, but none of them was mistaken in the common opinion they had of her. Not much later, there was a dispute among the goddesses over beauty, and Priam's son Alexander[44] was made judge. Hera offered him kingship over all Asia, and Athena offered military dominance, [42] but Aphrodite offered marriage to Helen. Overwhelmed by the sight of the goddesses and unable to make a determination concerning their physical appearance, Alexander was compelled to become judge only of their gifts, and he chose intimacy[45] with Helen before all the others. He did not focus on pleasure. Although pleasure is preferred over many things even by the intelligent, it did not stimulate him to this. [43] Rather, he desired to become Zeus' son-in-law in the belief that this was a much greater and finer honor than the kingdom of Asia. Even base men sometimes achieve great empires and dynasties, but no one in the future would

---

[43] The word for "opinion," *doxa,* could also mean "glory" or "reputation."

[44] He is also called Paris.

[45] Isocrates uses exactly the same word, *oikeiotēs,* as he used describing Theseus' desire for Helen (see above, 18).

be deemed worthy of such a woman. Moreover, he could leave his children no more noble a possession than to achieve for them that they would be descended from Zeus not only on their father's side[46] but also on their mother's. [44] He knew that other kinds of good fortune quickly disappear, but noble birth remains in the same family forever, so this choice would be for his entire family, but the other gifts would be only for his own time.[47]

[45] No intelligent person would find fault with this reasoning, but some have vilified him who have given no thought to what happened beforehand but have looked only at the result. It is easy for all to realize the ignorance out of which they utter these blasphemies concerning him. [46] Haven't they become laughable if they think that their own natural ability is more competent than that of a person selected by the gods? Surely the gods did not put an ordinary person in charge of determining a matter over which they found themselves in such great dispute. They clearly picked the best judge with as much seriousness as they had concern for the matter itself.[48] [47] We must examine what sort of man he was and judge him, not by the anger of those who lost out, but from the reasons all the goddesses had, when after deliberation they chose his insight. Nothing prevents even the innocent from suffering badly at the hands of the more powerful, but a mortal who has won the honor of becoming a judge of gods must be a person of outstanding intelligence. [48] I would be amazed if someone thought that he planned badly in choosing to live with her for whose sake many demigods were willing to die.[49] When he knew that the gods were quarreling over beauty, wouldn't he have been foolish to despise it himself, not to believe it the greatest of gifts when he saw that the goddesses were so serious about it?

[49] Who would have scorned marriage to Helen? When she was kidnapped the Greeks were just as upset as if all Greece had been

---

[46] Alexander could trace his ancestry to Zeus by going back seven generations.

[47] Helen and Alexander had no children. We may wonder whether Isocrates' readers are meant to reflect on this irony. At any rate, Isocrates' emphasis on Alexander successfully deflects interest away from the issue of Helen's culpability.

[48] The contest was over the goddesses' beauty, yet Isocrates has just said that Alexander was unable to judge this issue. See above, 42.

[49] Many of the heroes at Troy had divine parents. See below, 52.

pillaged, and the foreigners[50] were as proud as if they had conquered us all. It is clear how they both felt: although the Greeks had many complaints earlier about other matters, they remained peaceful, but over her they waged a war that was greater, not only in the magnitude of its passion, but also in its length and the extent of its preparations, than there had ever been before. [50] Although the one side could have returned Helen and been free of the troubles, and the other could have forgotten about her and lived securely for the rest of time,[51] neither was willing to do this. The Trojans saw their cities razed and their land pillaged in order not to hand her over to the Greeks. The Greeks chose to stay, growing old in a foreign land, never to see their families again, rather than leave her behind and return to their homelands. [51] They did this not because they were fighting for Alexander or Menelaus but for Asia and Europe. They thought that whichever land she physically inhabited would be the more prosperous.

[52] So great a longing (*erōs*) for the toils of that campaign befell not only the Greeks and foreigners, but also the gods, that they did not divert their mortal offspring from the struggles at Troy. Zeus knew the fate of Sarpedon,[52] Eos that of Memnon,[53] Poseidon that of Cycnus,[54] and Thetis that of Achilles. Nevertheless they encouraged them and sent them forth. [53] They thought that it was nobler for them to die fighting for the daughter of Zeus than to live and not face dangers on her account. Why should it be surprising that they thought this way about their children? They themselves had waged a much

---

[50] These are the *barbaroi*, non-Greeks. In classical times the *barbaroi* are almost invariably the Persians or other non-Greeks living under Persian rule. The traditional translation, "barbarian," is misleading. Although the Greeks were ethnically chauvinistic, they did not assume that non-Greeks were necessarily, or even likely, to be uncivilized or barbarian.

[51] In 67, below, Isocrates will say that Helen was responsible for Greece's not being enslaved, which seems to contradict what he says here.

[52] Sarpedon, a son of Zeus, was a leader of the Lycians who fought alongside the Trojans. His death at the hands of Patroclus is related in *Iliad* 16, where it is recognized that Zeus might have had the power to prevent it.

[53] Memnon was king of Ethiopia and the son of Eos (Dawn) and Tithonus. He was killed by Achilles.

[54] Cycnus was also killed by Achilles.

greater and more terrible battle, when they fought against the Giants.[55] Against them they fought together, but over Helen they waged war against each other.

[54] The gods thought this way quite reasonably, and I could use many superlatives about her. She had the most beauty, which is the most venerated, most honored, and most divine quality in the world. It is easy to understand its power: many things that lack courage or wisdom or a sense of justice may appear more honored than any of these qualities alone, but we will not find anything loved that has been stripped of beauty; everything is despised unless it has gained a share of this aspect (*idea*), and virtue is especially esteemed because it is the most beautiful of qualities. [55] One may also understand how much beauty excels over other things in the world from our attitudes toward each of them. We wish to obtain other things only if we need them, but spiritually we experience no further concern over them. A longing for beautiful things, however, is innate in us, and it has a strength greater than our other wishes, just as its object is stronger. [56] We distrust those who are foremost in intelligence or anything else, unless they win us over by treating us well every day and compelling us to like them. But we have goodwill toward beautiful people as soon as we see them, and we serve only them without fail, as if they were gods. [57] We enslave ourselves to such people with more pleasure than we rule others, and we have more gratitude to them, even when they impose many tasks on us, than to those who demand nothing. We criticize those who come under any other power and denounce them as flatterers, but we think that those who serve beauty are idealistic and industrious. [58] We feel such reverence and concern for this sort of quality that we disenfranchise those with beauty who have prostituted it and abused their own youth more than those who wrong the bodies of others.[56] Those who guard their youth undefiled by base

---

[55] Despite references to the Giants in Hesiod, *Theogony* 183–185, and Homer, *Odyssey* 7.59, there was no canonical account of the battle of the gods and giants, known as the Gigantomachy, before Apollodorus (1.6.1) and Ovid, *Metamorphoses* 1.151–162.

[56] It was illegal for Athenian citizens to prostitute themselves and then continue to perform as citizens by, e.g., speaking in the Assembly. The relevant laws are discussed in Aes. 1. *Against Timarchus.*

men, as if it were a temple, we honor for the rest of time as if they had done something good for the entire city.

[59] Why spend my time discussing human opinions? Zeus, the most powerful of all, has displayed his power in other things, but he thinks it right to become humble as he approaches beauty. He took the form of Amphitryon when he came to Alcmene.[57] He joined Danaë as a golden shower.[58] He became a swan when he fled into the bosom of Nemesis[59] and again likened himself to one when he wed Leda. Clearly he always pursues this quality of nature with craft, not with violence. [60] Beauty is so much more preferred among the gods than among us that they even pardon their wives when they are overcome by it. One might point out many immortal wives who have been overcome by a mortal's beauty. None has sought to have the event pass unnoticed, as if it were something shameful. They have wanted what they did to be exalted in song as something noble, rather than concealed by silence.[60] The greatest evidence of what I have been saying is that we would find that more mortals have become immortal because of their beauty than because of all other qualities (*aretai*).[61]

[61] Helen achieved more than other mortals just as she excelled

external
beauty
equals
back to internal
beauty

---

[57] Alcmene was the mother of Heracles; Amphitryon was her husband.

[58] Danaë was the mother of Perseus, the Gorgon slayer.

[59] In one version of the story of Helen, Zeus impregnated Nemesis, who laid an egg, which was then hatched by Leda, but this version would hardly flatter Helen, so it seems unlikely that Isocrates is alluding to it here, especially since he also mentions Zeus approaching Leda. In 16, above, however, he refers to Leda only as the mother of Castor and Pollux.

[60] The most famous story of a goddess overcome by desire for a mortal is that of Aphrodite, who falls in love with the Trojan prince Anchises. Their encounter is amusingly related in the *Homeric Hymn to Aphrodite,* in which Aphrodite herself also tells the story of Eos' love for Tithonus. Aphrodite's love for Adonis, the nymph Salmacis' love for Hermaphroditus, Demeter's affair with Iasion, and Echo's love for Narcissus might also be cited, but in fact none of these is characterized during their infatuations as anyone's wife. It is unclear whether Isocrates is being ironic or just sloppy.

[61] Besides Helen, only the Trojan prince Ganymede achieved widespread renown in antiquity for becoming immortal because of his beauty. Zeus took a liking to him and carried him to Olympus to serve as cupbearer for the gods.

over them in appearance. Not only did she win immortality, but she also gained power equal to the gods'. First, she brought her brothers into the company of the gods, although they had already been seized by fate, and, since she wished to make their transformation credible, she bestowed such conspicuous honors on them that when they are seen by those endangered at sea they rescue whoever reverently appeals to them.[62] [62] After this, she returned such gratitude to Menelaus for the hard work and dangers that he encountered for her sake that although the entire family of Pelopidae was destroyed,[63] the victims of irrevocable mishaps, not only did she preserve him from these misfortunes, but she made him a god instead of a mortal and established him as her companion and a partner on her throne for all time.[64] [63] I can also produce the city of Sparta, which gives active witness to these events by preserving her ancient rites prominently. Even now at Laconian Therapne they perform a traditional, holy sacrifice to both of them, not as heroes but as gods.[65]

[64] She also displayed her power to the poet Stesichorus:[66] when he began his ode by maligning her somehow, he arose deprived of his eyesight, but when he realized the cause of his misfortune, he composed what is called his *Palinode* (*Recantation*), and she restored his original physical ability. [65] Some of the Homeridae[67] claim that she

---

[62] After their death, Castor and Pollux became stars, the constellation Gemini. They were also associated with the phenomenon known as St. Elmo's fire.

[63] Isocrates must be thinking of Thyestes, Atreus, and Agamemnon, who all suffered miserably as a result of family jealousies. Pelops' son Atreus killed the children of his brother Thyestes and served them to him for dinner. Thyestes in turn cursed Atreus' family, and in time Atreus' son Agamemnon, the brother of Menelaus, was murdered by his own wife. However, not all the other Pelopidae were destroyed: Agamemnon's son Orestes, after avenging his father, also survived.

[64] Homer (*Odyssey* 4.561–570) sees Menelaus honored by the gods at the end of his life by being sent to the Field of Elysium. He says explicitly, however, that this is because Menelaus has Helen as his wife and is Zeus' son-in-law.

[65] This was the shrine of Helen and Menelaus known as the Menelaion, about 2.5 kilometers (1.5 miles) southeast of Sparta overlooking the Eurotas river. See Herod. 6.61 and Pausanias 3.19.9.

[66] A Greek lyric poet who was active about 600–550. The story of his palinode is also recalled in Plato's *Phaedrus* 243a.

[67] An early guild of rhapsodes devoted to reciting the poetry of Homer.

stood over Homer at night and directed him to write about those who had campaigned against Troy. She wanted to make their death more enviable than the life of others. They claim that Homer's poem has become so alluring and renowned among all in part because of his skill (*technē*), but most of all because of her.

[66] Inasmuch as she can both punish and reward, those privileged with wealth must propitiate and honor her with offerings, sacrifices, and other petitions, and philosophers must attempt to say something about her worthy of her attributes. It is fitting for the educated to make this sort of offering.[68]

[67] What I have left out is far more than what has been said. Aside from arts (*technai*) and philosophy and the other benefits that might be attributed to her and to the Trojan War, we may justly believe that Helen is the reason we are not enslaved to the foreigners. We shall discover that the Greeks formed a common mind and created a shared military force against the foreigners because of her, and that then for the first time Europe set up a trophy of victory over Asia. [68] As a result, we achieved such a transformation that while before her time foreigners who suffered misfortune could presume to rule Greek cities—Danaus seized Argos as an Egyptian exile,[69] Cadmus of Sidon reigned over Thebes,[70] the Carians settled the islands,[71] and Tantalus'

---

[68] Isocrates is clearly referring to his own work, but he is also urging other intellectuals to embrace traditional, panhellenic mythology in this way.

[69] Danaus was the brother of Aegyptus and king of Libya before fleeing from Africa to protect his fifty daughters from his brother's plan to marry them to his fifty sons. He settled in the Argolid, where he was eventually induced to allow the marriages but had his daughters kill their husbands on their wedding night. (See Aeschylus' *Suppliants*.) In Homer, the "Greeks" are often referred to as Danaäns after him.

[70] Cadmus came from Sidon in Phoenicia in search of his sister Europa, who had been kidnapped by Zeus in the form of a bull. He went to the oracle at Delphi and was told there to abandon his search and establish a city, which in time became Thebes, whose citadel was called the Cadmeia (see above, 31).

[71] Unlike the other people Isocrates mentions here, there are no significant myths associated with the Carian occupation of the Aegean islands. In fact, as Thucydides points out (1.4, 1.8), the Carians inhabited the islands before the Greeks and were driven out by them, settling in the southwestern area of Asia Minor.

son Pelops conquered the entire Peloponnesus[72]—after this war our nation made such progress that we took even great cities and much land away from the foreigners. [69] If, then, some people wish to elaborate this material and expand on it, they will not lack material to stimulate their praise of Helen beyond what I have said, but they will find many original arguments to make about her.

---

[72] Pelops came from Lydia, also in Asia Minor; the southern peninsula of Greece is called the Peloponnesus ("island of Pelops") after him (see above, 62).

11. BUSIRIS

INTRODUCTION

This speech has much in common with *Encomium of Helen* (10): besides both being epideictic speeches, they both lack any specific occasion, they both take on "unpopular" themes, and they both claim to be improvements on attempts made by others. But in Isocrates' mind they may also have differed significantly: he appears to take the *Encomium of Helen* very seriously throughout, but he admits in section 9 of the *Busiris* that the theme of this speech is not serious. The *Busiris* may also be much earlier; it is commonly dated to 391–385.

The speech is addressed to Polycrates (ca. 440–370), an Athenian living on Cyprus who became famous for his *Prosecution of Socrates* (cf. 4), against which the surviving defenses by Plato and Xenophon are said to have been written. He thus embraced a genre of paradoxical writing, in which the sophist might show off his dexterity by arguing unpopular causes. He is also said to have written an encomium of Clytemnestra, who is otherwise vilified for having murdered her husband Agamemnon. We know nothing about his defense of Busiris beyond what can be inferred from this speech.

Busiris was a king from Egypt's legendary past, and Isocrates takes him in some ways as a composite for Egyptian culture. The historian Herodotus (2.45) reports the tradition that Egyptians slaughtered foreigners entering Egypt and that they were killed by Heracles in turn, but he does not mention a king. Busiris' name does come out, however, in the versions told later by Apollodorus (2.5.11) and Ovid (*Ars amatoria* 1.647–652). The name is a Greek corruption of the Egyptian Bu-Osiris, meaning "the place of Osiris," that is, a temple dedicated to the Egyptian judge of the dead. Heracles' overcoming him is therefore an instance of the hero triumphing over death. But these details are deeply submerged before Isocrates takes up the story. Human sacrifice was abhorrent to the Greeks, even in their myths (like that of Iphigenia), and cannibalism was beyond the pale. This speech is especially interesting in revealing what Greeks generally thought of Egyptian civilization, both good and bad, and what Isocrates thought of the use that might be made of myth (or legend) and history.

II. BUSIRIS

[1] I learned from others of your fair-mindedness, Polycrates, and of the reversal in your life.[1] I have read some of the speeches you wrote, and I would have been most pleased to discuss frankly with you the entire program of education with which you are compelled to spend your time. I think that it is fitting for everyone who has been practicing philosophy longer and who knows it in more detail to be willing to offer this contribution (*eranos*)[2] to those who are suffering misfortune unjustifiably and so are seeking to earn a living from philosophy. [2] Since we have not yet met each other, if we ever happen to be in the same place in the future, we shall be able to converse at greater length about other matters, but for now, I thought I should relate to you by letter these matters in which I may be of service to you, while concealing them as much as possible from others.[3] [3] I am aware that most people who are admonished naturally regard it as no help but listen to what is said with reluctance to the extent that anyone examines their mistakes in detail. Nevertheless, those with goodwill toward people must not recoil from this hostility but should try to change the view of those who feel this way about those who give them advice.[4]

---

[1] Fair-mindedness (*epieikeia*) is one of Isocrates' central values. By saying this to Polycrates, he is indicating that he thinks Polycrates is worthy of being taught (cf. 13.21). We do not know what reversal Polycrates had suffered.

[2] On *eranos*, see 10.20n.

[3] Isocrates clearly kept a copy of his letter for himself, which made its way eventually into wider circulation.

[4] Views about unsolicited advice are unlikely to differ much now from antiquity. This opening should probably be read as largely ironic: Isocrates' "goodwill" masks what is essentially a polemic.

[4] Since I have noticed that you boast no small amount about your *Defense of Busiris* and *Prosecution of Socrates,* I will try to make clear to you that you really missed what is needed in both speeches. Everyone knows that those who want to eulogize people must point out more good attributes than they actually have, and those who want to prosecute them must do the opposite.[5] [5] You are so far from employing your speeches in this way that although you claim to be defending Busiris, you have not only not freed him from the defamation that he is already facing, but you have even implicated him in such enormous crimes that no one could invent any more terrible. Others who have attempted to malign him have only slandered him for sacrificing the strangers that visited him. You even accuse him of cannibalism. And when you attempted to accuse Socrates, you gave him Alcibiades as a student as if you wanted to make that a point of praise. No one had noticed that Alcibiades had been taught by Socrates, although all would agree that he was a really outstanding Greek.[6] [6] You know that if the dead could advise those who are talking about them, Socrates would be as grateful to you for your accusation as he is to any of those who normally praise him, but Busiris, even if he were very mild toward others, would still be so incensed by what you said that he would stop at nothing to get revenge. Isn't it more a matter for shame than self-respect to be liked more by those you have maligned than by those you have praised? [7] You have been so careless about avoiding contradiction that you say that Busiris aspired to the renown of Aeolus and Orpheus,[7] but you have not shown that he had any of the same

---

[5] Isocrates does not yet follow the scheme that Aristotle (*Rhetoric* 1.3) would make canonical, in which eulogy is contrasted not with prosecution (*katēgoria*) but with blame (*psogos*). In fact, Aristotle's scheme is probably artificial, there being no occasion for a speech of blame that corresponded with the funeral oration or oration at an athletic festival, where speeches of praise were delivered.

[6] Isoc. 16, a speech to be delivered by the younger Alcibiades, is largely devoted to praise of his father, the older Alcibiades referred to here. In Plato's *Symposium,* the relationship between Socrates and Alcibiades is made the object of an amusing description by Alcibiades. Alcibiades was one of the most controversial figures in Athenian history; many would disagree with Isocrates' opinion.

[7] Aeolus tried to help Odysseus return to Ithaca (Homer, *Odyssey* 10.17–27). Orpheus led his wife, Eurydice, up from Hades, though she had to return when he looked back at her at the last minute.

behavior that they did. In what respects would we put him beside what has been said about Aeolus? Aeolus sent strangers back to their homelands who had been shipwrecked on his land, but Busiris sacrificed and ate them, if we are to believe what you said. [8] Or should we compare his to Orpheus' deeds? Orpheus led the dead out of Hades, but Busiris destroyed the living before their appointed time. So I would be glad to know what Busiris would have done if he had actually despised them, since in admiration of their virtue he appears to have accomplished entirely the opposite. The oddest thing of all is that although you have taken genealogy seriously, you have dared to say that he aspired to be like those figures, whose fathers had not yet even been born.[8]

[9] In order that I do not appear to be doing what is easiest by attacking what you have said without presenting anything of my own, I will try to clarify my point for you briefly on the same theme[9] although it is not a serious one and calls for no exalted language, from which both praise and defense must be composed.

[10] Who could not speak easily about Busiris' noble family? His father was Poseidon, his mother Libya,[10] the daughter of Zeus' son Epaphus.[11] They say she was the first woman to become queen in a land named for herself. Despite the good fortune of having such ancestors, Busiris had no pride in these things alone but thought he should leave behind a memorial of his own excellence (arete) for all time.[12]

---

[8] The chronology of Greek mythology is notoriously confused. Nevertheless, according to Apollodorus, Busiris was killed by Heracles, who lived before the events of the *Odyssey*. Like Heracles, Orpheus belongs to the generation of the Argonauts. See below, 36–37.

[9] The same formula appears in 10.15.

[10] Libya is usually said to have been the mother not of Busiris but of Belus and Agenor, the kings of Tyre and Egypt. Apollodorus makes Busiris the son of Lysianassa, also a daughter of Epaphus.

[11] Epaphus was the son of Io, whom Zeus had turned into a cow in order to conceal his affair with her. According to Aeschylus, *Prometheus Bound* 850–851, he was born in Egypt after she was returned to mortal form.

[12] According to Aristotle (*Rhetoric* 1.3), the principal subject of a speech of praise is a person's *arete*. Along these lines, Isocrates has here signaled the purpose of his speech very clearly.

[11] He looked down on his mother's empire in the belief that it did not measure up to his own natural ability. After overpowering many peoples and acquiring a very large dominion, he established his kingdom in Egypt. He selected it as the outstanding place to live, not only of places he held then but of all places.[13] [12] He saw that the other places were neither conveniently nor happily situated by nature: some were overwhelmed by storms; others were destroyed by heat waves. But this land was set in the most beautiful area of the world, was able to provide a great many and a great variety of goods, and was fortified by the immortal wall of the Nile, [13] which itself provided not only a natural defense but also sufficient food. It was impregnable and difficult for enemies even to attack, yet it was easily navigable and useful in many ways for those living within it. In addition to what I said before, the Nile has given the Egyptians a godlike ability in agriculture. For while Zeus dispenses storms and droughts to others, each Egyptian has made himself master of both of these. [14] They have achieved such an abundance that the excellence and natural capacity of their land and the size of their fields allow them to harvest a continent, but in their export of surpluses and the import of necessities, they inhabit an island, because of the power of the river. It surrounds their land in a circle and flows through much of it, giving them the richness of both island and continent.[14]

[15] In sum, Busiris began where intelligent people must by acquiring the most beautiful spot possible and by discovering sufficient food for those around him. After this, he divided the people up: some he put in charge of religious matters; others he directed to crafts; others he compelled to practice warfare.[15] He thought that necessities and surpluses must be gained from the land and from crafts, but the safest protection for these was the practice of warfare and religion. [16] After he had calculated all the numbers of people in order to manage best the common affairs, he directed that the same people should always practice the same occupations. He knew that those who change oc-

---

[13] Like other Greeks in his day, Isocrates identified Egypt with the Nile delta, which exported much grain.

[14] In a speech delivered by Pericles (Thuc. 1.143), a similar description of island and continent is applied to Athens. Isocrates may be recalling it.

[15] Plato, *Timaeus* 24a–b, saw a similar scheme coming from Egypt.

cupations do not master even one of the jobs in detail, but those who remain continuously in the same occupation do each one superbly. [17] In consequence, we shall find that with regard to skills, the Egyptians excel over others with the same expertise more than other tradespeople excel over the unskilled. And as for the arrangement by which they preserve their kingship and the rest of their state, they do so well that the philosophers who attempt to discuss such things and are most highly regarded choose to praise the Egyptian state, and the Spartans manage their city best when they imitate some part of the Egyptians' practice: [18] for example, their rule that no one fit for battle may leave the country without the permission of the authorities, their common meals, and their physical training. Beyond this, since they lack none of the necessities of life, they do not disregard the public directives, nor do they practice other crafts, but they put their minds to weapons and military expeditions. All these practices have been taken from Egypt. [19] The Spartans have made such bad use of these practices, however, that since they are all made into soldiers, they choose to seize others' possessions by force. But the Egyptians live as people should: they do not disregard their own affairs, but they do not covet others' property.[16] One can see the difference between the two states from this: [20] if we were all to imitate the laziness and greed of the Spartans, we would quickly be destroyed both by the lack of daily necessities and by civil war, but if we were willing to adopt the Egyptians' customs and decided that some should work and the others should protect their property, each group would satisfy its own needs and live a happy life.

[21] In addition, one may reasonably suppose that Busiris was responsible for the cultivation of practical wisdom (*phronēsis*). He furnished the priests a healthy endowment through the revenues that came from sacrifices, soundness of mind (*sōphrosynē*) through the purifications set out under the laws, and leisure (*scholē*)[17] through exemp-

---

[16]This is a statement of a central Greek value, minding your own business. The Athenians were proverbially accused of meddlesomeness (*polypragmosynē*), taking an interest in others' affairs. After the Peloponnesian War, Sparta also took on a domineering role over other cities. Isocrates' view is aristocratic, implying criticism of those who involve themselves habitually in public affairs.

[17]A better translation might be "free time," since the Greeks did not imagine by *scholē* the sort of leisure that we might devote to tanning ourselves beside a

tion from the dangers of war and other work. [22] Living under these conditions, the priests discovered medicine to aid their bodies by employing not dangerous drugs but only those that are as safe as their daily food, and so beneficial that the Egyptians are by common agreement the healthiest and longest living of peoples. For their souls they developed the discipline of philosophy, which has the ability both to form laws and to investigate the nature of reality. [23] Busiris put older men in charge of the most important matters and persuaded younger men to disregard pleasure and pass their time in astronomy, arithmetic, and geometry. Some praise the powers of these activities as useful for certain tasks, while others try to show that they contribute most to virtue.[18]

[24] It is especially worthwhile to praise and admire the piety of the Egyptians and their service to the gods. Those who dress themselves up more than is justified, pretending to have wisdom or any other virtue, do harm to those they deceive. But those who have been such effective leaders in religious matters that the rewards and punishments of the gods appear greater than they really are, these people benefit human life most. [25] Indeed, by instilling in us a fear of the gods from the beginning, they cause us not to act like beasts toward one another. The Egyptians are so holy and solemn about these matters that oaths sworn in their sanctuaries are more credible than those sworn by others, and each believes that he will immediately pay the penalty for his transgressions. He will not escape detection for the present or defer his punishment to his children.

[26] They held these views with reason. Busiris established many different kinds of religious practice for them. He even enacted laws to revere and honor animals that are despised among us. He did not misjudge the animals' power, but he thought it necessary to accustom the crowd to abide by all the instructions of the magistrates, [27] and at the same time he wanted to test through visible means what conviction they had concerning invisible matters. He thought that those who made little of these things would perhaps despise greater ones also, but those who obeyed the rules in everything in the same way would demonstrate steadfast piety.

---

pool. As our cognate words "school" and "scholar" suggest, *scholē* for someone like Isocrates meant time to be devoted to study.

[18] Isocrates expresses similar views in 4.265 and 5.26–27.

[28] Someone without the impulse to hurry could go through many more admirable aspects of their holiness, which I am neither the only person nor the first to observe. Many people have done so now and in the past, including Pythagoras of Samos.[19] After he went to Egypt and became their student, he was the first to bring the rest of philosophy to the Greeks, but he was more clearly interested than others in their sacrificial rites and in the temple rituals. He thought that even if he got nothing more from the gods through these things, among men at least they would make him especially famous. [29] And this is what happened. He so exceeded others in fame that all the young desired to become his students, and older people were more pleased to see their children conversing with him than attending to their own affairs. We must believe this. Even now people admire those who claim to be his students more even when they are silent than those men who have the greatest reputation for speaking.[20]

[30] Perhaps you[21] will object to what I have said because I am praising the land, the laws, the piety, and even the philosophy of the Egyptians, but I cannot demonstrate that Busiris is their cause, although he is my subject. If someone else had responded in this way, I would have considered his criticism educated, but it is inappropriate for you to make this reproach.[22] [31] When you wanted to praise Busiris, you chose to say that he split the Nile apart to flow around his land and that he sacrificed and ate visiting foreigners, but you gave no reason to believe that he did these things. Now isn't it ridiculous that you are demanding from others what you do not provide even in the slightest? [32] You stray much further from credible speech than we do. I attribute to him nothing that is impossible, only laws and a constitution, which are the acts of good and noble men. But you make

---

[19] Pythagoras was one of the most influential figures in Greek philosophy, but he was also one of the most mysterious. He was born ca. 550 BC on the island of Samos and migrated to Croton in southern Italy. There he formed a society that was shrouded in secrecy but came to have many followers and did important work, especially in religion and mathematics.

[20] A reference to the secrecy of the Pythagoreans.

[21] Polycrates.

[22] It is common in lawcourt speeches to anticipate the opponent's arguments, but Isocrates' application of this technique here seems strained.

him the author of things no human would ever do: one is characteristic of the brutality of wild beasts, the other the work of divine power.
[33] Moreover, even if we are actually both speaking falsely, I have at
least employed those arguments that must be used when giving praise,
but yours suit those who malign, so you have clearly failed to provide
not only the truth of the matter but even the basic form (*idea*) that
praise requires.

[34] Besides this, if it were necessary to get free of your arguments
and investigate (*exetazein*)[23] mine, no one could justly assail them. If
someone else had clearly done what I claim happened because of Busiris, I would agree that I was extremely bold to attempt to change
people's views on matters everyone knows. [35] But as it is, since the
facts are open to interpretation and we can only speculate about them,
if we look at what is likely, who would suppose anyone more responsible for the institutions there than a son of Poseidon[24] who was
descended from Zeus on his mother's side? He acquired the greatest
power of anyone in his own time and became most renowned later.
Surely it is inappropriate for those who were inferior in every respect
to be recognized as authors of such great goods before he is.

[36] Indeed, it would be easy to show on chronological grounds
that the arguments of those who malign Busiris are false. They accuse him of murdering guests and say that he was killed by Heracles.
[37] But all writers agree that Heracles was four generations younger
than Perseus,[25] the son of Zeus and Danaë, and that Busiris was more
than two hundred years older than he.[26] Isn't it odd that someone who

---

[23] The rhetorical handbook that is known as the *Rhetorica ad Alexandrum* distinguishes investigative (exetastic) oratory as a distinct form of speech, which is
nevertheless used in all the other forms (*Rhet. ad Alex.* 5). Here Isocrates appears
to use the word "investigate" to mark off a part of his speech that will feature this
method.

[24] Theseus, the Athenian national hero, was also a son of Poseidon. See 10.18.

[25] The slayer of the Gorgon. His legend is the earliest of those of the Greek
heroes.

[26] In the *Prometheus Bound* (see above, 10n), there are supposed to be thirteen
generations between Io, who as Epaphus' mother should be Busiris' grandmother,
and Heracles, and six generations from her to Abas, the great grandfather of
Perseus.

wants to dispel this attack on him should leave aside this argument (*pistis*), which is so clear and powerful? [38] But the truth was of no concern to you. You followed the insults of the poets, who describe the offspring of the immortal gods doing and suffering more terrible things than the offspring of the most unholy humans. They have made the sort of statements about the gods that no one would dare make against his enemies.[27] They have not only reviled the gods for theft, adultery, and being slaves to humans, they have also told stories about their eating their children, castrating their fathers, tying up their mothers, and engaging in many other instances of lawlessness.[28] [39] The poets did not pay the penalty they deserved for these blasphemies, but they did not escape unpunished either. Some became wanderers begging for their daily needs; others were blinded. One fled his homeland and spent his life at war with his family.[29] Orpheus, who was especially associated with these stories, was killed by being torn apart.[30] [40] Therefore, if we are sensible, we will not imitate their stories. And when we make laws about defaming one another we will not make light of loose talk against the gods either. We will stay on guard and hold that those who say such things and those who believe them commit impiety equally.

[41] I believe that neither the gods nor their offspring share in evil. They have all the virtues by nature and have become leaders and teach-

---

[27] Isocrates' criticisms of the immorality attributed to the gods in traditional Greek mythology were anticipated by the sixth-century poet Xenophanes of Colophon (Gagarin and Woodruff 1995: 39). They were also shared by his contemporary Plato (see *Republic* 10). But whereas Xenophanes advocated rejecting mythology and Plato created whole new, sanitized myths, Isocrates reclaimed the traditional mythology and retold the stories in such a way that the gods' morality was restored.

[28] Hermes' theft of Apollo's cattle is portrayed in the *Homeric Hymn to Hermes*. The adulterous affair between Aphrodite and Ares appears in Homer, *Odyssey* 8.266–366. In Euripides' *Alcestis,* Apollo is said to have been enslaved to the mortal Admetus. In Hesiod's *Theogony,* Cronus castrates his father Uranus. Hephaestus confines his mother Hera, according to the poetry of Pindar and Alcaeus.

[29] Homer is often characterized as a blind wanderer. Isocrates himself reports the blinding of Stesichorus in 10.64. The exile may be Archilochus or Alcaeus.

[30] See Vergil, *Georgics* 4.

ers of the finest conduct for the rest of us. It is unreasonable to attribute the cause of our children's blessings to the gods but to believe that
they take no thought of their own. [42] If one of us were to suppose
himself master of human nature, he would not allow his slaves to be
depraved. Do we convict the gods of being so impious and lawless that
they ignored their own offspring? Polycrates, you think that you will
improve those with no relation to you if they attend your course, but
do you believe that the gods have no concern for the virtue of their
own children? [43] Indeed, according to your speech, don't they fail
in two most shameful ways? If they do not require their children to be
good, aren't their intentions worse than those of humans? And if they
want them to be good but don't know how to do it, don't they have
less power than the sophists?

[44] There are many things that someone might say to extend
Busiris' praise and defense, but I don't think I need to speak at great
length. I was not making a display (*epideixis*) for others, but I discussed these things because I wanted to show you how you should
handle each of them. The speech you composed is not a defense of
Busiris. Anyone would justly think it an admission of the charges.
[45] You do not free him from the accusations; you show that some
others also did the same things and thus invent a very easy excuse for
wrongdoers. It is not easy to discover an injustice that has never been
committed before, and if we believe that those who are convicted of
any of them have done nothing terrible whenever we find that others
appear to have done the same things, wouldn't we make easy defenses
for all of them and thus provide a great opportunity for those who
want to be depraved? [46] You would really appreciate the naiveté of
what you have said if you related it to yourself. Consider how you
would feel if serious and terrible accusations were made about you and
someone had spoken for you in this way. I know that you would hate
him more than your accusers. Isn't it really shameful to compose the
sort of defenses for others that would anger you if spoken on your
behalf? [47] Look at this also and go through it in detail: if one of
your students were led to do what you have praised, wouldn't he be
the most wretched of people living, or who ever have lived? What need
is there to write the sort of speeches whose greatest good would be to
persuade no one who hears them?

[48] But perhaps you would say that this has not escaped you, that

you wanted to leave behind an example for philosophers of how one must compose defenses regarding shameful accusations and difficult causes. Even if you did not know it before, I think it is now clear to you that someone would be rescued sooner by saying nothing than by making a defense in this way. [49] Moreover, it is also clear that philosophy, which is already greatly resented and in mortal danger,[31] will be hated even more because of speeches of this kind.

If you listen to me, you certainly will not compose worthless speeches in the future; and if you do, you will strive to say things that will not leave you with a worse reputation, will not corrupt your imitators, and will not debase education in public speaking.[32] [50] Do not be surprised that I attempt to advise you so forthrightly, even though I am younger and have no connection to you. I believe that to give counsel about such things is not the business of the oldest or those who are closest, but of those who know the most and want to help.

---

[31] This may be an allusion to Socrates and thus to Polycrates' epideictic speech attacking him.

[32] Lit. "*paideusis* concerning *logoi*," a circumlocution for what we call "rhetoric."

13. AGAINST THE SOPHISTS

〰〰〰〰〰〰〰〰〰〰〰〰〰〰〰〰〰〰〰〰〰〰〰〰〰〰〰〰〰〰〰〰〰〰〰〰〰〰〰

a pamphlet that is distributed.

INTRODUCTION

This short work gives a quick, opening snapshot of Isocrates' career as a teacher of politics, culture, and public speaking. It was probably written about 390. Its program shows a remarkable similarity to that of *Antidosis* (15), which was written thirty-five years later, but the goals of the two works are different. Later on, Isocrates will be on the defensive, defending his career and pleading for the importance of his contribution to Athenian life and politics. In this work he is more polemical; he wants to open up a space for himself and his teaching and distance himself from other teachers.

Unlike *Encomium of Helen* (10), to whose beginning this work is also similar, *Against the Sophists* does not name names—no doubt a conscious rhetorical strategy. But we can sometimes reconstruct the teaching systems of some of Isocrates' competitors from his criticisms: their use of mock debates, model speeches, and so on. Clearly Isocrates is assuming—perhaps he is also developing—some of the technical vocabulary that is used by other sophists, such as *kairos* and *to prepon* (13), *idea* and *enthymēma* (16), and *eidē* (17), although he disdainfully rejects other terminology (19). It has generally been thought that his statement of his own teaching method, which seems to be introduced in the final chapter, has been lost. This view has recently been challenged by Too, who argues that Isocrates purposefully did not express it; see also Papillon 1995.

13. AGAINST THE SOPHISTS

[1] If all those who undertook to teach were willing to speak the truth and not make greater promises than they plan to fulfill, they

would not have such a bad reputation among the general public. But as it is now, those who dare to make boasts with too little caution have made it appear that those who choose to take it easy are better advised than those who apply themselves to philosophy. Who would not hate and despise first and foremost those who spend their time in disputes,[1] pretending to seek the truth but attempting from the beginning of their lessons to lie? [2] I think it clear to all that it is not in our nature to know in advance what is going to happen. We fall so far short of this intelligence that Homer, who enjoys the highest reputation for wisdom, has written that the gods sometimes debate about the future—not because he knows their thoughts but because he wants to show us that this one thing (i.e., knowledge of the future) is impossible for human beings.[2] [3] Now these people have become so bold that they try to persuade the young that if they study with them they will know what they need to do and through this knowledge they will become happy.[3] And once they have established themselves as teachers and masters of such great goods, they are not ashamed to demand only three or four minas for them. [4] If they were selling some other property for such a small fraction of its worth, they would not dispute that their reasoning is faulty. And although they value all of moral excellence and happiness so little, nevertheless they still claim to be sensible teachers of others. They say they have no need for money, disparaging wealth as "mere silver and gold," but in their desire for a little profit they almost promise to make their students immortal. What is most ridiculous of all is [5] that they distrust those from whom they have to get this small profit—those to whom they intend to impart their sense of justice—and they deposit the fees from their students with men whom they have never taught. They are well advised to do this in regard to their security, but it is the opposite of what they teach. [6] It is all right for those teaching anything else to be careful over important

---

[1] I.e., eristic arguments. Plato discusses several kinds in *Sophist* 225–226.

[2] That the gods deliberate about the future shows that they do not know the future, and if the gods do not, how can humans? Aristotle (*Rhetoric* 2.23.4) uses this argument to illustrate the *topos* of "the more and the less," that is, *a fortiori* reasoning.

[3] According to Theophrastus, who is quoted by Athenaeus 567A, Cleomander of Cyrene promised to teach how to achieve good fortune (*eutychia*).

matters: nothing stops those who have become skilled at other things from being dishonest in their obligations. But isn't it irrational for men who impart virtue (*aretē*) and soundness of mind (*sōphrosynē*) to distrust their own students in particular? Surely men who were gentlemanly and just toward others would not wrong those who made them that way.

[7] When private citizens consider all these things and see that those who teach wisdom and impart happiness are themselves in great need and earn little from their students, that they are vigilant about inconsistencies in words but overlook those in actions, and further, that they pretend to know the future [8] but are incapable of saying or advising anything about what should be done at present, and that those who follow their own opinions (*doxai*) live more harmoniously and are more successful than those who claim to have knowledge (*epistēmē*), I think it is reasonable for them to despise such pursuits and to believe them idle and trivial and not a cultivation of the soul.[4]

[9] It is not only these teachers who deserve criticism, but also those who offer skills in political speeches.[5] They have no concern for the truth but think that their art (*technē*) consists of attracting as many students as possible by the smallness of their fees and the grandness of their instruction and of being able to earn something from them. They themselves are so senseless—and they assume others are as well—that they write speeches that are worse than private citizens might improvise, and they promise to make their students such good orators that they will miss none of the possibilities in their cases. [10] They do not attribute any of this power either to the student's experiences or to his native ability, but they say that the science of speeches is like teaching the alphabet. Although they have not investigated how either of these subjects works, they think they will be admired and that their teaching of speeches will appear to be worth more because of their exaggerated promises. They have a poor understanding that it is not those who make bold boasts about arts who make them great, but those who can discover the power there is in each art.

(margin, handwritten) not taking any *account* of what is promised

---

[4] Isocrates' views on opinion and knowledge run completely contrary here to those of Plato. See also 4.184, 4.262, and 5.9.

[5] Or "civic discourse" (*politikoi logoi*). See below, 20–21, 2.51, and 15.260.

[11] Rather than gaining great wealth myself, I would have preferred philosophy to have as much power as these people claim it does. Perhaps we would not have been left so far behind and enjoyed only the smallest part of its profits. But since it does not have such power, I wish they would stop talking nonsense. I see insults directed not only against those who are mistaken, but also that all the others who are connected in the same profession are attacked as well.

[12] I am amazed when I see these men claiming students for themselves; they fail to notice that they are using an ordered art (*tetagmenē technē*) as a model for a creative activity (*poiētikon pragma*). Who—besides them—has not seen that while the function of letters is unchanging and remains the same, so that we always keep using the same letters for the same sounds, the function of words[6] is entirely opposite. What is said by one person is not useful in a similar way for the next speaker, but that man seems most artful (*technikōtatos*) who both speaks worthily of the subject matter and can discover things to say that are entirely different from what others have said. [13] The greatest indication of the difference is that speeches cannot be good unless they reflect the circumstances (*kairoi*), propriety (*to prepon*), and originality, but none of these requirements extends to letters. So those who use such models would much more rightly pay than receive money, because they attempt to teach others although they themselves need much instruction.

[14] If I must not only criticize others but also clarify my own thought,[7] I think that every reasonable person would agree with me that many philosophers have remained private citizens, while others have become skilled speakers and politicians without ever having visited the sophists. Abilities in speaking and all the other faculties of public life are innate in the well-born and developed in those trained by experience. [15] Education (*paideusis*) can make such people more skillful and better equipped at discovery. It teaches those who now hit upon things by chance to achieve them from a readier source.[8] But it cannot fashion either good debaters or good speechwriters[9] from

---

[6] I.e., *logoi*, which could also be translated as "speeches" or "arguments."

[7] Isocrates cites the following sections in 5.194.

[8] Cf. Arist., *Rhetoric* 1.1, where similar views are expressed.

[9] This expression, *logōn poiētai*, occurs often in the work of Alcidamas, *Against the Sophists* 1, 4, 12. See Gagarin and Woodruff 1995: 276–289.

those who lack natural ability, although it may improve them and make them more intelligent in many respects.

[16] Now that I have gone this far, I wish to speak more clearly about these things. I contend that it is not all that difficult to gain a knowledge of the forms (*ideai*) that we use in speaking and composing all speeches, if a person surrenders himself not to those who make easy promises but to those who know something about them.[10] But to choose from these the necessary forms for each subject, to mix them with each other and arrange them suitably, and then, not to mistake the circumstances (*kairoi*) but to embellish the entire speech properly with considerations (*enthymēmata*) and to speak the words rhythmically and musically, [17] these things require much study and are the work of a brave and imaginative soul.[11] In addition to having the requisite natural ability, the student must learn the forms (*eidē*) of speeches and practice their uses. The teacher must go through these aspects as precisely as possible, so that nothing teachable is left out, but as for the rest, he must offer himself as a model, [18] so that those who are molded by him and can imitate him will immediately appear more florid and graceful than others. When all these conditions occur together, then those who practice philosophy will achieve success. But if any of the points mentioned is left out, the students will necessarily be worse off in this regard.

[19] I am sure that all the sophists who have recently sprung up and joined in the boasting—even if they now do so excessively—will be brought around to my view. But there remain those who lived before us, who dared to write the so-called *Arts* (*technai*),[12] whom we must not let go without criticism. They promised to teach lawcourt skills and picked out the most wretched of terms, which those opposing this education ought to have used, not those supporting it.[13] [20] In-

---

[10] Cf. 10.11.

[11] Plato may be ridiculing Isocrates at *Gorgias* 463a by having Socrates say that rhetoric is the activity of a "bold and conjecturing soul."

[12] We often refer to these *Arts* as rhetorical handbooks. Aristotle (*Rhetoric* 1.1 1354b24) also criticizes the *Arts* for concentrating on forensic oratory. Cole has argued that the early *technai* consisted principally of practice and demonstration texts.

[13] Presumably Isocrates has in mind the sort of terminology that Plato ridicules in the *Phaedrus* 266e–267a: "proofing" (*pistōsis*), "supplementary-

asmuch as it was teachable, these terms belong to a subject that could
be of no greater help for lawcourt speeches than for any others. Those
people were much worse than those who wallow in disputes. These
people go through such useless theories that if anyone followed them
in practice he would immediately be in deep trouble, but they do at
least profess to teach virtue and soundness of mind in these matters.
Those men, although they urged others to make political speeches,
had no concern for the speeches' other benefits but undertook to be
teachers of meddlesomeness and greed.

[21] Nevertheless, those who wish to follow the prescriptions of my
philosophy may be helped more quickly to fair-mindedness than to
speechmaking.[14] Let no one think that I mean that a sense of justice
is teachable;[15] I contend that there is no sort of art that can convert
those who by nature lack virtue to soundness of mind and a sense of
justice. But I certainly do think that the study of political speeches can
assist in encouraging and training these faculties.

[22] So that I do not appear to be destroying others' pretensions
while myself claiming more than is within my power, I think the reasons by which I was persuaded will easily make clear for others also
that these things are true.[16]

---

proofing" (*epipistōsis*), "refutation" (*elenchos*), "supplementary-refutation" (*epie-
lenchos*), "covert-allusion" (*hypodēlōsis*), "indirect-compliment" (*parepainos*) and
"indirect-censure in meter" (*parapsogos en metrōi*).

[14] Isocrates does not use the term "rhetoric" (*rhētorikē*), which appears in Plato
and Aristotle. Here he uses the word *rhētoreia* and appears to mean by it a rhetorical attitude of mind, speechmaking for its own sake. He clearly means it in an
unflattering way, associating it with meddlesomeness and greed.

[15] The question of the teachability of virtue was one of the central questions
for Plato. See especially his *Protagoras.*

[16] Since the last sentence seems to suggest that Isocrates is about to say something more about his own development of thought, it seems likely that the end-
ing of our text has been cut off. The pattern here seems to follow one that Isocrates uses in 10.15 and 11.9. But see Too 1995 and Cahn 1989, who offer different
explanations.

16. ON THE TEAM OF HORSES

INTRODUCTION

Like 20, this speech begins with only a reference to the witness testimony that supported the narrative of events lying behind the dispute. Much of what remains is a defense and praise of the life of the speaker's father, the famous Athenian general Alcibiades. He had been one of Athens' brightest lights and inspired the Athenians' (ultimately disastrous) expedition to Sicily in 415. But after his recall on charges of impiety, he fled, eventually to the Spartans, and gave them crucial advice about how to conduct the war against Athens. Nevertheless, after falling out with the Spartans, Alcibiades again found himself successfully leading the Athenians in battle from 411/10 until shortly before their fateful defeat at Aegospotami in 405, which led to the city's surrender. In his own voice, Isocrates presents a very favorable view of Alcibiades in 11.5 and one more equivocal in 5.58–61.

The speaker, who was also named Alcibiades, tells us that he had just been born when his father was first exiled in 415 (45). It is thought that the present lawsuit and the speech arose soon after he reached the age of majority in 397. The affair that gave rise to the lawsuit is also described by Plutarch in his life (*Alcibiades* 12) and by Diodorus Siculus (13.74), although they differ over the name of the accuser, Tisias or Diomedes.[1]

The speech begins with a short account of the present circumstances, in which the younger Alcibiades claims that he is besieged by

---

[1] Those interested in the career of Alcibiades may also consult Thuc. 6–8. For less favorable portraits of father and son, see Pseudo-Andocides 4 and Lys. 14–15.

those attacking him as a way to continue grudges against his father (1–3). Nevertheless, he takes up a defense of his father (4) and begins with the charges that arose against him in 415, which resulted from the profanation of the Eleusinian Mysteries and led him first into exile in Argos and then into league with the Spartans (5–11). The younger Alcibiades must then defend his father on the charge of treason, and he does so by identifying Alcibiades' actions with those of the democratic exiles who were also compelled to fight against Athens during the reign of the Thirty in 404/3 (12–15). When Alcibiades rejoined the Athenian cause in 411/10, he and the city had great success (16–21). The speech then turns to his private life (22–24), ancestry (25–28), his early successes as soldier and general (28–30), his marriage (31), his victories in the Olympic games of 416 (32–34)—where, curiously, no mention is made of the chariot team that led to the dispute in this case—and his other public services (35). Alcibiades is described as a loyal democrat (36–41) unlike Charicles, a kinsman of the prosecutor Tisias (42–44). Finally, the younger Alcibiades makes a plea on his own behalf, arguing the seriousness of the case for himself personally (45–50).

16. ON THE TEAM OF HORSES

[1] You have now heard the Argive delegates[2] and other knowledgeable people testify about the team of horses, that my father had them not by stealing from Tisias but by purchasing them from the city of Argos. But everyone is making a practice of malicious prosecution (*sykophantein*) against me in the same manner: [2] they bring suits over private charges, but their prosecutions involve the affairs of the city; they spend more time attacking my father than detailing their sworn charges; and they so despise the laws that they think it right to punish me for the injustices they claim you suffered from him. [3] I believe that accusations over public matters have no place in private contests, but since Tisias often criticizes me about my father's exile and takes your affairs more seriously than his own, I am compelled to make a defense in response to these things. I would be ashamed if I

---

[2] Athens had a long friendship with Argos, a city in the Peloponnesus that often stood against its powerful neighbor Sparta.

appeared to any citizen to give less thought to my father's reputation than to my own problems.

[4] A short account would be enough for the older men: they all know that the democracy was destroyed and that my father fled the city because of these same men. But for the sake of the younger people, who were born after these events and who have often heard his attackers, I shall begin the story earlier.

[5] When those who conspired against the people the first time and set up the Four Hundred³ saw that my father was vigorously opposed to their activities—although invited, he was not willing to join them and remained faithful to the majority—they thought that it would be impossible for them to change the established order until he was out of their way. [6] Since they knew that some in the city would be especially angered out of respect for the gods if anyone appeared to abuse the Mysteries,⁴ and that others would be angry if anyone dared destroy the democracy, they combined both charges and brought an impeachment to the Council.⁵ They said that my father gathered his club (*hetaireia*) for the purpose of revolutionary activities and that its members had performed the Mysteries while dining together at Polytion's house. [7] The city became tense because of the gravity of the charges and an Assembly was quickly gathered, but my father showed so clearly that his accusers were lying that the people would gladly have punished them. They selected him as general for the Sicilian expedition. After this, he sailed off in the belief that he had been cleared of the slander, but his enemies got the Council together, and, after they had won over the speakers for themselves, they stirred up the

---

³ A group of oligarchs who took control of government temporarily in 411/10.

⁴ These were the famous Eleusinian Mysteries, which were celebrated annually with a great procession from Athens to the nearby town of Eleusis, followed by secret festivities initiating people into the cult of the goddesses Demeter and Persephone. The secrecy of the proceedings was carefully guarded, and any private performance of them was a serious act of impiety.

⁵ There were different forms of impeachment (*eisangelia*), but the most notable was a public prosecution, brought to a deliberative body, such as the Council or Assembly, against public figures, either orators or generals, who were accused of "subverting the democracy" or "treason." Andocides (1.14 and 27) says the impeachment was brought by the Assembly; he is more likely to be correct.

matter again and suborned informers. [8] Why must it be a long story? They did not stop before they had recalled my father from the expedition and killed or exiled his friends from the city. Although he discovered the power of his enemies and the misfortunes of his associates and thought that he would suffer terrible things because they had not judged him when he was present but condemned him in his absence, he still did not think he should go over to the enemy. [9] He took great precautions to do no harm to the city by going to Argos to live quietly. But his enemies reached such a height of insolence (*hybris*) that they persuaded you to drive him out of Greece entirely and inscribe his name as a traitor and to send delegates and demand him back from the Argives. Not knowing how to handle the troubles that beset him and pursued on all sides, with no other refuge appearing available to him, at last he was compelled to flee to Sparta.

[10] This is what happened. But his enemies have so much insolence that although he was so illegally banished, they accuse him of doing terrible things and try to demonize him, as if he fortified Decelea,[6] instigated the islands to revolt,[7] and took a position as the enemy's teacher. [11] Sometimes they pretend to scorn him and say that he was no better than others, but now they are accusing him of everything that has happened and say that the Spartans learned from him how to wage war, even though they can teach others the art of war. If I had sufficient time I would easily show that he did some of these things justly and that he has been unjustly blamed for the others. It would be most terrible of all if my father received a reward after his exile, but I am punished because of his exile.[8]

[12] I think that it would be just for him to receive the fullest pardon from you. When you were banished by the Thirty, you experienced the same misfortunes as he. You should consider how each of

---

[6] During the last ten years of the Peloponnesian War (413–404), the Spartans garrisoned Decelea, a fortified position in Athenian territory.

[7] Chios in 412 was the most important island to revolt; it took with it several of the settlements on the coast of Asia Minor. See Thuc. 6.91.6 and 8.6.12 and Lys. 14.35–38.

[8] This argument seems slightly out of place here, since the narrative has not yet reached the point where Alcibiades was rewarded. See, however, Xen., *Hellenica* 1.4.13–17.

you felt and what thoughts you had: what sort of danger wouldn't you have endured in order to put an end to your living abroad, to return to your homeland and take revenge on those who expelled you? [13] What city, friend, or foreigner were you not willing to ask to help in regaining your city? What means did you not try in your attempt to return? Didn't you seize Piraeus and destroy the grain in the fields?[9] Didn't you damage the land, set fire to the outlying towns, and finally attack the walls? [14] You believed so strongly that it was necessary to do this that you were more angered at your fellow exiles who remained inactive than at those who caused your misfortunes. It is not reasonable, therefore, to criticize those who desired the same things as you or to regard as criminals those who went into exile and sought to return.[10] It would be much more reasonable to criticize those who remained and committed crimes that deserve exile. Do not begin your judgment of what sort of citizen my father was from the time when he had nothing to do with the city. [15] Look instead at the time before his exile, how he behaved toward the masses, how with two hundred hoplites he instigated the largest cities in the Peloponnesus to revolt from Sparta and become your allies,[11] what sort of dangers he posed for the Spartans, and how he led the Sicilian campaign. You owe him thanks for these things. But for what happened when he was in trouble you would be just in holding responsible those who banished him.

[16] Remind yourselves also how many benefits he brought the city when he returned, and how things were before you took him back.[12] The democracy had been destroyed, the citizens were in strife, and the soldiers were at odds with the officials in power. Both sides had reached such madness that neither had any hope of safety. [17] The democrats thought that those who ruled the city were greater enemies than the Spartans, and the oligarchs sent communications to those at Decelea[13] with the thought that it would be better to surrender their

---

[9] This argument also appears in Lys. 14.32–33, where it is refuted.

[10] These arguments appear in the mouth of Alcibiades himself in Thuc. 6.92.

[11] In 419 BC. This revolt, which included Argos and Mantinea, came to an end with the defeat of Alcibiades' coalition in 418. See Thuc. 5.52.2.

[12] Alcibiades was recalled in 411/10. See Thuc. 8.81.

[13] I.e., the Spartans.

homeland to the enemy than to share government with those fighting on the city's behalf. [18] This, then, was the thinking of the citizens: the enemy controlled the land and sea, you had no money, and the Persian king was supplying the Spartans;[14] in addition, ninety ships had come from Phoenicia to Aspendus[15] and were prepared to help the Spartans. With the city in these misfortunes and dangers, [19] the soldiers sent for him. He did not sulk at this situation, complain about the past, or deliberate about what was going to happen in the future. Straightaway he chose to suffer with the city whatever might come rather than enjoy the Spartans' good fortune, and he made clear to everyone that he was waging war against those who banished him, not against you, and that he longed to return to the city, not to destroy it. [20] Once he joined you he persuaded Tissaphernes[16] not to provide money to Sparta, stopped your allies from revolting, paid the soldiers from his own funds, returned the government to the people, settled the citizens' differences, and turned back the Phoenician ships. [21] It would be a large task to recount one by one the many Spartan triremes he seized after this, how many battles he won, how many cities he captured through force or made your friends through persuasion. Despite the many dangers that threatened the city during that crisis, the enemy never set up a victory trophy over you while my father was in command.[17]

[22] I know that I am leaving aside much of what he did as general; I have not spoken of it in detail because almost all of you recall what he did. But they recklessly and brazenly attack the private life of my father, and they have no shame about speaking so freely about a dead man, although they were afraid to do so when he was alive. [23] They have become so senseless that they think that they will gain a good reputation among you and among others if they can insult him as much as they can, as if everyone did not know that even the vilest men

---

[14] Xen., *Hellenica* 1.1.14, puts these thoughts in the mouth of Alcibiades himself.

[15] A city in Pamphylia on the southern coast of Asia Minor, a suitable staging point for entering the Aegean sea.

[16] The Persian governor in Asia Minor.

[17] In 6.111, Isocrates uses the same image, put into the mouth of a Spartan, as the concluding argument in the *Archidamus.*

can heap abuse not only on the best of men but even on the gods. [24] Perhaps it is foolish to be concerned about everything they have said. Just the same, I wish no less to describe my father's activities for you, beginning a little earlier with some recollections of our ancestors, so that you will know that for a long time the greatest and most noble of civic accomplishments have been ours.

[25] On the male side my father was a Eupatrid—it's easy to recognize their good birth from this name[18]—and on the female side he was an Alcmeonid, a family that has left a great memorial for its wealth. Alcmeon was the first citizen to win the chariot race at Olympia, and the Alcmeonids displayed their goodwill toward the people during the times of tyranny.[19] Although they were related to Peisistratus and were most closely associated with him of all the citizens before he came to power, they refused to share in his tyranny and chose to go into exile rather than see the citizens enslaved. [26] During the forty years of civil strife (stasis),[20] they were hated by the tyrants so much more than the other citizens were that whenever the tyrants defeated the Alcmeonids,[21] they not only razed their homes, but they also dug up their graves. The Alcmeonids were so trusted by their co-exiles that they continued to lead the people during the whole time of exile. In the end, my father's grandfathers on his father's and mother's sides, Alcibiades and Cleisthenes, took over generalship of the exile community, restored the people, and banished the tyrants. [27] They then established the democracy, as a result of which the citizens were so well educated in bravery that they fought and defeated the foreign-

---

[18] "Eupatrid" literally means "son of a good father." It is thus not properly the name of a family (genos) but was originally simply a designation for all aristocrats before the famous lawmaker Solon formalized Athens' class structure along economic lines in the sixth century. Alcibiades' father Cleinias was killed in 447, when Alcibiades was four years old (see below, 28). Alcibiades was then brought up by his mother's family.

[19] This was approximately 560–510, when first Peisistratus, and then his sons, Hippias and Hipparchus, ruled.

[20] The dating of events during the sixth century is notoriously difficult. It is unclear which forty years are being referred to.

[21] Peisistratus actually lost the tyranny and regained it twice before his grip on power became firm.

ers²² by themselves when they came against all of Greece. They also earned such a reputation for justice that the Greeks willingly put the command at sea in their hands, and they made their city so great in importance through its power and other assets that those who claim Athens is Greece's capital²³ and are accustomed to making such exaggerations as these appear to be speaking the truth.

[28] My father, in short, inherited from his ancestors a friendship with the people that was old, genuine, and founded on the greatest service. He himself was left an orphan—his father Cleinias was killed fighting the enemy at Coroneia²⁴—and Pericles became his guardian, who by common agreement was the most temperate, just, and wise of citizens. I think that this was one of my father's fine points, that he was born from such people and then raised, supported, and educated under men of such character. [29] At his scrutiny²⁵ he did not fail those men I have mentioned, nor did he think it right to live a life of indolence or to see in his ancestors' virtues the grounds for arrogance. From the beginning he was so ambitious that he thought he had to make himself a memorial of their deeds. At first, when Phormio selected the best men and led out a thousand Athenians to Thrace,²⁶ my father joined the campaign and so distinguished himself in its dangers that he was crowned and received a full suit of armor from the general. [30] Truly, what must a man do to deserve the highest praises? When he campaigns alongside the best from the city, shouldn't he win the prize for valor? And when he is in command confronting the strongest of the Greeks in every danger, shouldn't he show himself to be superior to them? My father did indeed accomplish the former as a young man, and he performed the latter when older.

---

²² I. e., the Persians and their subject allies, who attacked mainland Greece for the first time in 490, when they were repulsed at Marathon by the Athenians, without Spartan help. Herod. 5.66 mentions that with their liberty from tyranny won, the Athenians became even greater.

²³ Lit. "city-center" (*astu*), the urban core of the polis.

²⁴ In 447/6.

²⁵ At eighteen Athenian youths went through a scrutiny (*dokimasia*) before the Council, where they were questioned about their age, their parents' citizenship, and other matters before taking on their military service. Cf. *Ath. Pol.* 42.

²⁶ This was a campaign sent to Potidaea in 432. See Thuc. 1.64 and Plato, *Symposium* 220e.

[31] After this he married my mother.[27] I believe that in her he also received a prize of valor. Her father was Hipponicus, who was first among the Greeks in wealth and second to none of the citizens in birth. He was the most honored and admired man of his time, and he gave away his daughter with a very large dowry and the highest reputation. Everyone prayed to win this marriage and the leading citizens all thought themselves worthy of it,[28] but Hipponicus wanted to make my father his son-in-law and chose him above all.

[32] At about the same time, my father saw that the festival in Olympia was esteemed and admired by all people and that the Greeks made a demonstration there of their wealth, strength, and education, that the athletes were looked up to and the victors' cities became renowned. He reflected in addition that while the public services here in Athens bring credit to private individuals in the eyes of their fellow citizens, those at that festival bring credit to the city in the eyes of all Greece. [33] With these thoughts, although he was no less talented or physically strong than anyone, he disregarded the gymnastic contests because he knew that some of the athletes in them were ill born, dwelt in small cities, or were poorly educated. He tried his hand at horse-racing, which attracts only the most affluent—no base person would do it—and he surpassed not only his opponents but also all previous winners. [34] He entered more teams than even the greatest cities had previously raced, and they were of such quality that they came in first, second, and third.[29] Besides this, in his sacrifices and in his other expenditures on this festival he was so lavish and generous that the public resources of the other cities appeared less than his private resources. He concluded his festival observance (*theōria*) having made the good fortunes of those before him seem small in comparison to his own, having put a stop to the admiration given those who had gained victory during his time, and having left behind for those who would race

---

[27] We know from other sources that her name was Hipparetē, but the orators rarely give the name of respectable women, preferring circumlocutions like "the mother of x." Thucydides gave expression to this sentiment when he wrote (2.46), "The greatest glory of women is to be least talked about by men."

[28] Cf. the suitors of Helen (10.39–40).

[29] Although Euripides, who is cited by Plut., *Alcibiades* 11, agrees with this account, Thuc. 6.16.2 says that Alcibiades' teams were first, second, and fourth. The "competitor" in such races did not actually drive the chariot.

horses in the future no opportunity to surpass him. [35] I am reluctant to speak about his sponsorship of choruses (*chorēgiai*), athletic training (*gymnasiarchiai*), and triremes (*trierarchiai*)[30] here; he so distinguished himself in other respects that although those who have performed public services less well than he did praise themselves as a result, if someone requested a vote of thanks for my father for all his services, he would appear to be making speeches about small matters.

[36] I must not disregard political activity, just as my father did not neglect it. On the contrary, he was so much better a democrat than those with the highest reputations that while you will find that others stirred up strife for their own benefit, he took risks on your behalf. He was a democrat, but not because he was rejected by the oligarchy—he was in fact invited to join it. And although he often had the opportunity not only to rule with the other oligarchs but to have even more power than they, he was unwilling to do so. He chose instead to suffer injustice at the city's hands rather than betray the constitution. [37] As long as you continued to be a democracy, no one could have persuaded you of this with words. But the civil wars that have now occurred have clearly distinguished the democrats, the oligarchs, those who want a share in neither party, and those who claimed to belong to both. In these wars he was twice expelled by your enemies. The first time, as soon as they got him out of the way, they overthrew the democracy;[31] later, they had hardly enslaved you before they condemned him, the first citizen to be exiled.[32] This was how thoroughly the city profited from my father's adversities, [38] and he shared the city's misfortunes. And yet many of the citizens disliked him, suspecting that he was plotting a tyranny. They did not see this in his actions, but they thought that everyone aspired to take this step and that he was the most capable of carrying it through. Therefore, it would be just to give him thanks, because while he alone of the citizens was worthy of this charge, he believed others must have an equal share in the political order.[33]

---

[30] These three activities were all *leitourgiai*, liturgies or public services. See Series Introduction.

[31] In 411/10.

[32] 404/3.

[33] During the fifth-century Athenian democracy, one of the main mechanisms used against possible tyrants was the procedure of ostracism. Attempts were made

[39] Because so many things could be said about my father, I am at a loss what to mention at present and what I must leave out. What has not yet been said always seems more important to me than what I have said to you already. But I think it is clear to everyone that the man who has the most dedication to the city's prosperity must be the one who shares most in its fortunes, both good and bad. [40] When the city was doing well, which of the citizens was more prosperous, more admired, or more envied than my father? Who lost greater hopes, more money, or a finer reputation when it fared poorly? In the end, when the Thirty came to power, others fled the city into exile, but wasn't he banished from Greece entirely? Didn't the Spartans and Lysander[34] give the same priority both to killing him and to destroying your power in the belief that they would have no assurance from our city by knocking down its walls unless they eliminated the one man capable of rebuilding them?

[41] It is easy to recognize his dedication to you not only from the good he has done you but also from the wrong he has suffered because of you. I have shown that he helped the democracy, desired the same constitution as you, suffered wrong from the same people, was unfortunate at the same time as the city, thought the same people his enemies and friends as you, and at every turn ran risks, at your hands, because of you, on your behalf and together with you. [42] As a citizen he is unlike Charicles,[35] this man's in-law,[36] who wanted to be a slave to the enemy but demanded to rule his fellow citizens. He lived peacefully in exile but returned and treated the city badly. Indeed, how would Charicles have been a more wicked friend or less worthy

---

in 416/5 to ostracize Alcibiades, but he combined his power with that of others to have another man, Hyperbolus, ostracized. Until Hyperbolus' ostracism, only the most reputable of citizens had seen ostracism directed against themselves. It was thus, somewhat ironically, a mark of honor.

[34] The Spartan general who captured Athens and oversaw the tyranny of the Thirty.

[35] One of the Thirty, Charicles had been general in 414/3, was exiled and recalled. See Xen., *Hellenica* 2.3.2, and Lys. 12.55.

[36] I.e., of Tisias, the prosecutor against whom he is speaking. The Greek word *kēdestēs* refers to a connection by marriage, thus an "in-law," but it does not distinguish between "father-in-law" or "brother-in-law" or even "step-father."

enemy? [43] You are his in-law, Tisias, and you served on the Council during the time of the Thirty. Do you dare to recall the wrongs[37] of others? Aren't you ashamed to break the treaty that allows you to live in the city? Have you not considered that if ever it is decided to take revenge for what happened, you will be in more danger, and sooner, than I? [44] I don't suppose that they will punish me for what my father did and yet pardon you for the wrongs that you yourself committed. You will not be able to demonstrate the justification that he had. You were not banished from the city; you joined in the government. You were not compelled; you were willing. You did not act in self-defense; you took the initiative in injuring your fellow citizens. Therefore, you do not deserve a hearing of your defense from them.

[45] Perhaps when Tisias gets into trouble I will speak at greater length about his activities as a citizen. But I am asking you not to desert me to my enemies or to subject me to irreversible misfortunes. I have experienced enough misery. I was left an orphan as soon as I was born, when my father was exiled and my mother died. I was not yet four when I came into mortal danger because of my father's exile. [46] I was still a child when I was banished from the city by the Thirty. When those from Piraeus[38] returned and the others regained their property, I alone, because of the power of my enemies, was deprived of the land that the people had given us in compensation for expropriated property. After having suffered such great misfortunes in the past and having twice lost my possessions, now I am facing a suit for five talents. The charge concerns money, but I am in a struggle over my citizenship.[39] [47] Although the same penalties have been inscribed in law, the risk is not the same for everyone. Those who have money face a fine, but those without means like me face losing my civic rights, which I regard a greater misfortune than exile. It is much more challenging to live without civic rights among one's fellow citi-

---

[37] He uses the term for "recalling wrongs" (*mnēsikakein*), which was prohibited by the settlement of 403. This settlement allowed for a highly successful reconciliation between the oligarchs and democrats after the despotic rule of the Thirty in 404/3. See Introduction to 18.

[38] These are the democrats, who overcame the Thirty. See 18.2.

[39] If someone could not pay a fine to the state, he became a state debtor and lost his civic rights until he paid it.

zens than to be a metic[40] among others. [48] Therefore, I am asking you to help me, not to let me be viciously attacked by my enemies, be deprived of my homeland, and become infamous for my misfortunes. I would justly win your pity because of the facts themselves, even if I were incapable of stirring you with speech. You are required to pity those who are unjustly in danger, who are contesting over the most important matters, whose circumstances are unworthy of themselves or their ancestors, who have been deprived of a great deal of money, and who have experienced a great reversal in their lives.

[49] Although I have many grounds for complaint, I will be especially upset, first, if I am going to pay damages to this man from whom I ought to be getting them, and second, if I am going to be dishonored because of my father's victory at Olympia while I see others getting rewards because of it. [50] Beyond that, I will be upset if Tisias, who has done nothing good for the city, is going to have power in the democracy as he did in the oligarchy while I suffer badly under both governments, even though I have harmed neither. And I will be upset if you do everything else differently from the Thirty but hold the same view as they did toward me, and if I, who was once deprived of my city with you, am now going to be deprived of it by you.

---

[40] A metic (*metoikos*) was a noncitizen, usually still a Greek, resident in a city. In Athens there was a large metic population, which enjoyed considerable rights alongside the Athenians'.

17. TRAPEZITICUS

INTRODUCTION

The defendant in this case, Pasion, is the most famous banker (*trapezitēs*) of classical Athens. A former slave, he was also the father of Apollodorus, the author of several speeches later included with those of Demosthenes (see Trevett 1992). The acrimony into which the case must have brought Pasion apparently did no serious or long-term damage to his professional reputation. In time, he would even be granted citizenship for service to Athens. He died in 370/69. The prosecutor, who is the speaker, is a young man from the Bosporus (now the Crimea on the Black Sea in southern Ukraine), the son of a man, Sopaeus, who was very close to the region's ruler, Satyrus. The Bosporus was an important area for Athens, the source of much of its imported grain.

The speaker came to Athens, he tells us, to see the sights and conduct some trade, and he was introduced to Pasion by a Phoenician named Pythodorus. When Sopaeus temporarily fell out of favor with Satyrus, the son took steps to hide his money from Satyrus' agents in Athens. These steps included a feigned denial that he had money on deposit with Pasion and even a (false) admission that he was in debt to the banker. When he decided to leave Athens, he asked Pasion for the money back and was refused (8–9). The obvious person to consult was Cittus, who kept the books at Pasion's bank, but Cittus temporarily disappeared, and then his status was disputed, whether he was a free man or a slave, which confused whether the information he had could be gained from him though torture or not (11–17). For a time it appeared that a resolution would be reached, according to which both men would go to Satyrus and settle the matter before him (18–20). But accusations that Pasion had made against Menexenus, one of the speaker's confidants, that Menexenus had kidnapped Cittus, led to Menexenus bringing charges of his own against Pasion for slander (21–22). This complication nullified the arrangement between Pasion and the speaker, and Pasion then arranged, as the speaker claims, to have a slave alter the document that set out the conditions under which Pasion and the speaker would appear before Satyrus (21–23). The narration mostly complete, the speaker begins his proofs with that document, arguing that Pasion's version of the circumstances of its composition makes no sense of the motives of the two parties (24–34). He then anticipates that Pasion will argue that the speaker was in debt to Stratocles and had had a friend, Hippolaïdas, borrow from Pasion (rather than lending him money himself), so he explains these circumstances (35–44).

He also takes up the issue of motive again, pointing out that his original charge was made when he was in a straitened situation, when he is unlikely to have engaged in sykophancy (45–48; cf. 21.11–13). He then resumes his narrative with the report that in the end, Pasion finally sent Cittus to go with the speaker to Satyrus, but the two gave conflicting accounts to the king of why they had come to him, with the result that Satyrus sent a letter to the Athenians asking them to resolve the matter (51–52). The speaker then concludes his proof by recalling the torture that he proposed to perform on Cittus (53–55) and pointing out the services of his father and Satyrus to Athens in the past (57–58).

The speech can be dated to after 394, when Athens broke Sparta's naval dominance (36). It offers us many insights into Athenian banking and into Athens' relations with the kingdom of Bosporus (besides Trevett 1992, see E. Cohen 1992). There are also many glimpses of aspects of Athenian judicial procedure, such as private arbitration and the use of torture on slaves.

17. TRAPEZITICUS

[1] Judges, this trial is important to me. I am risking not only a lot of money but also the appearance of unjustly coveting another's possessions. That is what concerns me most. I will still have sufficient property even if I lose, but if I appeared to be making a charge over so much money with no right to it, I would be reviled for my whole life. [2] The most difficult thing of all, men of the court, is the sort of

opponents I am facing. Dealings with people at banks occur without witnesses,[1] and those who have suffered injustice at their hands must run a risk against people who have many friends, who handle lots of money, and who appear credible because of their trade. Nevertheless, despite these circumstances, I believe that I shall make it clear to all that I am being robbed of the money by Pasion.

[3] I shall relate to you as well as I can what happened from the beginning. My father, men of the court, is Sopaeus. All who sail to the Black Sea know that he is so closely connected to Satyrus[2] that he both rules a large area himself and has responsibility over Satyrus' entire empire. [4] But when I learned about this city and the rest of Greece, I desired to go abroad, so my father loaded two ships with grain, gave me money, and sent me off for trade and touring. When Pythodorus the Phoenician introduced me to Pasion, I began to use his bank. [5] Later, when a rumor reached Satyrus that my father was plotting against his rule and that I was associating with exiles, he arrested my father and wrote to those visiting here from the Black Sea to seize my money and order me to sail back. If I did none of these things, they were to demand it from you. [6] In these difficulties, men of the court, I told Pasion my troubles. Indeed, he behaved so agreeably toward me that I would have trusted him completely, not only about money but about everything else. I thought that if I surrendered all my money, I would run the risk, if something happened to my father, of losing everything, since I would be deprived of my money both here and there. But if I admitted having the money and did not surrender it after Satyrus' order, I would put myself and my father under the greatest suspicion in the eyes of Satyrus. [7] We discussed it

---

[1] This statement has occasioned much discussion (see E. Cohen 1992: 205–206). It represents a surprising exception to the regular presence of witnesses at all significant transactions. Cohen believes that it indicates the banks' involvement in a secretive economy that sought to avoid taxation. But it must be recalled that the bankers' primary role was as currency traders. If the speaker is referring to an Athenian law or custom that dealings with people at banks are to occur without witnesses, this may simply refer to currency transactions, not to deposits, whose acceptance was a secondary function for bankers.

[2] Satyrus reigned over the Bosporus area from 432/1 to 393/2. See Diodorus Siculus 14.93.

and decided to surrender the money that was visible[3] and not only to disclaim the money on deposit with Pasion but to appear to be in debt to him and to others on interest, that is, to do everything possible to persuade those men that I had no money.

[8] At that time, men of the court, I was thinking that Pasion was giving me all this advice out of goodwill for me, but when I had dealt with the representatives from Satyrus, I realized that he had designs on my money. When I wanted to collect my money and sail to Byzantium,[4] Pasion thought a very fine opportunity had come his way. A lot of money was on deposit with him—certainly enough to be worth some shamelessness on his part—and I had denied having anything before many onlookers. When asked, in plain view of everyone, I also admitted that I was in debt to others.[5] [9] In addition, men of the court, he thought that if I attempted to remain here, the city would hand me over to Satyrus; if I went somewhere else, my words would be of no concern to him; and if I sailed back to the Black Sea, I would be put to death along with my father. Calculating these factors, he decided to steal my money. He pretended to me that he was short of funds at the time and could not pay me back. But when I wanted to understand the matter clearly and sent Philomelus and Menexenus[6] to him to demand it back, he told them he had nothing of mine. [10] Beset with so many troubles from all sides, what thought do you think I had? If I was silent, this man would steal my money. If

---

[3] In Athens the usual distinction between visible (*phanera*) and invisible (*aphanēs*) property (*ousia*) was essentially like that between real estate, i.e., land, and personal property, cash and so on. In this case, however, since foreigners could not own land in Athens, there is no question of the speaker having had visible property in that sense. He must be referring simply to the cash and personal possessions that he would have had on his person or in his lodgings.

[4] It is curious that he does not suggest sailing directly to Bosporus. Byzantium is certainly on the route to Bosporus, and perhaps it was a transit point for travelers to the Black Sea, but it may be that Satyrus had less influence there than at Athens and that the speaker never intended to go further.

[5] He mentions Stratocles in 35–36, below.

[6] This Philomelus may be the student of Isocrates mentioned in 15.93. A Philomelus of Paeania is mentioned in Lys. 19.15 (cf. Dem. 21.174). Menexenus is probably the speaker in Is. 5, or his cousin. He is not the person portrayed in Plato's *Menexenus*.

I spoke up, I would still get nothing, and I would expose myself and my father to very serious allegations before Satyrus. So I thought it best to keep quiet.

[11] After this, men of the court, messengers came and told me that my father had been released and that Satyrus so regretted what he had done that he had given him the greatest assurances, had made his rule even larger than before, and had chosen to marry my sister to his own son. On learning this, Pasion knew that I would now act openly concerning my money, and he hid his slave Cittus,[7] who had thorough knowledge about the money. [12] When I went and demanded the man with the thought that he would provide the clearest test (*elenchos*) of what I was charging, Pasion made the most terrible claim: that Menexenus and I had corrupted and bribed him when he was seated at the bank[8] and had received six talents of silver from him. In order that there might be no test or torture[9] about the money, he claimed that we had hidden the slave and had then counter-charged him and demanded this slave, whom we ourselves had made disappear. As he said this with cries of anger and tears, he dragged me to the Polemarch,[10] demanded guarantors,[11] and did not release me until I supplied him guarantors for six talents. Please call witnesses of these events.

[WITNESSES]

[13] You have heard the witnesses, judges. Since I had already lost some money and faced shameful accusations about the rest, I left

---

[7] Cittus is also mentioned as a banker in Dem. 34.6

[8] Just as in English a "bank" may simply be something like a bench, in Greek a *trapeza* (lit. "four-footed") was also simply a table where the banker (*trapezitēs*) did business.

[9] Slaves could not appear in court as witnesses in Athens. With the assent of both sides, however, the answers they gave to questioning under torture (*basanos*) could be used to settle disputes. In 1.25, the verbal form of *basanos* appears in the word's original context as a "test" for metal.

[10] The Polemarch was the official in Athens who supervised suits involving non-Athenians. The charge was kidnapping, i.e., seizing a free person and carrying him off as a slave. Clearly it was serious.

[11] Or sureties, men who promised to pay if the accused did not.

for the Peloponnesus to investigate,[12] but Menexenus found the slave here. He seized him and demanded that he be tortured both about the deposit and about the charges this man was making about us. [14] Pasion then became so bold that he had the slave released on the grounds that he was free.[13] He had no shame or fear. Although he claimed the man had been kidnapped by us and that we had received so much money from him, he had him released into freedom and so prevented his torture. And what is most terrible of all is that when Menexenus had him give a guarantor for the slave before the Polemarch, Pasion supplied a guarantor for him for six talents.[14] Have the witnesses of these things step up.

[WITNESSES]

[15] Now after he had acted this way, men of the court, Pasion thought that his past actions had clearly been wrong and believed that he could make things right in the future. So he came to us claiming that he was ready to surrender the slave for torture, and we chose torturers and met at the Hephaesteion. I demanded that they whip the surrendered individual and rack him until he appeared to them to speak the truth. But Pasion here claimed that they had not been chosen executioners and he told them, if they wanted anything, to find it out verbally from the slave. [16] Since we disagreed, the torturers themselves refused to perform the torture and decided that Pasion should hand the slave over to me.[15] Pasion was so averse to the torture that he refused to obey them and hand him over, but he was ready to return the money if they convicted him.[16] Please call the witnesses of these events.

---

[12] It is unclear what he meant to investigate and why he went to the Peloponnesus.

[13] If Cittus were free, he could not be tortured. Giving a slave his freedom (or pretending to) was not an unheard of means of avoiding his torture.

[14] Pseudo-Dem. 59.40 presents a similar scenario, in which a surety is supplied before the status of an individual is decided before the Polemarch.

[15] I.e., to be tortured. Pasion was claiming that Cittus was not a slave. If he was free, the torturers might have got into serious trouble if they assaulted him.

[16] This entire episode is one of our most important sources regarding the evidentiary torture of slaves in Athens. But it is also atypical, perhaps the result of its

[WITNESSES]

[17] Now, men of the court, as a result of the meetings, everyone condemned his conduct as unjust and scandalous: first, after hiding the slave—who I claimed knew about the money—he charged that we had hidden him; then, when we seized the slave, he prevented his torture on the grounds that he was free; and later, when he surrendered him as a slave and chose torturers, he called for a verbal interrogation and did not allow an actual torture. Because of this he thought that he would find no safety if he came before you, and he sent a message and asked me to come and meet him at a sanctuary. [18] When we came to the Acropolis, he had covered his head and was crying. He said that he was compelled by lack of funds to deny what had happened and that he would try to return the money in a short time. He begged me to forgive him and to help cover up his misfortune so that it would not be publicly known that someone who took deposits had done such wrongs. Thinking that he regretted what he had done, I agreed and called on him to find a way, whichever he wished, so that it would turn out well for him and I would get my money. [19] Two days later we met and exchanged a pledge to keep silent about what had been done—a pledge that he broke, as you will realize as the story proceeds—and he agreed to sail with me to the Black Sea and there to return the gold to me so that he might discharge his obligation as far from this city as possible and that no one from here would know the manner of our settlement: when he sailed home he could say whatever he wanted. But if he failed to do these things, he would refer an arbitration to Satyrus on terms[17] that Satyrus would condemn him to pay one-and-a-half times the money. [20] After we wrote these things down and brought to the Acropolis Pyron,

taking place between a former slave, Pasion, and a non-Athenian. Usually the proposal is for the opponent of the slave's owner to perform the torture, not a third party. In this case, Pasion seems to have seen the torturers, or interrogators (*basanistai*), somewhat in the role of arbitrators, who might simply have verbally questioned the slave. He does seem to have given them the right to decide the dispute. But by forbidding the torture, Pasion seems to have avoided conceding that Cittus was a slave.

[17] A similar "arbitration on terms," where the arbitrator simply confirms terms already agreed upon by the disputants, is mentioned in 18.10.

a man of Pherae [18] who regularly sailed to the Black Sea, we gave him the agreement for safekeeping and ordered him to burn the document if we reached a settlement, and if not, to give it to Satyrus.

[21] Our affairs, men of the court, had been resolved in this way. But Menexenus was angry about the accusation that Pasion had made against him [19] and brought suit demanding the surrender of Cittus. He claimed Pasion should pay the same penalty for lying that Menexenus would have paid if he had been shown to have done any of these things. And Pasion asked me, men of the court, to settle things with Menexenus, saying there would be no advantage for him if, after sailing to the Black Sea and returning the money according to our agreement, he would still be made a laughingstock here. The slave, if he were tortured, would tell the truth about everything. [22] I thought that I should do whatever he wanted with regard to Menexenus but that he should do what we had agreed to do for me. At that time he was weak, unable to deal with his difficulties. He was afraid not only about the torture and the suit that had been brought but also that Menexenus might get hold of the document. [23] Since he was at a loss to discover an escape, he persuaded [20] the slaves of his guest-friend (*xenos*) [21] to alter the document that Satyrus was supposed to receive if Pasion did not reach a settlement with me. He had hardly accomplished this when he became the boldest of all people. He said he would not sail with me to the Black Sea and that he had no obligation to me. He called on me to open the document before witnesses. Why should I tell you the details, men of the court? We found written in the document that I had released him from all my charges.

[24] I have told you everything that happened as accurately as I can. [22] I think that Pasion, men of the court, will base his defense on

---

[18] Pherae was at this time the most important city in Thessaly, a fertile region in north central Greece.

[19] See above, 14.

[20] I.e., bribed.

[21] I.e., Pyron. The Greek word *xenos* refers to someone from another city with whom ties of hospitality and assistance have been established. The translation "guest-friend," while cumbersome, reflects the meaning in English better than any single word.

[22] So ends the narrative part of the speech. He continues by detailing proofs to support his case.

the altered document and rely especially on this. So give me your attention. I think that I shall make his depravity clear to you from the very same arguments.

[25] First, reflect on this: when we gave the guest-friend the agreement, according to which Pasion is claiming that he was released from the charges but I say that I was supposed to recover the gold, we called on the guest-friend to burn the document if we achieved a settlement between ourselves, but if not, to give it to Satyrus. We both agree that these were the terms. [26] So what encouraged us, men of the court, to direct that the document be given to Satyrus if we did not settle, if in fact Pasion had already been released from the charges and our affair had been concluded? Clearly we wrote this agreement with the thought that there were still outstanding matters between us that Pasion had to resolve with me according to the document. [27] Next, I can tell you, men of the court, the reasons why he agreed to return the gold. For when we were cleared of the allegations made to Satyrus and he could not conceal Cittus, who had thorough knowledge of the deposit, he thought that if he surrendered the slave to torture his wickedness would become apparent, [28] but if he did not do this, he would lose the case, and thus he wanted to reach a settlement with me. Ask him to show you what profit I gained or what danger I feared by releasing him from the charges. If he cannot show you any of these motives, isn't it more just to trust me rather than him about the document? [29] Indeed, men of the court, it is easy for everyone to recognize that since I was making the charges, if I feared testing[23] them, I could have waived the affair good-bye without making any agreement; but because of the torture and the trials that would come before you, Pasion could not be free of danger whenever he wanted unless he persuaded me, since I was making the charges. Therefore, I did not have to make the agreement about his release; he had to make one about returning the money. [30] It would be extraordinary if I had had so little faith in my case before composing the document that I not only released Pasion from the charges but also made an agreement about them and that I would want to come before you after I had com-

---

[23] The Greek word is the plural *elenchous*. The sentence structure makes clear that he means the torture of the slave and/or the trial before the judges, which would both serve to "test" his charges.

posed such a test²⁴ against myself. Really, who would plan his affairs this way?

[31] The greatest evidence of all that Pasion was not released in the written agreement but agreed to pay back the gold is that when Menexenus brought suit against him²⁵—before the document was altered—he sent Agyrrhius, a friend of both of ours, and asked me either to call off Menexenus or else cancel the written agreement I had made with him. [32] And yet, men of the court, do you think he would want to cancel this agreement, which he would use to expose us as liars? He did not use these arguments after he had changed the text; he sought refuge in it about everything and called on us to open the document. I will provide Agyrrhius himself as witness that at first he sought to cancel the agreement. Please come up.

[TESTIMONY]

[33] I think I have shown sufficiently that we made the agreement not as Pasion will try to tell you but as I have reported. It is not surprising, men of the court, that they altered the document. Not only have such things happened often before, but some of Pasion's associates have done much worse things. Who of you does not know that Pythodorus,²⁶ called the shopkeeper, who says and does anything for Pasion, last year opened the waterjars and plucked out the names of the judges²⁷ that had been submitted by the Council? [34] Really, if he dared physical danger for the sake of small gains by opening these jars in secret, these jars that have been stamped by the prytanies, sealed by the producers of the choruses,²⁸ guarded by the treasurers, and kept

---

²⁴ Like the torture and the trial before the judges, the agreement itself is now also described as a test (*elenchos*).

²⁵ See 18, where Menexenus is said to have brought charges in response to the alleged "kidnapping" of Cittus.

²⁶ Cf. Dem. 54.7.

²⁷ I.e., the names of the candidates to be judges for the Festival of Dionysus, where Athens' major dramatic competitions took place. Cf. Lys. 4.3.

²⁸ The prytanies were the fifty members of the five-hundred-member Council who had responsibility for the daily administration of the city for each of the ten months of the Athenian civic year. The chorus producers (*chorēgoi*) were wealthy Athenians who were given the responsibility for funding and organizing the chorus of a dramatic production.

on the Acropolis, why the need for surprise, when they stood to make so much profit, if they changed the text of a little document that was being kept by a guest-friend, either by persuading his slaves or by devising some other trick? I do not know what more needs to be said about these things.

[35] Already Pasion has tried to persuade some people that I had no money at all here, claiming that I had borrowed thirty staters[29] from Stratocles.[30] I think you should hear about this also, so that you may know what sorts of evidence inspired him to steal my money. When Stratocles was about to sail to the Black Sea, men of the court, and I wanted to get as much of my money as possible from there, I asked Stratocles to leave me his gold here and to recover it from my father in the Black Sea.[31] [36] I thought it would be a great advantage if the money were not risked at sea, especially since the Spartans ruled the sea at that time. I do not think that this is an indication favoring his argument that I had no money here. Rather, my dealings with Stratocles are the greatest evidence favoring my argument that I had gold on deposit with Pasion. [37] When Stratocles asked who would pay him back the money if my father did not follow my instructions and he did not reach me here after sailing back, I introduced Pasion to him, and Pasion agreed to pay him back both the capital and the accrued interest. But if no money of mine were on deposit with him, do you think that he would so easily have become my guarantor for so much money? Witnesses, please come up.

[WITNESSES]

[38] Perhaps, men of the court, he will present witnesses to you that before Satyrus' representatives I denied having anything except what I turned over to them, that he himself tried to claim my money

---

[29] Presumably staters from Cyzicus, which each had a value of approximately twenty-eight Athenian drachmas. See Series Introduction.

[30] The name Stratocles appears in Is. 11.8, in Dem. 43.42, and in the fragments of Lysias and Isaeus.

[31] I.e., the Bosporus. The Greek word *pontos* means simply "sea," i.e., the Black Sea, but in this speech it refers more particularly to the area controlled by Satyrus along the north coast of the Black Sea, much as "Lake Placid" refers not only to a lake but to a town near the lake.

since I admitted that I owed him three hundred drachmas, and that I allowed Hippolaïdas, a guest-friend and associate of mine, to borrow from him.[32] [39] Since I was put into the misfortunes that I have related to you, men of the court, having lost all my money at home and being forced to hand over what I had here to those who came, with nothing left unless I could secretly save the gold I had on deposit with Pasion, I admit I did acknowledge owing him three hundred drachmas, and I acted and spoke about other things in such a way that they might be persuaded that I had no money. [40] You will easily realize that this was not because I lacked resources but so that they might believe me. First, then, I shall present witnesses to you who know that I received a lot of money from the Black Sea and then those who saw me using this man's bank and finally those from whom at the time I had bought more than a thousand staters of gold. [41] In addition to this, when a special levy (*eisphora*) was imposed on us, of the foreigners I contributed the most when others did the registration, and when I was chosen registrar, I registered myself for the largest contribution, but I pleaded with my fellow registrars on behalf of Pasion, saying that he was using my money.[33] Witnesses, please come up.

[WITNESSES]

[42] In addition, I shall present Pasion's activity as support for this testimony. Someone denounced a trading ship,[34] for which I had lent a lot of money, on the grounds that it belonged to a Delian man. When I disputed this and demanded that the ship launch, those who wished to prosecute maliciously (*sykophantein*) swayed the Council in such a way that at first I was almost put to death without a trial,[35] but

---

[32] If the speaker had been solvent, he would have provided the loan himself.

[33] The *eisphora* was an extraordinary levy, which was imposed in times of war and other emergencies. Resident aliens ("metics") and foreigners were also compelled to pay.

[34] This was a *phasis,* a denunciation of someone holding property that belonged to the state.

[35] In the Athenian constitution, only a lawcourt had the power to sentence a man to death (*Ath. Pol.* 45.1), but this power had been usurped by the Council under the Thirty. See also Lys. 22.2.

finally they were persuaded to receive guarantors from me. [43] I asked Philip, a guest-friend of my father, and he appeared, but he feared a serious risk and left. Pasion, however, provided Archestratus[36] from the bank as guarantor of the seven talents for me. And yet, if he were losing only a small amount and knew that I had nothing here, he would surely not have become my guarantor for so much money. [44] It is clear that he called in the three hundred drachmas as a favor to me[37] and that he became my guarantor for seven talents with the thought that he had sufficient collateral in the gold that was on deposit with him. From the actions of Pasion, therefore, I have shown you, and you have heard from others who know, that I had a lot of money here and that it was on deposit at his bank.

[45] It seems to me, men of the court, that you will make the best decision about what we are disputing if you recall the time and the circumstances when I sent Menexenus and Philomelus to demand the deposit back and Pasion first dared to deny it. You will discover that my father had been arrested and his entire property confiscated. Because of my circumstances it was impossible for me either to remain here or to return to the Black Sea. [46] Now, is it more likely that in such difficulties I would make an unjust charge or that Pasion would be encouraged by the seriousness of our misfortunes and the amount of money to cheat me? Who has ever been such a sykophant that he would plot against another's wealth while facing physical danger himself?[38] With what hope or purpose would I have unjustly prosecuted this man? Did I think he was immediately going to give me money out of fear of my power? Neither of us was in this situation. [47] Did I think that by coming to trial, even contrary to justice, I would have an advantage before you over Pasion? I was not even prepared to remain here since I was afraid Satyrus would demand me back from you. Would I make myself hateful to the one man in the city with whom I had been especially close in order to achieve

---

[36] Archestratus was an Athenian citizen and had owned both the bank where Pasion worked and Pasion himself, when Pasion was still a slave.

[37] I.e., in order to help deceive Satyrus' representatives.

[38] Much the same argument appears in 21.14.

nothing? Who of you thinks I should be condemned for such madness and stupidity?

[48] It is worth considering, men of the court, the strangeness and unbelievability of Pasion's arguments at each point. When I was in such a situation that I could not have brought suit against him even if he had conceded that he was stealing my money, at that point he accuses me of attempting to charge him unjustly.[39] But when I was released from the allegations before Satyrus, and everyone thought he would lose the suit, at that time, he says, he released me from all the charges. What could be more illogical than this?

[49] Perhaps it is only on these points and not on the others that he is clearly saying and doing contradictory things. But he claimed that his slave, whom he himself had hidden, had been kidnapped by us. He registered this same slave in his property assessment as a slave along with his other servants, but when Menexenus demanded him for torture, he had him released, claiming he was free. [50] In addition, while stealing my deposit, he dared to charge us on the grounds that we had six talents from his bank. Whoever tries to lie about such conspicuous matters, why should you believe him about matters he conducted one-to-one?

[51] In the end, men of the court, after he agreed to sail to Satyrus and do whatever he decided, he played a trick in this also. He refused to sail himself, although I invited him to do so many times, but he sent Cittus instead. When Cittus got there he claimed he was a free man, a Milesian by birth, and that Pasion had sent him to inform Satyrus about the money. [52] On hearing both of us, Satyrus decided not to give judgment on dealings that arose here, especially since Pasion was not there and was not about to follow Satyrus' judgment. But Satyrus thought that I had been done such an injustice that he called together the shippers[40] and asked them to help me and not to

---

[39] See 21.15.

[40] The *naukleroi*, merchants residing in Bosporus. Some of them may have been Athenian citizens. Others were metics who resided normally in Athens. Some may even have been slaves, like Lampis in Dem. 34, who worked independently of his owner, but Satyrus would not have been interested in addressing slaves, since their voice would have carried little weight in Athens.

allow me to be wronged. He also composed a letter to the city and gave it to Xenotimus, the son of Carcinus,[41] to carry. Please read it to them.

[LETTER]

[53] Although I have so many claims on justice, men of the court, I think the greatest evidence that Pasion is stealing my money is that he was not willing to surrender for torture the slave who knew thoroughly about the deposit. What test would be stronger than this about dealings with those at banks? We certainly do not use witnesses for them. [54] I see that in both private and public matters you acknowledge nothing more credible or true than torture. You recognize that witnesses can be suborned even about what has not transpired, but tortures clearly indicate which side is telling the truth.[42] Knowing this, Pasion wanted you to infer from probabilities about this case rather than have clear knowledge. Surely he could not say that he would be at a disadvantage in the torture and that for this reason it was unreasonable for him to hand over the slave. [55] You all know that if the slave had denounced him, he would have been abused by this man in the worst way humanly possible for the rest of his life; but if he had held firm, he would have been set free and had a share of what this man stole from me. But although Pasion would have had such a great advantage, he knew what he had done, and so he put up with standing trial and facing other charges[43] just so that there would be no torture concerning this case.

[56] Therefore, I ask you to recall these things and vote against Pasion, not to condemn me of such depravity that although my home is by the Black Sea and I have so much property that I can help others, I would come here to prosecute Pasion maliciously by accusing him of lying about his deposits.

[57] It is also worth considering Satyrus and my father, who all this time have regarded you above all Greeks and have often allowed you

---

[41] A Carcinus gained fame as a general in 432/1; see Thuc. 2.23.

[42] An argument almost exactly the same as this one is found in both Is. 8.12 and Dem. 30.37.

[43] I.e., those of Menexenus.

to import grain although they were sending the ships of other merchants away empty because of the scarcity of grain. In private dealings also, in which they have served as judges, you have come away not only with an equal share but with more. [58] Therefore, it would not be reasonable for you to make light of their letters. I ask you therefore to vote according to justice both about me and about them and not to think that the false words of Pasion are more credible than mine.

18. SPECIAL PLEA AGAINST CALLIMACHUS

INTRODUCTION

From the speech itself the dating of 402 BC seems most likely. It is one of several speeches (by Andocides, Lysias and even, perhaps, Plato's *Apology of Socrates*) that result from attempts to settle scores after the Peloponnesian War and the brief but tragic tyranny of the Thirty that followed it (404–403). The Athenians were remarkably successful in bringing an end to the civil strife that had plagued the city during the several years of Athens' decline at the end of the war and especially during the tyranny. One of the mechanisms of this success was a treaty between the oligarchs, who had supported the Thirty, and the democrats, who had been driven into exile but eventually returned and regained control of the city. The treaty included an oath to be sworn by everyone "not to recall past wrongs." Of course, there were some who attempted to get around the oath.

This is the first speech that we have that results from a special plea (*paragraphē*), an innovation in Athenian judicial procedure that was designed to put teeth into the treaty and its oath. Indeed, this appears to be the first case in which it was employed. The special plea is essentially a counter-charge by the defendant that the prosecutor's charge is inadmissible. As is explained in 2–3, it reverses the order of who speaks, putting the prosecutor on the defensive and increasing the risk he takes in bringing his suit. It is uncertain what happened in cases in which the special plea failed: some argue that this also decided the original case (for the prosecutor); others claim that another trial was held on the original charge. Several more *paragraphē* speeches are found among the speeches of Demosthenes (32–38), but they all deal with commercial matters.

The events that gave rise to the case are quickly related (5–8): Callimachus is on a vendetta against those who took a role in the confiscation of some money from him. Our speaker thought that he had settled with him through an arbitration (10), but Callimachus resurrected the case (12). The rest of the speech consists of several interwoven themes: anticipations of Callimachus' arguments (13–15, 35–41), descriptions of the speaker's impeccable record (16–18, 58–68), discussion of the treaty and oath of settlement (19–34, 42–46), and attacks against Callimachus' character (47–57). The speech offers several interesting lines of argumentation concerning probability, the nature of law and treaties, and the idea of judicial precedent (which did not have the binding force that it has in common-law systems today).

18. SPECIAL PLEA AGAINST CALLIMACHUS

[1] If any others had already disputed over such a special plea (*paragraphē*), I would begin my words with the case itself. But as it is now, we are compelled to speak first about the law according to which we have come to court, so that you may cast your vote with an understanding of what we are disputing, and none of you will be surprised that I am speaking before the prosecutor even though I am the defendant.

[2] When you came back from Piraeus,[1] you saw that some of the citizens were eager to bring malicious prosecutions[2] and were attempting to break the treaties.[3] Since you wished to stop them and to

---

[1] The tyranny of the Thirty was overcome by democratic forces that stationed themselves for a time in Piraeus, Athens' port, about seven kilometers (four to five miles) from the city itself. "Those in Piraeus" came to mean the democrats, as opposed to "those in the city."

[2] The Greek is the verb *sykophantein*, and so the person bringing a malicious prosecution is known as a sykophant (see below, 3, and Series Introduction; cf. also now Christ 1998).

[3] The treaty included an oath of resolution (see the introduction to the speech) for past wrongs.

show others that you did not make this treaty under compulsion but because you thought it would benefit the city, on Archinus' suggestion you enacted a law that if anyone should bring a suit contrary to the oaths, the defendant could make a special plea: the magistrates would introduce this issue first, and the man who brought the special plea would speak first. [3] Whoever lost would pay a one-sixth penalty, so that those who dared to recall past wrongs (*mnēsikakein*) would not only be convicted as perjurers but would also be penalized immediately, without awaiting punishment from the gods. Therefore, with such laws in force, I thought it would be terrible if I allowed this sykophant to risk only thirty drachmas, while I myself am contending over my entire estate.

[4] I shall show that Callimachus is not only bringing a suit contrary to the treaty, but also lying about his charges and, in addition, that we have already had an arbitration concerning them. I wish to relate to you the facts from the beginning: if you learn that he has suffered nothing wrong from me, I think that you will both support the treaty more gladly and become angrier with him.

[5] The Ten who succeeded the Thirty[4] were in office when I happened to be walking with Patrocles, a close friend of mine, who held the office of *basileus*.[5] Patrocles was an enemy of Callimachus, who is now prosecuting me, and he confronted him as Callimachus was carrying some money. He seized him and claimed that Amphilochus[6] had left this money, that it had become the state's. (Amphilochus had been one of those in Piraeus.[7]) [6] When Callimachus disputed this and a terrible argument ensued, many others came running up,

---

[4] As the Thirty began to lose ground to the democratic forces in Piraeus, they elected a board of Ten to continue in government. This board was quickly replaced by another board of Ten, however, which sued for reconciliation. *Ath. Pol.* 38.3 mentions that a Rhinon of Paeania was a member of this second board; cf. below, 6.

[5] The *basileus* ("king") was one of the nine annually selected magistrates who had responsibility for the Athenian legal system. His special areas included religious matters and homicide. See *Ath. Pol.* 57.

[6] The manuscripts and editors disagree about this name. Some manuscripts read "Philon," while editors have proposed "Pamphilus."

[7] I.e., a democrat.

including, by chance, Rhinon, one of the Ten. So Patrocles immediately denounced[8] Callimachus before him for having the money, and
Rhinon took them both to his colleagues. They referred the matter to
the Council, and when the decision came down, it was resolved that
the money was the state's. [7] After this, when the exiles returned from
Piraeus, Callimachus accused Patrocles and brought charges that he
was responsible for his misfortune. After forcing Patrocles to pay ten
minas of silver and giving him a release, Callimachus brought a malicious prosecution against Lysimachus. And after he received two hundred drachmas from him, he began to make trouble for me. At first
he made an accusation, claiming that I had cooperated with those
men, but in the end he came to such a point of shamelessness that he
blamed me for everything that had happened. Perhaps he will dare to
make the same allegations even now.

[8] I shall present witnesses to you, first those who were present
from the beginning, who will say that I did not seize him or touch the
money, then Rhinon and his colleagues, who will say that it was not I
but Patrocles who made the denunciation before them, and finally the
councilors, who will say that Patrocles was the prosecutor. Please call
the witnesses of these things:

[WITNESSES]

[9] Although so many people had been present at the events, this
man here went himself into the crowds and sat in the shops making
speeches about how I had mistreated him and stolen his money, as if
no one knew the truth. Some of his associates approached me and
advised me to settle my differences with him, not to prefer defamation
and risking a great deal of money, not even if I really had faith in my
case. They said that many things come out contrary to expectation in
the courts [10] and that your verdicts were more a matter of luck than
justice, so that it would be more profitable for me to pay a small
amount and be released from serious charges than to pay nothing and
risk so much. Why should I go through the details for you? They did
not leave out much of what is commonly said in such cases. In the

---

[8] This was a *phasis*, a "denunciation of a man who is illegally withholding
property which belongs to the state" (Todd 1993: 389).

end I was persuaded—everything I say to you will be true—and I gave him two hundred drachmas. But in order that he could not bring a malicious prosecution again, we submitted an arbitration on terms[9] to Nicomachus of Batē.[10]

[WITNESSES]

[11] At first Callimachus abided by the agreement, but later he plotted with Xenotimus—the man who destroys our laws, bribes our courts, insults our officials, and causes all sorts of trouble[11]—and brought a suit against me for ten thousand drachmas. When I presented a witness who said that the suit was inadmissible since there had been an arbitration, he did not bring suit against the man[12] [12] because he knew that if he did not receive one-fifth of the votes, he would owe the one-sixth penalty. But he persuaded the official and brought the same suit again in the belief that he would risk only the court fees.[13] Since I was at a loss about how to deal with these troubles, I thought it would be best to bring a case before you in which the risk was equal for both sides. And this is what happened.[14]

[13] I hear that Callimachus intends not only to lie about the allegations but to deny that there was an arbitration. He is preparing to argue that he never referred the arbitration to Nicomachus, whom he knew to be an old friend of ours, and that it is unlikely that he would have been willing to settle for two hundred drachmas instead of ten

---

[9] Athenians preferred to settle their disputes privately by seeking out a private arbitrator and empowering him to impose a settlement rather than go to court. Here they apparently chose Nicomachus not to settle their dispute but to confirm terms that they had already reached (cf. 17.19). In 14, below, the speaker says that they were not in dispute before him.

[10] We know nothing more about this Nicomachus. Some expression calling for the witnesses has probably fallen out of the manuscripts at this point.

[11] Despite his apparent notoriety, we know nothing else about Xenotimus.

[12] Presumably it would have been a suit for false testimony.

[13] Athenian law recognized the principle of not allowing the same issue to be tried twice (see Dem. 24.54), which would add rhetorical weight to the speaker's claim.

[14] This passage suggests that the special plea is based not on the treaty and settlement but on the arbitration settlement.

thousand. [14] But consider, first, that we were not in dispute at the arbitration. We referred it on terms, so he did nothing odd if he chose Nicomachus as arbitrator. It would have been much odder if he had agreed on the terms and then opposed the arbitrator. Second, if he was actually owed ten thousand drachmas, it is unlikely that he would have given a release for two minas, but since he was accusing me unjustly and prosecuting maliciously, it's no wonder he was willing to accept this amount. Furthermore, if he made me pay a small amount after making large accusations, this is no evidence for him that an arbitration did not take place, but much rather evidence for us that even in the beginning his allegation was unjust. [15] I am surprised if he thinks that he knows that it is unlikely for him to have been willing to accept two hundred drachmas instead of ten thousand, but he does not believe that I would realize—if I wanted to lie—that I must say that I had paid more than this. I think that just as it would have been an indication for him that the arbitration did not take place if he had convicted my witness for false testimony, so it is evidence for us that I am speaking the truth about it that he clearly did not think it worthwhile to proceed against him.

[16] I believe that even if there had not been an arbitration and there were no witnesses to what was done and we had to consider just the probabilities, it would still not be difficult for you to reach a just verdict. If I dared to wrong others as well, you would likely condemn me for wronging him also. But as it is, I shall be shown to have caused no one monetary loss, nor have I put anyone in physical danger,[15] nor have I erased anyone from the list of those having citizenship, nor have I inscribed anyone on the list with Lysander.[16] [17] And yet the viciousness of the Thirty impelled many to do these sorts of things. It is not just that they did not stop those who committed crimes; they actually ordered some people to do wrong. But I, at any rate, will not be found to have done any such thing during their rule. This man claims that he was a victim of injustice when the Thirty had been thrown out, when Piraeus had been taken, when the people (*dēmos*)

---

[15] He means that he has not prosecuted anyone in a case in which the penalty would have been a fine or bodily harm, such as exile or execution.

[16] Thus taking away their civic rights; see 21.2 and below, 61.

were in power and there were discussions about a reconciliation. [18] Do you think that anyone who conducted himself properly during the Thirty would put off his injustice until those who had earlier done wrong were feeling regret? What is most terrible of all is the thought that although I did not think it right to punish any of my existing enemies, I would attempt to harm this man, with whom I had never had any dealing at all.

[19] I think that I have shown sufficiently that I am not responsible for the confiscation of Callimachus' money. But you will also learn from the treaties that he has no right to bring suit concerning what happened then, even if I did everything he says. Please take the text:

[TREATY]

[20] Did I put my trust in a small point of justice when I made my special plea? Does the treaty explicitly release those who have informed against someone (*endeixis*) [17] or made a denunciation (*phasis*) [18] or who have done anything like this? And have I not been able to show that I have not done these things, or any other wrong? Please read the oaths as well:

[OATHS]

[21] Isn't it terrible, men of the court, that although these are the terms of the treaty and such oaths have been sworn, Callimachus thinks so much of his own words that he thinks he will persuade you to vote contrary to them? If he saw that the city regretted what it had done, we should not be surprised at him. But as it is, you have shown in your legislation that you believe that the treaty is very important. [22] When Philon of Coele was indicted for dishonesty on a delegation and he had no defense to make in the matter, he simply cited the treaty. You resolved to release him and made no judgment in the matter. While the city does not think it right to punish even admitted wrongdoers, this man dares to bring a malicious prosecution against those who have done nothing wrong. [23] Indeed, it has not escaped

---

[17] Although the exact nature of the *endeixis* is unclear, it seems closely associated with *apagōgē* (summary arrest).
[18] Cf. 17.42 and 18.5.

him that although Thrasybulus and Anytus, the most powerful men in the city,[19] have lost a great deal of money and know who listed their property,[20] nevertheless they do not dare to bring suit against them or recall past wrongs. Even though in other matters they can more easily get their way than others can, concerning matters covered by the treaty, at any rate, they consider themselves equal to others. [24] And it is not only these men who have thought this way. None of you has dared to bring such a suit either. It would be terrible if you observed your oaths regarding your own affairs but attempted to transgress them in regard to this man's malicious prosecution, if you required private agreements to be publicly binding but allowed anyone who wished to destroy the city's treaty. [25] What someone would find most amazing would be if you established these oaths regarding the reconciliation, when it was unclear whether they would benefit the city, so that even if it were not beneficial, you would have to abide by your agreements, but you transgress the oaths now, when they have turned out so well for you that even if there had been no pledge, it would still be worthwhile to guard the existing constitution. [26] And while you get angry at those who say that we must repeal the treaty, you let this man here, who dares to transgress its written terms, go free. You would be doing something that is unjust, unworthy of you, and inconsistent with what you decided before.

[27] Consider that you have come to pass judgment on very important matters. You will cast your votes concerning a treaty, and it has never been profitable to violate treaties, either for yourselves in relation to others or for others in relation to you. They have such a power that most things in life, for both Greeks and foreigners, exist through treaties. [28] Because of our trust in them we visit one another and trade for whatever each happens to need. With them we conduct our transactions among ourselves and we settle both private

---

[19] Thrasybulus was the leading military person among the democratic exiles during the rule of the Thirty; he subsequently played a prominent part in reviving Athens' imperial ambitions. Anytus is best known as one of the principal accusers at Socrates' trial in 399; he was also a prominent democratic politician.

[20] The listing of property was known as *apographē* and was part of the process whereby the state seized some or all of an individual's assets that were owed to it.

animosities and the city's wars. This is the one common thing that all people use continually, so it is incumbent on everyone to support them, especially you. [29] Only recently, although we were defeated in war and were in the hands of our enemies, and many wanted to destroy the city, we took refuge in oaths and treaties.²¹ If the Spartans dared transgress them, every one of you would have been upset. [30] And yet, how can anyone accuse others, when he is guilty himself? If we were mistreated in violation of the treaty, who would think we were suffering injustice if we ourselves appeared to give it no importance? What pledges will we find to offer others if we so capriciously break those we made to ourselves? [31] It is worthwhile remembering these things also: while our ancestors accomplished many noble things, the city has won renown not least from these settlements. You can find many cities that have fought nobly in war, but no one could point to a city better advised with regard to civil strife (*stasis*). [32] Moreover, of those activities that carry risk, one might ascribe the greatest part to luck, but no one would attribute the credit for our moderation to anything other than our intelligence. So it is not right for you to betray this reputation.

[33] Let no one think that I am exaggerating or overstating the matter because I have made these arguments while a defendant in a private suit. This contest is not just about the money described in the suit. For me it is about this, but for you it is about what I was saying a little earlier. About this no one could speak worthily or propose a sufficient penalty. [34] This suit differs from others in that while others are of concern only to the litigants, this one involves a danger to the entire city. You are judging this case after swearing two oaths, one that you customarily swear for other suits,²² and this one, which you swore for the treaty. If you decide this case unjustly, you will transgress not only the laws of this city but also the common laws of all people. So it is not right to base your vote about these matters on

---

²¹ At the end of the Peloponnesian War in 404 the Athenians capitulated according to terms that saved the city from utter destruction. See Xen., *Hellenica* 2.2.20 and 2.4.43.

²² This was the so-called Heliastic Oath, which all those who might be impaneled on juries swore each year. A text of the oath is preserved in Dem. 24.149–151.

favor (*charis*), a sense of fairness (*epieikeia*), or anything else, other than the oaths.[23]

[35] I don't think even Callimachus will deny that it is necessary, beneficial, and just for you to decide about the treaty in this way. But I believe he will complain about his present poverty and the misfortune he has experienced. He will say that he will suffer terrible and cruel hardships if under the democracy he is to pay a one-sixth fine on the money he lost during the oligarchy, if he was compelled to go into exile then because of his property, and now, when he ought to be receiving justice, he will lose his civic rights.[24] [36] He will accuse those involved in the revolution in order to get you angry. Perhaps he has heard that when you do not catch the guilty, you punish whoever happens by. But I think this is not your policy, and I believe it is easy to counter the arguments that I have just mentioned. [37] With regard to his complaints, you should be helping, not those who show that they are very unfortunate but those who clearly speak more justly than their opponents about what they have sworn in their suit. About the one-sixth fine, if I were to blame for this situation, you would reasonably show sympathy for him inasmuch as he was about to be fined. But as it is, he is the sykophant, so you may assume that he is saying nothing with justice. [38] Next, you must reflect that all those who returned from Piraeus could tell the same stories that he has, but none of them has dared to bring such a suit. Indeed, you ought to hate such people and regard them as bad citizens, those who have experienced the same misfortunes as most have but think it right to exact different punishments from the others. [39] Besides, it is possible for him even now, before making trial of your judgment, to drop the suit and be released from the entire matter. Indeed, isn't it illogical for him in this danger to seek to gain your pity, when he controls the situation he has put himself in, and when even now he can avoid any risk? [40] If he mentions what happened under the oligarchy, demand that he not

---

[23] This is almost the only occasion in all Attic oratory in which a speaker makes explicit reference to arguments based on such extralegal considerations. In his *Rhetoric* (1.13–15), Aristotle outlines a theoretical basis for such argumentation.

[24] He will say that he will be fined one-sixth of ten thousand drachmas and suffer the loss of his civic rights (*atimia*) because he is unable to pay.

accuse those whom no one will defend. Demand instead that he show that I, the person you must vote on, took the money. Demand not that he show that he has suffered terribly, but that he substantiate that I caused it, the one from whom he is demanding to recover his losses. [41] He could show in a trial against any citizen that he has been treated badly. Indeed, you must give weight not to accusations that can be directed toward those who have done no wrong, but to those that can be made only against those who have committed injustice. In response to those arguments, then, this is perhaps sufficient, and it will be possible now to raise my own objections.

[42] Consider this, even if I seem to be saying the same thing twice: many people are paying attention to this suit not out of concern for our affairs but because they think that it is a judgment concerning the treaty. If you decide justly, you will allow them to live in the city without fear. If not, how do you think those who stayed in the city will feel if you show that you are angry at all alike who gained a share in the citizenship? [43] What will people think who are conscious of some small wrong on their part when they see that not even those who conducted their public lives properly obtain justice? How much turmoil must we expect, when some people are encouraged to bring malicious prosecutions by the thought that you share their views, and others fear the present constitution on the grounds that it no longer provides them a refuge? [44] Wouldn't it be right to fear that if the oaths are destroyed we may again be in the same situation that compelled us to make the treaty? Surely you do not have to learn from others the benefit of concord and the evil of civil strife. You have experienced both to such a degree that you would be the best to teach others about them.

[45] So that you do not think that I am spending a long time on the treaty because it is easy to say many just things about it, I appeal to you to recall this one point when you cast your votes: before concluding it we were at war, one group holding the city,[25] the other having captured Piraeus; we hated each other more than the enemies that were left us by our ancestors. [46] But since we gave each other pledges and joined together in unity, we have run our city nobly and

---

[25] Lit. "the circle," i.e., of the city, which was enclosed by walls.

for the common good, as if no misfortune had happened to us. Previously, everyone thought that we were very ignorant and unfortunate, but now we have the greatest reputation in Greece for happiness and soundness of mind. [47] Therefore, it is right to punish those who transgress the treaties not only with the prescribed penalties,[26] but with the most extreme, since they are responsible for the greatest evils, especially those who have lived as Callimachus has. While the Spartans waged war on you continuously for ten years,[27] he did not offer himself for even one day to follow the generals' orders. [48] He passed that time running away and hiding his property. And when the Thirty came to power, then he sailed back to the city. He says he's a democrat, but he was so much more eager than the rest to participate in that regime[28] that even though he suffered badly, he decided not to withdraw but chose to be besieged together with those who had done him wrong rather than participate as a citizen with you, who had suffered injustice together. [49] He continued to participate in that government until the day you were about to attack the wall. Then he left, not out of disgust with what was going on then but because he feared the coming danger, as he made clear later. For when the Spartans came and the democrats were surrounded in Piraeus, again he escaped from there and lived in Boeotia. Therefore, he ought to be inscribed among the deserters rather than named among the exiles.[29] [50] Although he acted this way toward those in Piraeus, toward those who remained in the city, and toward the city in general, he does not like getting an equal share with others. He seeks to have more than you, as if he alone suffered injustice or were the best of citizens or experienced the worst misfortunes because of you or was responsible for the most benefits to the city.

[51] I would like you to know him as well as I do, so that instead

---

[26] The one-sixth penalty that has been mentioned before, in 3, 12, and 35, above.

[27] During the last ten years of the Peloponnesian War (414–404), the Spartans kept a permanent garrison in Athenian territory at Decelea. Before that, they had only invaded during the campaigning season.

[28] I.e., the oligarchy of the Thirty.

[29] I.e., the democrats who fled into exile from the Thirty.

of being upset by his losses, you would begrudge what he has left. But as it is, not even twice as much water[30] would be enough to discuss the others he has plotted against, the sorts of private suits (*dikai*) and the public suits (*graphai*) he has brought, or all those with whom he has associated and against whom he has given false testimony. [52] When you have heard just one of the things he has done, you will easily understand the rest of his depravity. Cratinus[31] once disputed a plot of land with Callimachus' brother-in-law. After a fight broke out between them, Callimachus and his brother-in-law hid a servant and alleged that Cratinus had smashed her head in. They claimed the slave had died from the injury and brought a suit for murder against him at the Palladium.[32] [53] When Cratinus discovered their plot, he kept quiet for some time so that they would not alter the situation or discover different arguments but would be caught in the act of wrongdoing. When Callimachus' brother-in-law had conducted his prosecution and Callimachus had testified that the slave was indeed dead, [54] Cratinus and some friends went to the house where she was hidden, took her by force, brought her to the court, and showed her off alive to everyone present. As a result, the brother-in-law received not a single vote of the seven hundred judges, although fourteen witnesses had testified to just what he had said. Please call witnesses of these things:

[WITNESSES]

[55] Who could prosecute this man's activities as they deserve? Who could find a greater example of injustice, sykophancy, and depravity? Some acts of injustice might not reveal entirely the character of those doing injustice, but from acts such as these it is easy to comprehend the wrongdoer's entire life. [56] Whoever testifies that the living have died, what do you think he would refrain from doing? Whoever is so depraved in regard to others' affairs, what would he not dare regarding his own? Why must you trust this man when he is speaking on his

---

[30] I.e., twice as much time. Speeches in the Athenian lawcourts were timed by a waterclock (*klepsydra*). See *Ath. Pol.* 67.

[31] We know nothing more about Cratinus or this incident.

[32] The Palladium was the court for cases of unintentional homicide and for the murder of slaves, metics, and foreigners. See *Ath. Pol.* 57.3.

own behalf, this man who is a proven perjurer on behalf of others? Who has ever had his false testimony more clearly exposed? You judge others on the basis of what is said, but the judges saw for themselves the testimony of this man—that it was false. [57] And after committing crimes like this, he will try to say that we are lying! That's like Phrynondas[33] criticizing someone for cheating, or Philourgus, who made off with the Gorgonion,[34] claiming that others were temple robbers. Who is more likely to offer a witness to events that did not happen than this man, who himself dares to testify falsely for others?

[58] It is possible to make many accusations against Callimachus, since he has conducted his public life in this way. But for myself, I shall leave aside all my other services to the city[35] and mention just one to you, for which you would not only justly be grateful to me, but which you might use as evidence regarding this entire case. [59] When the city lost its ships in the Hellespont and was stripped of its power,[36] I distinguished myself so much from most of the trierarchs that I was one of the few to save my ship, and of these I alone sailed back to Piraeus and did not stop performing my trierarchy.[37] [60] The others gladly took the release from their services and felt disheartened at the situation. They regretted what they had spent and were concerned to hide what they had remaining. They thought that the common interest was lost and looked out only for their own affairs. But I did not have the same thought as they did. After I persuaded my brother to be joint trierarch, we paid the sailors from our own resources and continued to harass the enemy. [61] In the end, when Lysander[38] promised the death penalty if anyone imported grain to you, we were so devoted

---

[33] A notorious cheater. See Aristoph., *Thesmophoriazusae* 861.

[34] A golden relief sculpture of the Gorgon's head was affixed to the shield of Athena's statue in the Parthenon.

[35] Wealthy Athenians were regularly assigned services (*leitourgiai*) to be performed for the city, such as sponsoring a chorus for a dramatic festival. It is typical in Athenian lawsuits for the speaker to mention which ones he has done.

[36] This is a euphemistic reference to the Athenian defeat at Aegospotami in 405.

[37] A trierarchy was one of the public services assigned to wealthy Athenians. It involved funding and commanding a warship, called a trireme.

[38] The Spartan commander. See above, 16.

to the city that while others did not dare import even their own grain, we seized the grain that was intended for the Spartans and brought it to Piraeus. For this you voted to crown us and to proclaim in front of the statues of the eponymous heroes[39] that we were responsible for great services.

[62] Surely you should not regard as democrats those who have been eager to participate in public life when the *dēmos* is in power, but those who were willing to take risks for you even when the city was experiencing misfortune. Surely you should not be grateful if someone has suffered badly, but if he has done you a service. And surely you should pity the poverty not of those who have lost their money but of those who have spent it on you. [63] It shall be clear that I have been one of these. I would be the most unfortunate of all if, after I have paid out much of my own money for the city, I should then appear to be plotting against others' money and giving no thought to the ill repute that I would gain among you, I who clearly regard not only my property but even my life as less important than my good reputation among you. [64] Who among you would not regret—if not immediately then soon—if you saw that the sykophant had become rich while I was deprived of what was left from my services to the city? Do you want to see the man who never took a risk for you become greater and more powerful than the laws and the treaty, [65] while I, who was so passionate about the city, am considered unworthy to obtain justice? Who would not criticize you, if you are persuaded by Callimachus' words and convict us of such depravity, even though you once decided to crown us for the brave acts we performed when it was not so easy as it is now to win this honor? [66] Our situation is just the opposite of others': they remind the recipients of the gifts they received, but we ask you to recall that you have given us a gift, so you have evidence of everything that has been said and of our character. [67] It is clear that we made ourselves worthy of this honor, not so that we might seize other people's property during the oligarchy but so that when the city was saved, other people would have their own

---

[39] These were the statues of the heroes for whom each of the ten Athenian tribes were named. Situated in the marketplace (*agora*), they were a common place for public notices and proclamations.

property and there might be a debt of gratitude to us among the mass of citizens. We are requesting this gratitude[40] now, not in an attempt to get more than is just but to show that we are doing nothing unjust, ⟨and that you are⟩[41] abiding by your oaths and the treaty. [68] It would be terrible if the treaty were effective in releasing from punishment those who have done injustice but ineffective for us, who have done good. It is right for you to guard your present good fortune with the consideration that treaties have created more civil strife in other cities but concord in yours. Recall this and vote for what is both just and advantageous.

---

[40] The word for gratitude, *charis,* is the same one that was translated as "favor" in 34, above. There Isocrates says that the judges should disregard appeals based on it.

[41] Sections 67–68 contain many problems in the manuscripts, which indicate a short gap of two or three words at this point.

19. AEGINETICUS

INTRODUCTION

This speech is unique in having been composed for presentation in a lawcourt outside Athens. In Athens, the dispute would be called a *diadikasia,* which occurs when two parties make a claim to an inheritance. But this dispute takes place on the island of Aegina (an independent *polis* in the Saronic Gulf about twenty-five kilometers [fifteen miles] south of Piraeus, Athens' port), and that is where the speech is to be presented. It is therefore impossible to determine which aspects of Athenian law might also apply in this case. In fact, the issue of what city's laws do apply is addressed in 12–15.

The speaker bases his claim on his posthumous adoption by the deceased, Thrasylochus, and his betrothal to Thrasylochus' sister. This was not uncommon: if a man lacked a son, he would often adopt someone into his family, even another man his own age, since the preservation of the male family line was deemed crucial. But the speaker's claim has been challenged on the ground that there is a living, natural heir.

After an introduction (1–4), the speaker begins his narrative by recounting the life of Thrasyllus, Thrasylochus' father, who made a substantial amount of money as an itinerant seer (5–9). He then relates his close relationship to Thrasylochus (10–11) and the laws under which Thrasylochus adopted him (12–15), which (he says) is all he really needs to do to demonstrate his case. Nevertheless, he continues by detailing his extraordinary services to Thrasylochus and the misfortunes into which they led him (16–29), contrasting them with the mistreatment Thrasylochus received from the speaker's opponent (30–33). He then anticipates the arguments of his opponent, which are based on the validity of the will (34–35) and the speaker's status (36–37), and details his friendship with Thrasylochus' brother, Sopolis (38–41). Lastly, before making his final appeal, he imagines what Thrasyllus might have thought of his becoming heir (42–51).

The speech has a lengthy narrative section, which gives an intriguing glimpse into the everyday life of exiled Greeks living an unsettled life, moving from one city to another. The political events related in 18–20 suggest a date after 393, perhaps 391 or 390. (Cf. Xen., *Hellenica* 4.8.7 and Diodorus Siculus 14.18.)

19. AEGINETICUS

[1] I used to believe, men of Aegina, that Thrasylochus had planned his affairs so well that no one would ever come forward to oppose the instructions he left in his will. But since my opponents have had the idea of disputing the will, even though it was arranged in this way, I am compelled to attempt before you to win what is just. [2] My experience has been the opposite of most people.[1] I see that others take it badly when they face risks over something unjustly, but I am almost thankful to these people for having brought me to trial here. If the affair had remained untried, you would not have known what behavior of mine led to my being the heir of his property. When you learn what I did, you will see that I would justly have earned an even greater gift than this.

[3] My rival for the money, mind you, should not have tried to obtain from you the property Thrasylochus left behind; she should have treated him well and thus earned the right to sue for it. But as it is, she is so far from feeling regret for mistreating him during his lifetime that now that he is dead, she is trying to invalidate his will and desolate his household. [4] I am surprised also at those acting on her behalf,[2] if they think that their risk is a good one because they will pay nothing if they are not successful. I think it is a serious penalty if they are exposed as contesting unjustly, since they will appear worse in your

---

[1] A commonplace found, e.g., in Lys. 16.1–2, 24.1 and Is. 2.1

[2] Since women could not appear in court in Athens, it seems likely that men are representing her here in Aegina also.

eyes. You will recognize the wickedness of these people directly from their actions when you have heard the facts to the end. I shall begin my narration from the point where I think you will most quickly learn what we are disputing.

[5] Thrasyllus, the father of the man who left the will, received no property from his ancestors. He became a guest-friend (*xenos*)[3] of Polemaenetus the seer and then became so close to him that when Polemaenetus died, he left his books on divination to him and gave him part of his property, which exists even now. [6] Thrasyllus took these resources and practiced the craft of divination.[4] He became a traveler, lived in many cities, and was intimate with different women, several of whom gave birth to children he never regarded as legitimate. Indeed, during this time he also got to know the mother of this woman.[5] [7] When he had acquired a lot of property and longed for his homeland, he left that woman and the others, sailed to Siphnos, and married my father's sister. Thrasyllus himself was the wealthiest of the citizens, but he knew that our family was foremost in birth and other honors. [8] He so appreciated the friendship of my father that when his wife died childless, he once more married a cousin of my father, since he did not wish to dissolve his close relationship with us. But he had not been married long when he experienced the same bad luck with this wife as he had with the first. [9] After this, he married a woman from Seriphos from a family that was much more worthy than the city itself.[6] From her were born Sopolis, Thrasylochus, and a daughter, who is now my wife. Thrasyllus, in short, left only these legitimate children and had made them heirs of his property when he died.

[10] Thrasylochus and I took over a friendship from our fathers,

---

[3] A *xenos* or "guest-friend" was someone from another city with whom one had formed a special friendship through the offering and receiving of hospitality. It was, and is, an important, widespread and long-lasting social institution in Greece.

[4] Note that divination is not connected closely to religious observance; it is a trade.

[5] His opponent, who has challenged his right to the inheritance.

[6] The smallness of Seriphos was proverbial (cf. Plato, *Republic* 329e, and Plut., *Themistocles* 8).

the strength of which I mentioned a little earlier, and we made ours still stronger than theirs. While we were children, we thought more of each other than of our brothers, and we did not perform a sacrifice, a festival observance, or any other celebration without each other. When we became men, we never came in conflict, but we shared private concerns, had similar feelings about the affairs of the city, and enjoyed the same friends and guest-friends. [11] What need is there to speak of our closeness at home?[7] Not even as exiles did we want to be separated. In the end, when he became emaciated and weakened over a long time, since his brother Sopolis had died before him and his mother and sister were not yet at hand, I nursed him in his loneliness with such care and loyalty that he thought he could not render thanks worthy of what I had done. [12] Nevertheless he did all he could: when he was badly off and had no hope of living, he called witnesses, made me his son, and gave me his sister and property.[8] Please take the will:

[WILL]

Please read the law of the Aeginetans also. It was necessary to make the will according to it since we were metics[9] there.

[LAW]

[13] According to this law here, men of Aegina, Thrasylochus made me his son. I was a fellow citizen and a friend, I had been born no worse than any Siphnian, and I had been educated and brought up just as he had. Therefore, I do not know what more he could have done according to the law, which prescribes that only people of the

---

[7] I.e., on Siphnos.

[8] The sister of Thrasylochus became an *epiklēros,* a woman upon whom the estate devolved. It was common in Athenian law that a man who inherited an estate through adoption would also be obliged to marry the deceased's sister or daughter. See Is. 3.68 – 69.

[9] A metic was usually a resident foreigner, although manumitted slaves also had this status. Since Greek cities did not generally grant citizenship to outsiders even if they had been resident for many years, or even generations, sizeable metic populations existed in many cities, especially those, like Athens, that had a large import-export trade.

same status be adopted. Please take the law of Ceos, which governed our city.¹⁰

[LAW]

[14] Men of Aegina, if indeed my opponents were opposing these laws but had the law that was in effect among them¹¹ as legal support, I would have less reason to be surprised at them. But as it is, their law is similar to those that have been read. Please take the document.

[LAW]

[15] What is left for them, when they themselves admit that Thrasylochus left the will and that none of the laws supports them? They all support me. First there is the law among you who are to decide the case,¹² then there is that of Siphnos, the home of the man who left the will, and finally there is that in effect among those who are disputing the case. What do you think they would not do, when they are seeking to persuade you that you must invalidate the will, although the laws are this way and you have sworn to vote according to them?

[16] I think that I have demonstrated my case itself sufficiently. But so that no one may think that I possess the inheritance on the basis of weak pretexts and that this woman is being deprived of the money after treating Thrasylochus fairly, I want to talk about these matters as well. I would be ashamed on behalf of the deceased if you were not all convinced that he did these things not only according to the laws but justly also.¹³ [17] I think that the demonstrations of this are easy. This woman and I were so different that although she bases her claim on birth, she spent the whole time angrily quarreling with Thrasylochus, with Sopolis, and with their mother, while I shall be shown to have been the most worthy friend, not only of Thrasylochus and

---

¹⁰ Ceos was an island near Siphnos. The Siphnians presumably took over the Cean law code and so acknowledged its source.

¹¹ In Troezen, see below, 31.

¹² I.e., the law of Aegina.

¹³ Here he signals extralegal argumentation. To the extent that he can show Thrasylochus' goodwill toward himself, he does strengthen the legal argument that the will is genuine, not forged, but the thrust of his argumentation is that he is not merely standing by the letter of the law.

his brother, but also with regard to the property itself that we are disputing.

[18] It would be a big task to discuss events long past, but when Pasinus seized Paros,[14] it happened that most of their[15] property was deposited there with guest-friends of mine. We had thought that this island would be especially secure. Since they were at a loss and thought that the property was lost, I sailed by night and brought out their money by risking my life. [19] The land was being garrisoned, and some exiles from our country had seized the city. On a single day they murdered with their own hands my father, my uncle, my brother-in-law, and three cousins in addition. Nevertheless, none of these things diverted me, but I sailed off determined to take the same risk on their behalf as I would for myself. [20] After this, when we were exiled from Siphnos with so much upheaval and fear that some people even neglected their own families, I was not content in these troubles to be able to rescue my family. I knew that Sopolis was away and that Thrasylochus was in a weakened state, and so I helped him evacuate his mother, his sister, and all his property. Now, who has more right to this property than the one who helped to save it then and who has received it now from its legitimate owners?

[21] What has so far been mentioned are the times I took risks but suffered nothing adverse. But I can also talk about times when in helping him I fell into the greatest misfortunes. When we went to Melos[16] and he saw that we intended to remain there, Thrasylochus asked me to sail with him to Troezen[17] and not to desert him for any reason. He spoke of his physical weakness and of his many enemies there and said that without me he would be unable to carry on his own affairs. [22] My mother was afraid because she had learned that there was disease at Troezen, and our guest-friends advised us to remain in Melos, but we decided that we should follow Thrasylochus' wishes. Later, when we had just arrived at Troezen, we were afflicted by such sickness that I myself almost died, and I buried my sister, a girl of fourteen,

[14]Neither the date of this event nor the identity of Pasinus is known.
[15]Thrasylochus and his brother.
[16]Another island, near Ceos and Siphnos.
[17]A city on the coast of the northeastern Peloponnesus, near the island of Aegina.

less than thirty days afterward, and my mother not five days later. How do you think I felt after this reversal occurred in my life? [23] Up to that time I had not experienced misfortune, but now I had experienced exile, lived as a metic among others, and lost my property. In addition, I saw my mother and sister banished from their homeland and die in a foreign land among strangers. Therefore, no one could justly begrudge me if I enjoyed some benefit from the affairs of Thrasylochus, since it was in order to please him that I took up residence in Troezen and suffered misfortunes that I shall never be able to forget.

[24] Moreover, they will not be able to say that I stuck with Thrasylochus through all these things while he was well off but left him in his misfortune. At that time I showed still more clearly and substantially my goodwill for him. When he had settled in Aegina and was enfeebled by the sickness from which he died, I took such care of him as no one to my knowledge has given another. Most of the time he was quite sick but still able to get around. But for six months straight he lay on his bed. [25] None of his relations saw fit to share in these hardships. No one came to see him except his mother and sister, and they did more harm than good. (They were weakened from Troezen, so that they themselves needed care.) Just the same, although the others felt this way about him, I did not object or leave. I cared for him with the help of one slave. [26] None of the other servants could endure it. Thrasylochus was by nature difficult and his illness made him still more bad-tempered, so it is no surprise that they did not remain. It is much more surprising that I could endure caring for such a disease. He suffered from an abscess much of the time and was unable to move from his bed. [27] He suffered so badly that we did not pass a day without tears. We wept continually over our hardships together, our exile, and our loneliness. These things never let up. It was impossible to leave or to appear unconcerned. To me that would have been more terrible than the troubles we already had.

[28] I would like to be able to make clear to you how I treated him, for I think that then you would not even allow my opponents a voice. But it is difficult now to describe how very difficult his care was, its great hardships with their unpleasant tasks and requirement for constant attention. You yourselves see how much sleeplessness and misery accompanies the care over such a disease over such a long time. [29] I was in such a bad way that all my friends who came to me said they

feared I would also succumb, and they advised me to take care of myself. They said that most of those who had cared for people with this disease had themselves also perished. To them I replied that I would really prefer to die than to see Thrasylochus die before his time because of a lack of care.

[30] Although this woman knew daily how he was doing and the trip would have been easy for her, she never bothered to look in on him through his long infirmity, but she has dared to dispute with me over his belongings after I have acted this way. Now they are trying to call him "brother," as if by addressing the deceased more familiarly she does not make the wrong she has done seem that much worse and more terrible. [31] When he was about to die, she saw our fellow citizens who had been in Troezen sailing to Aegina to join in his burial, but she did not stir herself at that time. She has been so crude and depraved that she did not see fit to come to the funeral, but within ten days after that she came to dispute his remaining property, as if she were a relative of his money but not of him. [32] If she will agree that she had such great animus toward him that her behavior was reasonable, then he would not have been badly advised if he wanted to leave his property to his friends rather than to her. But if there was no disagreement between them and yet she was so unconcerned and wicked toward him, she would much more justly be deprived of her own property than inherit his. [33] Consider that she had no part in his care during his illness, and when he died she thought he was unworthy of the customary rites; he received both of these because of me. Surely it is just that you cast your votes not for those people who claim to be related to him by birth but have in fact acted like his enemies, but much rather for those who have no family designation but have shown themselves more closely related in times of misfortune than his blood relatives.

[34] They say that they do not doubt that Thrasylochus left the will, but they claim that it is not right or correct. But, men of Aegina, how would someone plan his affairs better or more advantageously? He has not left his household without an heir, and he has returned gratitude to his friends. He has not only put his mother and sister in charge of their own possessions, he has married his sister to me and made me his mother's adopted son. [35] Would he have done better if he had put no one in care of his mother, if he had not thought of me,

if he had left his sister to chance and had seen the name of his family disappear? [36] But perhaps they will argue that I was unworthy to be made Thrasylochus' son and to receive his sister in marriage. All the Siphnians would testify that my ancestors were foremost of the citizens in birth, wealth, reputation, and everything else. Who was thought worthy of higher offices or contributed more money or produced finer choral productions (*chorēgiai*) or performed the other public duties (*lēitourgiai*) more magnificently?[18] From what family in Siphnos were more kings[19] born? [37] Even if I had never spoken to him, therefore, Thrasylochus would likely have wanted to give me his sister, and I, even if I had none of these distinctions but were the lowest of citizens, I would have a just claim on the greatest rewards because of the benefits that I rendered him.

[38] I believe, moreover, that in making his will this way he would also have pleased his brother Sopolis. Sopolis also hated this woman and thought she was hostile to his interests; he regarded me as his most important friend. He made this clear in many ways, but especially when our fellow exiles decided to storm the city[20] with the help of mercenaries. After he was chosen to lead with full powers, he selected me as his secretary and made me treasurer of all the money; and when we were about to go into danger, he placed me at his side. [39] See how advantageous this was for him. Our attack on the city was unsuccessful, and the retreat did not turn out as we had wished. Since he was injured, unable to walk and barely conscious, I carried him off to the ship on my shoulders with the help of my servant, so that he often declared to many people that I alone was responsible for his rescue. [40] Indeed, what could have been a greater favor than that? When he died after sailing off to Lycia, however, this woman was performing sacrifices and celebrating festivals only a few days after the message

---

[18] These were duties taken on by the rich in lieu of taxation. Mentioning them in Athenian courts is a common way to demonstrate nobility and patriotism. The same was presumably true also in Aegina.

[19] Presumably this was only a religious office, like that of the *basileus* ("king") in Athens, who was the magistrate responsible for legal cases having religious significance, such as homicide and impiety.

[20] Siphnos.

arrived. She felt so little shame dishonoring the dead man in this way in the presence of his brother, who was still living. But I mourned him just as the law requires for family members. [41] I did all these things because of my character and my friendship toward them, not for the sake of this trial here. I never thought that these men would be so unfortunate that by both dying childless they would create this test of how each of us behaved toward them.

[42] You have heard in essence how this woman and I behaved toward Thrasylochus and Sopolis. But perhaps they will turn to the one argument that remains for them, namely, that Thrasyllus, the father of this woman, would believe he was being wronged—if the dead have some perception of what is happening here—if he saw his daughter deprived of his money and me inheriting what he had acquired. [43] I think we should not discuss those who died long ago but those who have just now left their estate. Thrasyllus left those he wanted in charge of his property. It is just that Thrasylochus be given the same privilege by you and that not she but those whom he designated in his will should become the successors of his estate. However, I do not think that I am evading the judgment of Thrasyllus. [44] I think he would be the harshest judge of all for her, if he learned how she had treated his children. He would be far from angered at you for voting according to the laws, but he would be much more angry if he saw the wills of his children invalidated. If Thrasylochus had given his property to my family, they would be able to criticize him. But as it is, he has adopted me into his family, so that they have received no less than they have given.[21] [45] Besides, Thrasyllus would be more likely than anyone to favor those who base their claim in the dispute on a gift. He himself learned his craft from Polemaenetus the seer and received his money, not by birth but because of merit, so I don't suppose he would feel jealous if someone who had treated his children well were deemed worthy of what he himself got. [46] You must recall what I said at the beginning: I showed you that he regarded our closeness as so important that he married first my father's sister and then my father's cousin. To whom would he sooner have given his daughter

---

[21] I.e., they have acquired a new son by adoption and thus kept the estate in the family.

in marriage than to those people from whom he thought fit to receive a wife? From what family would he more gladly see a son adopted by law than that from which he sought to have children by nature?

[47] Therefore, if you grant me the estate, you will meet with approval from Thrasyllus and from everyone else who has an interest in these matters. But if you are deceived by this woman's persuasion, you will do not only me an injustice but also Thrasylochus, who left the will, Sopolis, and their sister, who is now my wife, and their mother, who would be the most unfortunate of all women if she were not only to endure the loss of her children but this also were added: that she should see their decision rendered invalid and their house become empty [48] while this woman rejoices over her misfortunes by being granted the money, and I am unable to win justice, even though I treated her sons in such a way that if anyone should look at me not in relation to this woman but in relation to those who have ever based their case on a testamentary gift, I would be found inferior to no one in my treatment of my friends. Indeed, such people as myself ought to be honored and held in high esteem, not stripped of gifts given them by others. [49] It is also right to support the law that allows us to adopt children and to plan for our estates. Consider that this law takes the place of children for those who are alone. Because of this law, relatives and those with no connections care for each other.[22]

[50] So that I may stop talking and spend no more time, look how important and just are the claims I have in coming before you: first, a friendship with those who left the estate, a friendship that is old, was handed down by our fathers, and has continued the whole time; then there are the many great services, which I rendered even in bad times; in addition there is the will, which has been admitted by our adversaries themselves; and finally, the law, which supports the will and which is approved by all the Greeks.[23] [51] The greatest evidence of this is that while the Greeks differ on many other matters, they agree about this. So I beg you, recall these and the other points I have made and vote justly; be the sort of judges for me that you would want to meet yourselves.

---

[22] This sort of argument appears also in Is. 2.13 and Dem. 20.102.
[23] See also Is. 2.24.

20. AGAINST LOCHITES

INTRODUCTION

It is commonly believed that the beginning of this speech, which would have contained the narrative of events, has been lost. But it is possible that the speaker, who makes a point of his poverty, was able to afford only this short, prepared speech. The testimony of witnesses, together with his own improvised connecting comments, may have provided the bulk of the narrative. It was the function of this text, then, only to underline the importance of the affair. The speaker seems to attempt to obscure whether the speech arose from a *graphē hybreōs* (a public suit for *hybris*, "wanton violence") or a *dikē aikeias* (a private suit for assault). The emphasis at the beginning of the speech on who struck the first blow and the later reference (19) to the prosecutor's receiving personal compensation suggest that this case was a *dikē*, but most of his arguments deal with *hybris*.

There are several interesting arguments in this speech; some of them would shock a modern jurist. It opens with a discussion of the importance of legislation restricting physical assault (1–3), touching at several points on the intent of the legislators. It also casts an eye on the recent tyranny of the Thirty, "the oligarchy" (4, 11), which helps to date the speech to approximately 402–400. The speaker anticipates his opponent's argument concerning the seriousness of the case by arguing that even minor transgressions are indications of serious moral depravity and that it is for the latter rather than the former that Lochites should be punished (5–9), a surprising legal principle indeed, as if simply being depraved, without acting out that depravity, were punishable. He then restates this argument, substituting the character of those involved with the tyranny for the seriously depraved, even though Lochites is too young ever to have been involved with the

Thirty (10–14). The rest of the speech develops an argument about equality in justice, in which the speaker attempts to make the judges identify themselves with him (15–22).

20. AGAINST LOCHITES

[1] That Lochites did indeed strike me and started the fight[1] all who were present have testified to you. You must not think this wrong similar to others, nor should you assign equal punishment for injuries to the person as for property damage. You know that the body is the most personal concern for all people: we have established laws and we do battle over its freedom; we desire democracy and we do everything else in life for its sake. Therefore, it is reasonable to restrain with the greatest punishment those who do wrong in this regard, which you take very seriously.

[2] You will find that those who have enacted our laws have been especially mindful about our bodies. First, they have created both private and public suits[2] without a preliminary deposit for this wrong alone, so that to the extent that each of us may be able and willing, he may punish those who injure him. Next, while in other charges the wrongdoer is liable to prosecution only by the victim, in a case of *hybris* ("violent assault"), inasmuch as it is a matter of public concern, any citizen who wishes may bring a written charge (*graphē*) to the Thesmothetae[3] and come before you. [3] The legislators thought that the act of striking each other was so terrible that even for verbal abuse they enacted a law requiring those who say something forbidden to owe damages of five hundred drachmas. Indeed, what degree of punishment must be inflicted on behalf of victims of physical abuse, when you appear to be so angered on behalf of victims of mere verbal abuse?

[4] It is amazing if you believe those who committed *hybris* during

---

[1] "Started the fight" is an archaic legal expression that goes back to Draco's law, more than two centuries earlier.

[2] On regular, private suits (*dikai*) and "written," public charges (*graphai*), see Series Introduction. Since *dikai* by this time were also written down, the original, terminological distinction does not accurately describe the practical, judicial distinction.

[3] The Thesmothetae were the six annual magistrates whose primary responsibility was administration of the lawcourts. See *Ath. Pol.* 59.

the oligarchy deserve death, but you let those doing the same things during the democracy go unpunished. They should rightly receive a greater punishment, for they are showing their depravity more clearly. If someone dares transgress the laws now when it is not tolerated, what would he have done then when those in control of the city were even thanking those who committed such wrongs?

[5] Perhaps Lochites will try to make light of the matter, disparaging my prosecution and saying that I suffered nothing serious from the blows, that I am making more of a fuss about what happened than it deserves. If there had been no *hybris* attached to what he did, I would not have come to you. But as it is, I have come to obtain justice from him not for any injury resulting from his blows but for the outrage and indignity he inflicted. [6] About these matters, free people should be especially indignant and inflict the greatest retribution. I see that when you condemn someone for temple robbery or theft, you do not set the penalty according to the size of what they take. You condemn all alike to death and believe it just that those who attempt the same acts should be restrained by the same punishments. [7] Surely you must hold the same principle regarding those committing *hybris:* examine not whether the beating was severe, but whether the law was broken; punish them not just for what happened to result in this case but for their entire behavior; take into consideration that small pretexts have often resulted in great evils, [8] and that because of those who dared to strike blows in the past, some people have become so angry that they have resorted to assaults, killings, exiles, and the greatest misfortunes. None of these things happened in this case, not because of the man defending it—for his part, they were all done—but nothing irrevocable occurred because of luck and the strength of my character.

[9] I think that you would be properly angered at this act if you went through for yourselves how much greater this crime is than others. You will find that other acts of injustice do harm to only a part of life, but *hybris* degrades all our activities. Many homes have been destroyed and many cities ruined because of it. [10] But why must I spend time talking about others' misfortunes? We ourselves have twice seen the democracy destroyed, and we have twice been robbed of freedom,[4] not by those guilty of other forms of depravity but because of

---

[4] In 411/10 and 404/3.

men who despised the laws and wished to be enslaved to the enemy and to commit *hybris* against their fellow citizens. [11] Lochites happens to be one of these. Even if he is younger than those who held power then, he has the character of that government. These were the natures that betrayed our empire to the enemy, razed the walls of our homeland, and executed fifteen hundred of our citizens without trial.

[12] It stands to reason that you should recall those events and punish not only those who harmed us then but also those who now wish to treat the city in this way. Just as those who are expected to be depraved are more dangerous than those who have already done wrong, it is better to discover how to avert future crimes than to obtain justice for those already committed. [13] Don't wait until they have banded together and seized upon a crisis in order to harm the entire city, but when they are handed over to you on a pretext, punish them for this in the belief that when you arrest someone demonstrating his complete depravity in a minor incident, you've had a piece of good luck. [14] It would be best if some sign or other were affixed to base people so that they might be restrained before they injured any citizen.⁵ But since they cannot be recognized before they victimize someone, when they are discovered, then everyone must hate such people and regard them as public enemies.⁶

[15] Consider too that the poor have no share in threats to property, but everyone has the same interest in outrages to the body, so when you punish thieves, you benefit only the wealthy, but when you check those committing *hybris,* you are helping yourselves. [16] For this reason, these must be thought the most important of trials, and while in other private dealings the penalty must be only as much as the prosecutor deserves, for *hybris* the defendant must pay enough that he will stop his present brutality. [17] If you take away the property of those who act like young thugs toward citizens, and if you believe that no

---

⁵ This image recalls a similar sentiment that is expressed in Euripides' *Medea* 516–519.

⁶ The legal principles expressed in this paragraph go far beyond anything else expressed in Greek (or modern) law, where punishments are made to fit crimes that have already been committed, not those that may only be anticipated. Certainly one aspect of incarceration is that it prevents future crimes, but a person punished for carrying a knife is not treated as if she has already committed murder.

punishment is sufficient for those who commit bodily harm but suffer only a monetary fine, then you will do everything that good judges must. [18] And in the present case, you will decide correctly, you will make the other citizens more orderly, and you will make your own lives more secure. It is characteristic of judges who have good sense to vote justly with regard to other people's affairs and at the same time to determine their own affairs well also.

[19] Let not even one of you think it right to reduce the award because you have observed that I am poor, one of the many.[7] It is unjust to make the penalty less for little-known victims than for the famous, to think that the impoverished are worse than those who have much. You would be dishonoring yourselves if you thought such things about citizens.

[20] Moreover, it would be most terrible of all if in a democratic city all people should not enjoy the same good fortune, if we thought that we all deserved to hold office yet robbed ourselves of justice under the laws, if we were willing to fight and die for our constitution yet allotted more in our voting to those who have property. [21] If you listen to me, you will not treat yourselves this way. You will not teach the young to despise the mass of citizens. You will not suppose that trials concern only others, but each of you will cast his vote as if he were judging on his own behalf. Those who dare to transgress this law, which was established on behalf of your bodies, do injustice to everyone alike. [22] Therefore, if you are sensible, call on one another and signal your anger to Lochites. You know that all such people despise the established laws but believe that these decisions of yours are the real laws.[8]

I have said what I can about the case. If someone present has something to say on my behalf, let him come up here and speak.

---

[7] We may wonder whether this argument is not disingenuous inasmuch as most of the judges would also have been relatively poor. But it seems likely that Athenian judges, like modern jurors, were probably slightly intimidated by wealth. The speaker thus makes a circuitous attempt to make the judges identify and sympathize with him.

[8] This argument not only contains a rhetorical commonplace but identifies a reality of the Athenian legal system, that the panel of judges was free to decide issues of both fact and law without any accountability, regardless of the wording and intent of the laws. The speaker thus reminds the jurors with this argument that they have sworn to decide cases according to the law.

21. AGAINST EUTHYNUS, WITHOUT WITNESSES

᪥᪥᪥

INTRODUCTION

This speech, which was composed a short time after the tyranny of the Thirty in 404/403, illustrates how tangled personal relationships became at that time. It was written for a man named Nicias, who attempted to liquidate and hide his assets from the tyranny. He gave some of his money (he says it was three talents) to a relative named Euthynus for safekeeping, but Euthynus allegedly failed to return one-third of it later. The suit Nicias has brought is thus a *parakatathēkēs dikē,* a suit to recover a deposit, and it shares many of the same lines of argumentation as 17, which also concerns a deposit. The orator Lysias is said to have written a speech on behalf of Euthynus in response to Nicias.

The words "without witnesses" were already added to the title in antiquity. The speech lacks the support of any witness testimony, which is quite unusual. The Athenians attempted to have almost everything witnessed that might ever be the subject of a lawsuit, whether marriages, commercial transactions, or acts of violence. (According to 17.2 and 53, deposits with bankers were an exception.) In this case, the haste and confusion of events may have prevented Nicias from providing witnesses. A result of the absence of witnesses is that the speech relies heavily on arguments from probability, and it ends abruptly, without a proper conclusion. It is possible, however, that the speech was one of a number of speeches presented by friends of Nicias in his support; one of the other speeches may have incorporated all the witness testimony.

The speech was delivered by a *synēgoros,* a co-pleader who seems to have been closely familiar with both Nicias and Euthynus. In general, Athenians pleaded their own cases in court, but such co-pleaders sometimes speak in place of or in addition to the litigant. From what we know of Isocrates' diffidence regarding the delivery of speeches, it seems unlikely that Isocrates himself is the *synēgoros* here.

21. AGAINST EUTHYNUS, WITHOUT WITNESSES

[1] I lack no excuse for speaking on behalf of Nicias here: he is my friend, he is in need, he has been wronged and he is unable to speak for himself,[1] so I am compelled for all of these reasons to speak for him.

[2] Now, I shall relate to you as briefly as I can the origin of his dealings with Euthynus. During the rule of the Thirty, his enemies were trying to remove his name from the list of citizens and inscribe it on Lysander's list.[2] In fear of these developments, Nicias here leased out his property, sent his slaves out of the country, brought his furniture to me, gave three talents of silver to Euthynus for safekeeping, and went to live in the country. [3] A little later, he wished to sail away[3] and asked for his money back; Euthynus returned two talents but denied having the third. Since Nicias could do nothing else at that time, he took his complaints to his friends and told them how he had been treated. Nevertheless, you must understand that he held this man in such high esteem and so feared the political situation that he is the sort of person who would have preferred to keep silent and be out a bit rather than appear now to be making an accusation when he had lost nothing.

[4] This, then, is what happened. The case puts us at a loss: no one—no free person, no slave—was present when Nicias deposited the money or when it was returned, so it is impossible to learn about

---

[1] Isocrates gives no indication why Nicias is unable to speak for himself, but it adds to Nicias' credibility as an innocent that he can be said to be so incapable of functioning in the public sphere. It ties in with the argument he uses in 5, below.

[2] Lysander was the Spartan general who had captured Athens. Xen., *Hellenica* 2.3.17–19, and *Ath. Pol.* 37, both of which report the events of this period, do not mention a list of proscribed individuals. They were presumably simply those left off the reduced list of 3,000 "citizens," which the Thirty prepared.

[3] I.e., to go into exile, as did many of the opponents and victims of the Thirty.

it by torturing slaves[4] or from free witnesses, but we must argue, and you must judge, who is telling the truth on the basis of evidence (tekmēria).[5]

[5] I think everyone knows that those who are clever at speaking but have no money attempt to bring malicious prosecutions (sykophantein) most often against those who are unable to speak for themselves but capable enough of paying them money. Nicias, however, has more money than Euthynus, and he is a poorer speaker, so he would not attack Euthynus unjustly for this reason. [6] Rather, someone might conclude from this very fact that it is much more likely that Euthynus took the money and is denying it than that Nicias did not give it and is making a false charge. Clearly everyone who acts unjustly does so for the sake of profit. Those who commit fraud already have the profit on account of which they do wrong, whereas those who make false accusations do not know whether they will even get anything. [7] Besides this, when affairs in the city are unstable and there are no court proceedings, there is no advantage for the latter in making accusations and no fear for the former in committing fraud.[6] So there would be nothing surprising, when even those who took out loans before witnesses are denying it, that Euthynus would deny having stolen what he received from Nicias when they were all alone; but it is unlikely that Nicias would think he would get something by making a wrongful accusation, when not even those who are rightly owed money can recover it.

[8] What's more, it is easy to see that Nicias would not proceed

---

[4] Slaves could not testify as witnesses before a lawcourt. The Athenians attempted to guarantee the truth of what they said by having them tortured through an out-of-court agreement called a "challenge" (proklēsis).

[5] According to the rhetorical theory of Aristotle (Rhetoric 1.2), tekmēria were "sure signs" or "certain indications," in the same way that having a fever is a "sure sign" that you are ill. Like the other orators, Isocrates is being less technical here. He means by tekmēria the circumstantial evidence from the case that is to be combined with arguments from probability. He is certainly not referring to documents or anything else that might commonly be introduced as "evidence" in modern courts.

[6] Of course, Nicias' formal accusation was not made until after the democracy had been restored.

against Euthynus, even if nothing prevented it, but it was possible, and he wanted to bring a malicious prosecution. Those who wish to do such things do not begin with their friends;[7] they proceed together with their friends against others and accuse those they neither respect nor fear, those who, they see, are wealthy but isolated and unable to act. [9] It was just the opposite, however, for Euthynus. He happens to be a cousin of Nicias, and he can both speak and act more ably than Nicias. And while he has little money, he has acquired many friends. So there is no one against whom Nicias would be less likely to act. And it seems to me, from my knowledge of their relationship, that Euthynus would not have wronged Nicias if he could have defrauded as much money from anyone else.

[10] Now the case was quite basic for them:[8] for in making an accusation, it is possible to choose anyone, but in defrauding, it is impossible to choose anyone other than a depositor. So if he had wanted to bring a malicious prosecution, Nicias would not have proceeded against this man, but in attempting fraud, Euthynus did not have anyone else.

[11] The following is the greatest evidence (*tekmērion*), and it is sufficient in every way: the accusation was made when the oligarchy had been established,[9] when these two men were in such a position that even if Nicias had been accustomed to bringing malicious prosecutions, he would then have stopped, but even if Euthynus had never thought of doing wrong, he would have been motivated to do so. [12] Euthynus was gaining honor for his crimes, but Nicias was threatened because of his money. You all know that at that time it was more dangerous to be wealthy than to do wrong. Some took others' possessions, while the rest lost what was their own. The city was in the hands of people who did not punish criminals but arrested those who owned anything; they thought that the wrongdoers were trustworthy and the wealthy their enemies. [13] So Nicias had no interest in getting

---

[7] The Greek word for friend, *philos,* may include everyone with whom a person is closely associated, both friends and family.

[8] Editors have seen corruption in the text here.

[9] He means here the informal accusation that Nicias made to his friends (see above, 3), not the formal accusation before the magistrate that led to the trial in court.

another's property by malicious prosecution; he wanted only to do nothing wrong and suffer no harm. Someone with as much power as Euthynus' could defraud someone of what he got from them on deposit and accuse those to whom he had made no loan. But those who were in Nicias' situation were compelled to surrender their loans to their debtors and to pay off those making malicious prosecutions. [14] Euthynus himself would testify to you that I am speaking the truth. He knows that Timodemos had this man Nicias give him thirty minas, not by accusing him of debt but by threatening to bring him into court. Now how likely is it that Nicias would be so foolish as to bring a malicious prosecution against others when his own life was in danger? [15] That he would plot against others' possessions when he was unable to safeguard his own? That he would add other opponents to his existing enemies and make wrongful accusations against those from whom it would be impossible to obtain justice even if they admitted defrauding him? That he would seek to gain more when he could not even remain on a par? That he would hope to recover what he had never lent when he was being forced to pay back what he had not taken?

[16] What I have said about these matters is enough. Perhaps Euthynus will say—as he said before¹⁰—that if he had tried to do wrong, he would never have returned two-thirds of the deposit and defrauded Nicias of the other third, but whether he intended to act unjustly or decided to be just, he would have had the same thought about all the money. [17] I think you all know that all people who engage in wrongdoing think about their defense at the same time, so it is no wonder that Euthynus did wrong in this way for the sake of this line of argument.¹¹ I could certainly point out others who accepted money on deposit and returned most of it but stole a small part. They acted unjustly in small transactions but became just in great ones, so Euthynus is neither the only one nor the first to have done such things. [18] You must also consider that if you accept such arguments from speakers, you will establish a new law about how to

¹⁰ It is unclear whether this was at a preliminary hearing or at an attempt at arbitration.

¹¹ I.e., if he only stole one-third of the money in order to use this apparent illogicality as a point in his defense.

commit injustice: [12] for the rest of time people will return some money but keep the rest. It will be profitable for them to use what they return as evidence, if they intend to escape punishment for what they defraud.

[19] Examine also how easy it is to make arguments on behalf of Nicias that are similar to Euthynus' defense speech. For when Nicias recovered the two talents, no one was present, so if indeed he wished and it seemed worthwhile to him to bring a malicious prosecution, clearly he would not have admitted recovering the two talents but would have used the same argument about all the money: Euthynus would be in danger of losing even more money, and, at the same time, he would not have the two talents to use here now as evidence.

[20] Finally, no one can show any reason whatsoever why Nicias would have made this accusation unless it were true, but it is easy to see Euthynus' reasons for doing injustice this way. When Nicias was in difficulties, all his relatives and friends had heard that his money had been deposited with Euthynus. [21] So Euthynus knew that many were aware that the money was in his keeping, but no one knew how much, so he thought that if he reduced the amount, he would not be discovered, but if he stole everything, he would be obvious. And so he preferred to take a sufficient amount and be left with a defense rather than return nothing and be unable to make a denial.

---

[12] In the *Rhetoric* (1.1.6), Aristotle warns against judges learning about matters of law from the speakers. Usually this argument is put in the form found in Aeschylus' *Eumenides* 490–507, that an acquittal will give *carte blanche* to future criminals.

PART TWO

Translated by Yun Lee Too

INTRODUCTION TO PART TWO

The speeches contained in Part Two, *Evagoras* (9), *To Nicocles* (2), *Nicocles* (3), *Areopagiticus* (7), and *Antidosis* (15), are texts that characterize Isocrates as teacher. Together these five speeches show that "teacher" in classical Athens need not mean "sophist," the figure caricatured in Aristophanes' *Clouds* and in the dialogues of Plato as the unscrupulous charlatan who makes promises and then disappoints and charges enormous fees for his lectures and displays. Isocrates' pedagogical identity demonstrates that rhetorical teaching—teaching that is articulated in rhetorical texts—may be an important mode of political activity, albeit one that is quite distinct from the contemporary political scene as conducted through litigation and sykophancy. Teaching is a responsible act, ensuring that rulers and ruled know their obligations to each other and to their community, that the community knows its origins and authority, and that it realizes the debt owed to the culture of speech and its practitioners.

The first three are the corpus' Cyprian speeches.[1] They testify to Isocrates' didactic project as one that concerns itself with teaching not

---

[1] For this grouping of the three texts, see Forster 1912. Usher (1990: 6) suggests that Isocrates may have become acquainted with Evagoras through Timotheus, the son of Conon. It seems probable that when Evagoras and Conon became political allies (see 9.51–57), the former took on Isocrates as his son's teacher. There is a fourth Cyprian speech, *To Demonicus* (1), included in the Isocratean corpus (translated in Part One, above). Its authenticity, however, has been doubted by scholars for the reason that it lacks originality, although the conventionality of its material might be understood as an appeal to traditional wisdom and knowledge; see Too 1995: 58 n. 53.

just private citizens but also orators, generals, kings, and monarchs (from whom he received great wealth) to appreciate, protect, and further Greek, and particularly Athenian, interests (see 15.30). *Evagoras* and *To Nicocles* concern the instruction of a ruler; here Isocrates uses encomium and gnomic sayings in advising Nicocles on how to rule. In the third work, *Nicocles*, Isocrates treats the obligations of the ruler's subjects; he assumes the speaking voice of the king, perhaps to make the point that the former pupil (see 15.40–41, 67–72) has assimilated his teacher's voice.[2] Together the three Cyprian speeches suggest that ideally authority in the ancient Greek world is knowing both how to rule and how to be ruled (cf. Arist., *Politics* 1277a25–29).[3]

The two longer speeches, *Areopagiticus* and *Antidosis*, characterize their author specifically as the teacher *of Athens*. Both of these works place in the forefront Isocrates' conservative ideology to a greater or lesser extent, offering Athens' past as a corrective paradigm for a present that is morally and politically chaotic. *Areopagiticus* is a speech that offers a historical lesson in the virtues of Athens' ancestral constitution and its institutions, above all the Areopagus Court. The institution ensured that young men were socialized in the responsibilities and values of a historical democratic community that are now sorely lacking in contemporary Athens, and the speech instructs in how the Court's restoration might be to the city's advantage.

Isocrates' longest speech, speech 15, also offers the author's most extended lesson. The *Antidosis* takes the form of a legal defense to offer its audience instruction in the value of philosophy, that is, the culture of discourse, for the community. Its teaching concerns the service provided by the culture of speech (*logos*), not rhetoric as currently practiced in the lawcourts and Assembly but as enacted by Athens' great historical leaders, Solon, Pericles, Themistocles, and implicitly, their direct descendant, Isocrates himself. It is a speech that asks its Athenian audience to give the credit for who they are as a community to *logos* and to the responsible teachers of *logos*.

---

[2] See Livingstone 1998: esp. 270–280.

[3] *To Nicocles* and *Nicocles* are especially significant texts in the history of education. In the Renaissance, they were translated into Latin, English, French, and German as paradigms for the genre known as the "instruction of princes." See Highet 1949: 122–123 and also Tatum 1989: 5–6.

9. EVAGORAS

INTRODUCTION

Evagoras, generally dated to 370, is an encomium written for a festival held by the king Nicocles to commemorate his deceased father, Evagoras. The subject of the speech was ruler of Salamis in east Cyprus, and his life is largely known from this speech.

Evagoras claimed to be a descendant of Teucer, who had founded and named the colony after his own Greek city. As king, Evagoras made Salamis a Hellenic outpost, encouraging settlement of Greeks in his kingdom (9.47–50). He was a friend of the Athenian general Conon and supported Greek military undertakings, including the decisive Athenian victory at the battle of Cnidus in 394. In 390 Evagoras turned his attention to enlarging his kingdom in Cyprus and caused Soli, Amathus, and Citium to appeal to Persia for help. Long-term war with Persia ensued, resulting in Evagoras' eventual retreat into Salamis and his recognition of the Persian ruler Artaxerxes as overlord. Evagoras died in 374 or 373 (Diodorus Siculus 15.74).

Evagoras is an interesting work from the perspective of literary history. Isocrates opens the work with the observation that a prose encomium such as this does not have the advantage of poetry's literary devices. He does so to suggest that he will demonstrate with this work that prose can be used just as effectively for an encomium as poetry (see 9.8–11 and Too 1995: 34). (Xenophon subsequently used this speech as the model for his encomium of the Spartan king Agesilaus.[1])

---

[1] See Momigliano 1971: 49–50. *Evagoras* may be the earliest prose encomium of a leader, although Aristotle claims that there was an earlier encomium for the Thessalian Hippolochus (*Rhetoric* 1368a17).

The speech covers the various topics that are, or would become, conventional for the genre of encomium: the subject's glorious genealogy and ancestry (12–20), his birth (21), his youth (22–23), his virtues (23–24), his accomplishments with emphasis on his moral and intellectual virtues (25–40), his concern to govern humanely (41–64), and his legacy (71–81) (see Arist., *Rhetoric* 1366b32–1367b36 for discussion of the genre).

Isocrates may implicitly be making the case for a new post-epic heroism, in which the fourth-century nonmaterial virtues, such as those celebrated in sections 25–40 of the speech, are privileged over and above the physical qualities, for example, strength and speed, of the traditional hero. If so, this ostensibly political heroism has a particular function as far as its immediate audience, the Cypriot king Nicocles, is concerned. Aristotle declares that praise and advice have a common, or shared, form (*eidos*), since, although their styles are distinct, their topics are generally interchangeable (cf. *Rhetoric* 1367b37–38; also see Quintilian, *Institutio Oratoria* 3.7.28). The eulogy of Evagoras thus serves as political instruction for Nicocles by offering him an example for imitation (*mimēsis;* cf. 75–76), and lends support to the author's statement that he writes only "political discourse" (cf. 15.45–46).

The instruction offered through encomiastic discourse is not necessarily a faithful representation of the past and its persons. Isocrates treats historical fact loosely in this work—a license that the epideictic genre has always claimed for itself—in order to embellish and to emphasize what is praiseworthy (cf. 11.4). For example, he lengthens the reign of the Phoenician dynasty in Salamis to make Evagoras' coup appear more remarkable,[2] while he decides not to treat the king's death.[3] If deliberately favorable to Evagoras, Isocrates is careful to avoid the charge that in writing this encomium he is merely seeking to win Nicocles' favor and to enrich himself (sections 1–4; cf. 3.1), but he argues that the speech should be regarded as a gift, one that demonstrates and enacts language's ability to represent the achievements of its subject better than sculpture (sections 73–77).

---

[2] Forster 1912: 19.

[3] Isocrates' former pupil Theopompus reports that he was killed by a eunuch named Thrasydaeus; see Diodorus Siculus 15.74 and Forster 1912: 20.

9. EVAGORAS

[1] Nicocles, as I saw you honor your father's tomb not only with a multitude of beautiful gifts, dances, songs (*mousikē*),[4] and gymnastic contests, and in addition, with competitions involving horses and tri-remes, leaving no room for anyone to outdo you in these matters, [2] I thought that, if the dead know anything about what occurs here, Eva-goras gladly receives these tributes and rejoices in seeing your concern for him and your lavish expenditure, but he would be thankful above all else if someone could give a deserving account of his activities and of the dangers he undertook. [3] We shall discover that ambitious and noble men not only wish to be praised for such things but that they prefer to die gloriously rather than to live,[5] that they are concerned about honor rather than livelihood, and that they do everything pos-sible to leave behind an immortal memory of themselves. [4] Expen-ditures produce none of these things but are (merely) a sign of wealth. Those who participate in music and other contests—some demon-strating their powers, others their skills—gain more recognition for themselves. But a fine speech (*logos*) that recounts Evagoras' deeds would make his excellence (*aretē*) ever-remembered among all men.

[5] Others should have praised the good men among their contem-poraries to ensure that those who could glorify the deeds of others would employ the truth concerning them, since they were speaking about them to those who knew the facts[6] and so that the youth would strive harder to achieve virtue, knowing that they, rather than those inferior to them, would be praised. [6] As it is, who would not become discouraged when he sees that those who lived at the time of the Tro-jan War and earlier are celebrated in song and on the tragic stage but realizes that he will never be thought to deserve such praises, not even if he should surpass their virtues? Envy is responsible for this, and envy

---

[4] The Greek word *mousikē* is a term that covers not just music but also litera-ture; it is sometimes translated by "culture." In accounts of ancient education, it often stands in opposition to *gymnastikē*, which denotes physical training.

[5] From Homer onwards, fame (*kleos*) was regarded as recompense for death, especially in heroic circumstances. Isocrates reflects this view at 2.37, 4.84, 5.35, 8.94, and 15.109.

[6] For the concern that the details of an encomium should be verifiable, see also sections 21 and 66.

is only good in that it is the greatest evil for those who possess it. For, some individuals are so grudging that they take more pleasure in hearing praise for those of whose existence they are uncertain than for those from whom they have benefited. [7] But sensible men must not become slaves to those with such perverse thoughts but must disregard them and accustom others to hear about those whom it is just to praise, particularly as we know that progress in the arts and in all other things is not due to those who adhere to the status quo but to those who make improvements and dare always to change things that are wrong.

[8] I know that what I am about to do is difficult—praising a man's excellence through a speech (*logoi*). The greatest proof of this is that those who concern themselves with philosophy (*philosophia*)[7] venture to speak on many other subjects of every different kind, but none of them has ever attempted to write on this matter. I have great sympathy for them, for many decorations (*kosmoi*) have been granted to poets. [9] They can write of gods interacting with humans, conversing and fighting alongside whomsoever they wish, and they can portray this not only with conventional language but also with borrowings, new terms, and metaphors, not neglecting anything but embellishing their compositions with every figure (*eidos*). [10] Such devices do not exist for prose writers; they must use with precision only words and arguments in current use and must keep to their topic. In addition, the former compose everything with meter and rhythm; the latter have no share in these things which have such great grace that they persuade their audiences by their fine rhythms and proportions, even if the style and arguments are inelegant.[8] [11] One might recognize their power from the following (consideration): if some well-regarded poem were to keep its words and ideas while losing its meter, it would appear to fall far short of the opinion we now have of it. Still, although poetry has such a great advantage, we must not hesitate to attempt prose speeches to see if good men may be praised by such speeches just as well as by those who celebrate them in songs and meter.

[12] Although many people are already aware of Evagoras' birth

----

[7] For "philosophy" (*philosophia*), see the Introduction to Isocrates and the Glossary for this volume.

[8] Cf. Gorgias, for whom the only difference between poetry and prose is that poetry (*poiēsis*) is speech (*logos*) possessing meter (*metron*) (*Helen* 10).

and his ancestors, it seems to me appropriate first of all to give an account of them for the sake of others, so that everyone may know that he himself fully lived up to the greatest and finest examples left to him as his inheritance. [13] It is agreed that the noblest of the demigods are offspring of Zeus,[9] and of these, everyone would grant first place to the Aeacids.[10] Among other families we will find some who excel and others who are inferior, but all the Aeacids have become renowned among their contemporaries. [14] Aeacus was the son of Zeus and the ancestor of the Teucrid family. He was so outstanding that during a period when the Greeks were suffering from drought and many men had perished, when the suffering became unbearable, the leaders of the cities came and pleaded with him. They thought that through his family's connections and his piety he would very quickly discover from the gods a relief for their present evils. [15] When they were saved and had received what they asked for, they set up a temple belonging to all the Greeks in Aegina where Aeacus had made his prayer.[11] During this time, as long as he was among men, he continued to enjoy the finest reputation, and when he departed this life, he is said to have the greatest honors, sitting beside Pluto and Korē.[12]

[16] Aeacus' children were Telamon and Peleus. The former distinguished himself fighting with Heracles against Laodemon;[13] Peleus distinguished himself in the battle against the Centaurs[14] and after

---

[9] Demigods are mortal offspring of gods and mortals, among whom number Achilles (offspring of the goddess Thetis and the mortal Peleus) and Aeneas (offspring of the goddess Aphrodite and the mortal Anchises).

[10] "Aeacid" means "descendant of Aeacus"; the most famous Aeacid was Achilles, the grandson of Aeacus.

[11] The temple was called the Aeaceum or sometimes the Panhellenion. It is attested by Pindar, *Nemean* 5.53 and *Olympian* 13.109 and Pausanias 2.29–30.

[12] Korē is also known as Persephone. Aeacus became a judge of the underworld with Minos and Rhadymanthus.

[13] Laodemon built Troy with the help of Poseidon. Isocrates refers to a Greek expedition against Troy in the generation before the more familiar Trojan War; see Forster 1912: 80–81.

[14] The reference is probably to the fight of the Lapiths and Centaurs at the marriage of Perithoüs. There is another story that tells how the Centaurs found Peleus sleeping on Mt. Pelion without his sword, but he managed to get to safety with the help of Chiron; see Apollodorus 3.13.3.

achieving fame during many other trials, married Thetis, daughter of
Nereus—a mortal joining with an immortal. And they say that of all
mortals who have lived until now, only at his nuptials was the wedding hymn sung by the gods.[15] [17] To each of these two were born
sons—to Telamon, Ajax and Teucer; to Peleus, Achilles—and these
sons gave the greatest and clearest evidence of their excellence. They
were leaders not only in their cities or in the regions where they lived,
but when the Greeks sent an expedition against the barbarians and
many were assembled on each side[16]—indeed, no one of note was
missing—[18] Achilles showed himself superior to all in these dangers. After him, Ajax was the best; and Teucer too was worthy of their
kinship and second to no other. After he captured Troy, he went to
Cyprus and settled Salamis, giving it the same name as his former
fatherland.[17] He left behind a family that now rules there.

[19] Thus from the beginning Evagoras had from his ancestors an
enormous inheritance. When the city had been established in this
fashion, the descendants of Teucer initially held the kingship. Later a
fugitive, arriving from Phoenicia,[18] was trusted by the then king and
received great power, but he was not grateful for it. [20] He mistreated
the man who had taken him in, and being clever at seeking his own
advantage, he deposed his benefactor and himself seized the throne.
Having no faith in what he had done and wishing to make his own
position secure, he barbarized the city and made the whole island slave
to the Great King.[19]

[21] When conditions were such and the descendants of that man
were in power, Evagoras was born. I elect to omit the rumors, prophe-
cies, and dreams about him, which made him appear superhuman,

---

[15] The *hymenaeus* or wedding song receives its name from the wedding god
Hymen. It was sung as the bride was led to the groom's house. Catullus narrates
the marriage of Peleus and Thetis in poem 64.

[16] The reference is to the Trojan War.

[17] According to Isocrates, Teucer names the town of Salamis east of Cyprus
after the island Salamis near Athens in the Saronic gulf.

[18] There is no information on the identity of this fugitive. The arrival of the
fugitive who wreaks havoc was a motif of ancient historical writing (see, e.g.,
Herod. 1.34–45).

[19] I.e., the Great King of Persia, Artaxerxes II (Mnemon) (404–361 BC).

not because I disbelieve what has been said. Rather in order to make clear to everyone how far I am from fictionalizing when I speak of what he accomplished, I will even avoid the facts if they are known to only a few and are not common knowledge among all citizens. Thus I shall begin to speak about him from what is generally agreed.

[22] As a child he had beauty, strength, and restraint, which are the most suitable virtues for his age. Witnesses could testify to each of these virtues: to his restraint, the citizens who were his fellow students; to his beauty, all those who saw him; and to his strength, all the contests in which he defeated his contemporaries. [23] When he became a man, all these qualities increased, and in addition, he gained courage, wisdom, and justice not in moderation, like others, but each of these to a superlative degree. He excelled in the virtues of body and soul to such a degree [24] that, when those who ruled at the time saw him, they were terrified and feared for their power. They thought that such an individual could not conduct his nature as a private citizen; when they considered his character, they were confident that if anyone else dared to harm them, Evagoras would come to their aid. [25] And although these opinions were so different, they were right about both of them. He did not remain a private citizen, and he also did not harm them, but the god (*daimōn*) planned that he should assume the kingship in a dignified manner and that someone else should undertake the necessary preparations that involved impiety.

[26] Thus the gods allowed Evagoras to assume power in a manner that was respectful of the gods and just. One of the royal family hatched a plot, killed the tyrant, and tried to arrest Evagoras, thinking that he would not be able to maintain power unless he had him out of the way,[20] but Evagoras fled this danger and found safety in Soli in Cilicia.[21] [27] He did not take the same view as others who fall into such misfortunes. When others are forced from power, even from tyranny, they are disheartened by their bad fortune. Evagoras, however, gained such confidence that, although he had previously been a

---

[20] The potentate was Abdemon. According to Diodorus Siculus, he came from Citium in Cyprus (14.98); but Theopompus identifies Abdemon as a Tyrian and a friend of the Persian king (Fr. 111).

[21] Soli was an Athenian colony southwest of Tarsus in Cilicia and is distinct from the Phoenician town Soli in northwest Cyprus.

private citizen, when he was forced into exile he thought he had to become monarch. [28] He despised the usual wanderings of an exile, the pleas to others to help him return, and the cultivation of men worse than himself. Instead, he took as his starting point this principle, which those who wish to be pious must adopt—to act only in defense and not to initiate aggression.[22] He chose a course by which he would either become king, if he succeeded, or die, if he failed. He summoned his men, whom people say at the most were fifty, and with these prepared his return. [29] From this one might observe his nature and the reputation he held among others.

Although he was about to sail with this (small) number to such a great undertaking and with all dangers at hand, he did not lose heart, nor did any of those he had summoned think to shrink from the dangers. They all adhered to the agreement as if they were following a god, and Evagoras held to his decision as if he had an army greater than his opponents' or had foreknowledge of the outcome. [30] This his actions make clear. When he landed on the island,[23] he did not think he had to take a secure position and then, with his own safety assured, sit around to see if some of the citizens would help him. Rather, immediately that very night, just as he was, he tore down a little gate in the wall, and leading his companions through this, he attacked the palace. [31] Why should I spend time speaking of the confusion at such moments, the fear of the other men, and his exhortations? He was opposed by the monarch's supporters, and the other citizens were spectators. Fearing the rule of one and the virtue of the other, [32] they held their peace. He did not stop fighting, whether one man against many or with a handful of men against all the enemy, until he had taken the palace. Then, he punished his enemies and helped his friends,[24] and furthermore, he restored the ancestral

---

[22] There is no contradiction with the representation of Evagoras as an individual who avoided aggression if the attack on the palace (cf. 30) is seen as a defensive act.

[23] I.e., Cyprus.

[24] Helping one's friends and harming one's enemies is a traditional Greek virtue. Plato presents it as the standard understanding of justice (*dikaiosynē*) (*Republic* 332ab).

honors to his family and established himself as monarch (*tyrannos*) of the city.[25]

[33] So if I mention nothing else and conclude my speech here, from this, I think, one can readily recognize the virtue of Evagoras and the greatness of his deeds. Nevertheless, I think both will become clearer from what remains to be said. [34] Although many monarchs have ruled from the beginning of time, it is clear that none have acquired this honor more nobly than he. If I compare Evagoras' deeds with each one of these, my speech would perhaps be unsuitable for this occasion (*kairos*), and there would not be sufficient time for it. But if I choose only to consider the most famous of these, I will make my point just as well and will treat the matter more succinctly.

[35] Who would not prefer the risks that Evagoras underwent to those who inherit their fathers' kingdoms? There is no one so complacent as to prefer to accept power from his ancestors rather than possess it as he did and leave it to his children. [36] The especially well known ancient instances of rulers who were restored to power are those related by the poets, who not only report the finest events, but compose new ones in addition. Even so, none of them has composed a story about anyone who undertook such terrible and fearful dangers [as Evagoras] and regained his rightful place. Most have been depicted as acquiring their kingdoms by good fortune, others as overcoming their enemies with trickery and devious strategies.

[37] Among those, and perhaps all, who lived later, the majority particularly admire Cyrus, who captured the kingdom of the Medes and took possession of it for the Persians.[26] But his defeat of the Median army by the Persian force was something that many Greeks and barbarians could have easily done, whereas Evagoras clearly accomplished most of what has been reported through his own mental and physical ability. [38] Furthermore, while it is not apparent from Cyrus' expedition that he would have withstood the perils of Evagoras, from what the latter did it is clear to everyone that he would easily have undertaken Cyrus' endeavors. In addition, Evagoras accomplished ev-

---

[25] Also see Diodorus Siculus 14.98 for Evagoras' rise to power.

[26] See Xen., *Cyropaedia*, a work that narrates the Cyrus' education and subsequent career, and Herod. 1.130.

erything in a pious and just manner, while some of Cyrus' results were gained impiously. The former destroyed his enemies, but Cyrus killed his mother's father.²⁷ Accordingly, if some should wish to judge not the magnitude of the outcome but the virtue of each, they would rightly praise Evagoras more than Cyrus.

[39] If I have to speak concisely and openly without reservations or fear of envy, no mortal, demigod, or immortal will be found to have acquired kingship in a finer, more remarkable, or more pious manner than Evagoras. If anyone really does not believe this, he would be completely convinced if he should undertake to investigate how each one became ruler. Then it will be clear that I have not just been boasting but have courageously spoken about Evagoras as a result of the truth of the matter. [40] If he had only distinguished himself in small matters, he would fittingly deserve correspondingly small words. As it is, all would agree that kingship is the greatest, noblest, and most intensely coveted of divine and mortal goods. This man possessed it in the finest way; which poet or literary artist²⁸ could find praise worthy of his actions?

[41] Then, although he was outstanding in this, he will not be found deficient in other respects. First of all, he was naturally gifted in intellect and had the ability to succeed in most things, yet he did not think he should treat things lightly or act impulsively, but he spent the most time investigating, thinking about, and planning matters. He thought that if he prepared his thoughts carefully, his regime would also fare well; and he was amazed at others who prepare their souls in the service of other affairs but do not think about the mind itself. [42] He had the same conviction when it came to political affairs. Because he saw that those who take greatest care over matters worry least, and that true freedom from care lies not in idleness but in success and endurance, he left nothing unexamined, but he knew political affairs and each citizen so thoroughly that no one who plotted against him or was decent escaped his notice, and all got their just deserts. He neither punished nor honored citizens on the basis of what

²⁷ Cyrus' maternal grandfather was Astyages. No other source attests Cyrus' killing of Astyages, although he does rebuke Astyages at Xen., *Cyropaedia* 1.3.10.
²⁸ "Literary artist," lit. "inventor of speeches" (*logōn heuretēs*), is a phrase that Isocrates uses elsewhere (at 5.144) to describe the prose writer.

he heard from others, but he made judgments about them from what he himself knew. [43] He involved himself in such concerns, and he did not err at all in matters that arose every day, but he governed the city so piously and humanely that those who visited the island did not envy Evagoras his power as much as they envied his subjects for being under his rule.

The whole time he did no injustice to anyone and honored those who were good. He ruled all stringently and punished transgressors lawfully. [44] He required no advisers and instead advised his friends. He often gave way to his associates but always defeated his enemies. He was formidable, not because of his stern face but because of the principles by which he lived. He was not disorganized or inconsistent in anything but maintained his agreements in deed and word alike. [45] He was proud not of the things he acquired by good fortune but of those he acquired by his own efforts. He made his friends subordinate to him by favors and enslaved others by his generosity. He intimidated not by being harsh toward many, but because his nature far surpassed that of others. He controlled his pleasures and was not led by them. He gained considerable leisure by few labors but did not neglect great labors for the sake of small leisures. [46] On the whole, he lacked none of the necessary requisites for monarchs, but he selected the best from each form of government. He was democratic in his service of the people; public-minded (*politikos*) in his government of the whole city state; a military strategist in his management of dangers, and an absolute ruler by excelling in all these qualities. That Evagoras had these qualities and more than these is easy to learn from his deeds themselves.

[47] Upon becoming king, he found the city reduced to barbarism through Phoenician rule: it did not welcome Greeks, it knew no crafts, engaged in no trade, and possessed no harbor. He remedied all these deficiencies and, in addition, considerably enlarged the city's territory. He built walls around it; he constructed triremes, and he increased the city with other structures to such a degree that it was outdone by no Greek city. He made it so powerful that many of those who previously scorned it now feared it.

[48] Cities cannot accommodate such great growth unless they are organized by someone with principles such as Evagoras had and as I tried to describe a bit earlier. As a result, I am not afraid of seeming

to exaggerate his qualities but rather of falling far short of his actual deeds. [49] For who could attain such a nature that he could not only make his city more worthy but also bring the whole area surrounding the island to gentleness and moderation? Before Evagoras came to power the citizens were so unwelcoming and hard to handle that they thought the best rulers were those who were the most savage toward the Greeks. [50] Now things have changed so much that they compete to see who will be considered the most friendly to the Greeks (*philhellēnes*), and the majority of them marry our women to produce children. They delight in Greek goods and Greek institutions rather than in their own, and more of those who concern themselves with music and other aspects of education spend time here than in their former cities. No one would fail to agree that Evagoras deserves credit for all these things.

[51] The greatest proof of his character and piety is this. Many distinguished Greeks left their own countries to live in Cyprus because they thought that Evagoras' kingship would be easier to bear and more lawful than their constitutions at home. It would be a large task to name all the others,[29] [52] but who does not know that Conon,[30] who was first among the Greeks in many virtues, when his city came upon hard times, out of all the options available to him, chose to come to Evagoras because he thought that Evagoras would give him the greatest physical security and would help his city most quickly. Although Conon had many earlier successes, in this matter he seemed to have

---

[29] Athenian exiles who took refuge in Cyprus include Conon (405–397), Andocides (399; see And. 1.4), and Nicophemus (see Lys. 19.36).

[30] Conon left Athens after the city's defeat by the Spartans under Lysander at Aegospotami in 405. One might speculate that following the fate of the generals at Arginusae, who were condemned to death by the people of Athens, the general left for Cyprus to avoid having to face the populist democratic rule at Athens, a sentiment with which the oligarchical Isocrates was no doubt sympathetic. This may well account for his favorable treatment of Evagoras. Conon was also the father of the general Timotheus, one of Isocrates' more prominent pupils, who was disgraced and whose reputation is defended at 15.101–139. Elsewhere, at 4.12, Isocrates refers to the naval success of Conon and the campaign of Timotheus at Cnidus (394) as being responsible for Athens' position of power in Greece; also cf. 9.56.

planned best of all. [53] For as a result of his arrival in Cyprus, he accomplished and received the most good. First of all, as soon as he and Evagoras met, they regarded each other more highly than those who were already their intimates. Next, they continued to agree in other matters and held the same opinion regarding Athens. [54] They saw it oppressed by the Spartans and experiencing a major change, and they found this painful and hard to bear. Both did what was appropriate.

Conon was an Athenian by birth, and Evagoras was made a legal citizen on account of his many generous benefactions. As they were considering how they might liberate the city from her misfortunes, the Spartans soon provided the opportunity (*kairos*). Ruling the Greeks by land and sea, they acquired such an insatiable appetite that they tried to damage Asia as well. [55] Conon and Evagoras seized the opportunity when the generals of the Persian king were at a loss as to how to deal with the situation. They taught them not to engage the Spartans on land but at sea, reasoning that if they formed a land army and succeeded this way, it would benefit only the mainland, but if they had prevailed at sea, all Greece would share in this victory. [56] And so it happened. The generals accepted their advice and organized a fleet. The Spartans fought at sea and lost their supremacy. The Greeks were freed, and Athens again received part of its ancient glory and became leader of the allies. This was accomplished with Conon as general,[31] although Evagoras had some share in this and provided most of the military force. [57] For these reasons, we accorded them the highest honors and erected statues of them near the statue of Zeus Soter, and near each other, a memorial to both and to the greatness of their benefaction and friendship with one another.[32]

The Persian king did not have the same opinion of them; rather, the greater and worthier their deeds, the more he feared them. I will give you another account of Conon;[33] but as for Evagoras, the king

[31] Conon returned to Athens to lead the Athenian and Persian fleets with Pharnabazus at Cnidus in August 394. The joint fleet destroyed Sparta's naval power and reestablished Athens' military power. See 4.65.

[32] The statues were erected in the Ceramicus or the Potters' District, close to the Royal Portico (*stoa basileios*); see Pausanias 1.3.2.

[33] See 5.62–64; also 4.12.

did not attempt to hide how he felt toward him. [58] He was clearly more preoccupied with the war in Cyprus than with all the others, and he considered Evagoras a greater and more difficult antagonist than Cyrus, who had competed with him for the throne.[34] This is the greatest proof. When he heard of Cyrus' preparations, he disregarded him to such a degree that Cyrus nearly reached his palace unnoticed as a result of his neglect. Yet he was so afraid of Evagoras that even while he was deriving benefits from him, he tried to go to war against him. This action was unjust, but his plan was not entirely illogical. [59] The king knew that many Greeks and barbarians had grown from lowly and base conditions to conquer great dynasties. He perceived that Evagoras' ambition, his reputation, and his activity were increasing significantly, that he had an unrivaled nature, and that fortune (*tychē*) was his ally. [60] Thus he was not angry about what had happened; rather, he feared for the future. He not only feared for Cyprus but waged war against Evagoras for much larger reasons. He was so concerned about this expedition that he spent more than fifteen thousand talents on it.[35]

[61] Nevertheless, although Evagoras was outmatched in all aspects of military resources, he pitted his intellect (*gnōmē*) against such superior equipment and proved himself far more amazing in this matter than in the others I have already mentioned. When they allowed him to live in peace, he ruled only his own city. [62] When he was forced to go to war, he and his son and ally Pnytagoras were so successful that he gained control of almost the whole of Cyprus, pillaged Phoenicia, forcibly captured Tyre, caused Cilicia to revolt from its king, and destroyed such a large number of the enemy that many Persians in remembering their misfortunes recall his virtue. [63] In the end, he gave them their fill of war so that the kings who were not normally in the habit of compromising with those who revolted until they became masters of their persons gladly made peace and gave up this custom,

---

[34] This is the younger Cyrus, whose attempt to win Persia from his brother Artaxerxes II is treated in Xen., *Anabasis*.

[35] Diodorus Siculus 15.2.1–2 tells us that Artaxerxes prepared for war against Cyprus with 300,000 men and more than 300 triremes. Evagoras formed an alliance with Acoris, king of the Egyptians, gained financial support from Hecatomnus, who ruled Caria, and forged other alliances to defeat Persia.

leaving Evagoras' rule unaffected. [64] Although the Spartans were at the peak of their reputation and power at the time, the King took away their rule within three years,[36] but when he had been at war with Evagoras for ten years, he left him in control of what he had before entering into war. The most marvelous thing of all is that the city, which Evagoras had taken from another despot with fifty men, could not be defeated by the Great King who had so much power.

[65] Could anyone illustrate Evagoras' courage, intellect, or his whole virtue more clearly than through such actions and dangers? Clearly, his achievement surpassed not only other wars but also the war of the heroes, which all men praise in song. For all the Greeks together captured only Troy, but he, with only one city, fought a war against all Asia. If as many people wished to praise him as praised the heroes, he would have acquired far greater fame than they. [66] Which of the heroes will be found to have accomplished such deeds if we take away the myths (*mythos*) and examine the truth? Who else was responsible for such great political transformations? He turned himself from a private citizen into a monarch; he restored his whole family to appropriate honors after it was driven from power; his citizens, who were barbarians, he made Greek again; [67] he made them warriors instead of cowards and famous instead of unknown. He took over a place that was completely inhospitable and uncivilized in every respect and made it gentler and kinder; and in addition to having entered into hostility with the King, he defended himself so well that the Cyprian War has become everlastingly famous. And when he was the King's ally, he made himself so much more useful than the others [68] that, it is agreed, he contributed the majority of the resources to the naval battle at Cnidus. After the battle, the King became lord of all Asia, and the Spartans were forced to fight over their own territory instead of ravaging Asia. The Greeks achieved autonomy instead of slavery, and the Athenians increased so much that those who previously ruled them came to offer them the empire. [69] If someone were to ask me what I think was Evagoras' greatest achievement—his concern over and

---

[36] The battle of Cnidus took place from summer 397 to August 394. Forster (1912: 104) sees it as a vast exaggeration on Isocrates' part to regard the victory at Cnidus as destroying Spartan power.

preparations against the Spartans which had the result just mentioned, or the last war, or his recovery of the kingship, or his whole management of affairs—I would not know what to say, for whatever I turn my thought to always seems to be the greatest and most wonderful of his achievements.

[70] Accordingly, if any of our predecessors have become immortal as a result of their virtue, I think Evagoras was also worthy of this gift. I cite as evidence the fact that the remainder of his days were more fortunate and more blessed by the gods than theirs were. We will discover that most of the demigods, even the most renowned, encountered great misfortunes, but Evagoras continued from the beginning to be not only the most admirable but also the most blessed. [71] In what respect did he lack good fortune? He had ancestors like no one else, except someone in the same family shared his. Also he surpassed others in both body and intellect to such a degree that he was worthy to rule not just Salamis but the whole of Asia as well. He acquired his kingdom in the finest manner and continued to live in it. Being a mortal, he left an immortal memory of himself. He lived for just enough time that he was not without a share of old age, but he also did not suffer the maladies of advanced age.[37] [72] In addition, although it seems to be especially rare and difficult to have both many children and good children, he did not lack either, for it also came his way.[38]

The greatest thing of all is that, of his descendants, he left behind none who were addressed as a private citizen. One was called king,[39] others, princes and princesses. If any poets employ hyperbole with regard to any figure from the past, and say that he was a god among men, or a mortal spirit (*daimōn*), all such phrases would suitably be said about Evagoras' character.

[73] I am sure I have left out a lot in speaking of Evagoras, for I am

---

[37] Evagoras died in 374 or 373. In keeping with encomiastic license, Isocrates omits mention of Evagoras' violent end, possibly resulting from a palace intrigue. See Arist., *Politics* 1317b4, and Theopompus (Fr. 111), who relates the ruler's death at the hands of a eunuch named Thrasydaeus.

[38] For the blessing of many children, see Herod. 1.30.4.

[39] Namely, Nicocles. See speeches 2 and 3.

past my prime, when I should have produced this eulogy more precisely and with greater care.⁴⁰ Nonetheless, even now, to the extent that my powers permit, he is not without praise.⁴¹ Nicocles, I think that statues of bodies are fine memorials, but that images of deeds and of character (*dianoia*) are worth much more, and one can observe these only in skillfully produced speeches.⁴² [74] I prefer these, first because I know that noble men are not so much esteemed for their physical beauty as honored for their deeds and intellect. Second, statues necessarily remain among those who set them up, but speeches can be conveyed throughout Greece, published in gatherings of men of good sense, and can be welcomed by those whose respect is worth more than that of all others. [75] In addition to these things, there is the fact that no one would be able to make their own body resemble a statue or a painting, but it is easy for those who wish to take the trouble and are willing to be the best to imitate the character and thoughts of others that are represented in speeches.

[76] For these reasons I have tried especially to write this speech, thinking that it will be by far the best encouragement for you, your children, and Evagoras' other descendants if someone assembled his virtues, arranged them in a speech, and passed them down to you to study and practice. [77] For we exhort people to pursue philosophy by praising others so that by emulating those who are praised they will desire the same way of life as theirs. But in addressing you and your family, I use as examples not others' but your own kin, and I advise you to pay attention so that you will be able to speak and act as well as any Greek. [78] And don't think that I am criticizing you for not caring, just because I often admonish you about the same things. Both I and others have not failed to notice that you first and alone among tyrants in the midst of wealth and luxury have attempted to engage in

---

⁴⁰ The date of the *Evagoras* is uncertain, although scholars tentatively place it between 370 and 365, when the author would have been in his late sixties and early seventies.

⁴¹ On the encomiastic convention of exaggerating an individual's good qualities, see 11.4.

⁴² Isocrates returns to the theme he began the speech with to give the work a neat framing (1–5).

philosophy and to labor and that you will make many kings emulate your education and desire this way of life, while abandoning that which they currently pursue.

[79] Nevertheless, although I know these things, I do and will continue to do what audiences do in athletic contests. They encourage not the runners who are lagging behind but those straining for victory. [80] It is my task, and that of your other friends, to say and write such things as will incite you to strive for these things you already now desire. You should not neglect anything but now and in the future take care and discipline your soul so that you will be worthy of your father and your other ancestors. Everyone should regard intellect as very important, but this is especially the case for you who have control of many affairs of greatest importance. [81] You must not be content if you happen already to be better than those around you, but you should be upset if with such a nature as yours, having descended originally from Zeus and most immediately from a man of such excellence, you do not far outstrip others, even those who are of the same position of honor as you. It lies in your power not to fail in this. Provided you remain with philosophy and continue to give as much to it as you do now, you will soon become the person you ought rightly to be.

2. TO NICOCLES

INTRODUCTION

Isocrates justifies writing *To Nicocles* by noting that, where ordinary individuals have many sources of instruction and correction—for example, laws, poetry, friends, and enemies—because of their social status and power, monarchs have none to teach them (2. 2–5). Kings are, however, precisely the people who require instruction more than any other. Isocrates writes within a particular didactic genre, the instruction of rulers, for which there were precedents in earlier literature (e.g., Homer, *Odyssey* 1.253–305, Hesiod, *Works and Days* 202–214 and 239–267, and the Solon-Croesus exchange at Herod. 1.30–33).[1] The presentation of material in the form of a catalogue of maxims shows the influence of Hesiod (cf. 15.68). Moreover, the advice that the rhetorician offers to his addressee seems to be largely generic in that it deals with nothing specific to Nicocles' particular situation, with the result that the speech may be viewed as a discourse on good monarchy in general.

Elsewhere, the author summarizes the theme of the speech as being advice to the king Nicocles on how to rule his citizens, and he describes its style not as his most elegant but as disjunctive, for the work is comprised of a set of discrete pieces of advice (15.67–69). His intention in composing the work, he retrospectively declares, was to demonstrate that he could deal with leaders as well as ordinary people without engaging in flattery and to ensure that the king's government was well intentioned to its people (15.69–70).

---

[1] See, e.g., Lattimore 1939; Martin 1984.

Cyprus was a hellenized community as a result of Evagoras' efforts and support of Athenian military enterprises, and one observes that recognizable Hellenic ideologies and discourses underlie *To Nicocles*. Although the author is offering advice to a monarch,[2] his counsel at times appears to be a blueprint for precisely the sort of conservative democracy that he espouses in other speeches (especially speeches 7 and 15). The encouragements to observation of the laws, gentleness (*praotēs*), moderation (*sōphrosynē*), and especially, outspokenness (*parrhēsia*), as well as the vocabulary by which these are articulated, might all be readily transferred to a democratic context. Moreover, the rhetorician advises his addressee to treat public and private interests as interrelated, as they are ideally in a democracy (see 2.21, 3.48 – 64, and Thuc. 2.60 – 64).

Isocrates is careful to avoid the perception that he is a sophist, a figure popularly perceived and depicted as someone who makes exaggerated promises to teach subjects of which he has little knowledge in order to satisfy his greed. He presents his knowledge and advice as a gift, not a means of extorting payment, from its recipient (see 2.1 – 4, 54).

In addition to the text with notes by Forster 1912, there is a recent edition with commentary by Usher 1990.

2. TO NICOCLES

[1] It seems to me, Nicocles, that those accustomed to bring to you, who are kings (*basileis*), garments, bronze, wrought gold, or any other such possession which they themselves need and you have in abundance are evidently not giving gifts but trading, and they are much more skilled at selling these things than those who are acknowledged as traders. [2] I thought that the finest, the most useful, and above all, the most fitting gift for me to give and you to receive would be if I were able to define what sort of activities you should aspire to and which ones you should avoid in order to govern your city and kingdom in the best possible way.

---

[2] Nicocles is interchangeably referred to as a *basileus* (king) and a *tyrannos* (tyrant), without any obvious negative connotations implied by these words.

Many things educate ordinary citizens: above all, the lack of luxury and the need to plan for one's livelihood each day; [3] then, the laws by which each individual lives as a citizen; next, outspokenness (*parrhēsia*) and open permission for friends to rebuke and for enemies to attack each other's faults. In addition, some of the earlier poets left behind precepts on how to live. From all these, it is reasonable that citizens will become better men. [4] But the situation of monarchs (*tyrannoi*),³ who need education more than others, is very different, and when they come to power, they are never admonished. This is because most men do not come near them, while those who do spend time with them do so to gain favor.

Moreover, kings have control over the greatest wealth and the most important matters, but since they do not use their advantages well, many have debated whether it is preferable to choose the life of the ordinary citizens who are reasonably well off or that of monarchs. [5] When people consider their honors, their wealth, and their power, all think monarchs equal to the gods; but when they consider the fear and danger, and when they review events and see that some have been destroyed by those who should least have done so, others have been forced to wrong those closest to them, and still others experiencing both, they again think it is preferable to live in any way other than to rule all Asia afflicted by such misfortunes.

[6] The cause of this inconsistency and confusion is that people regard monarchy as a priesthood which could be held by any man, although it is in fact the greatest of human activities and requires a substantial amount of vision. On each specific issue at hand, it is the task of those continually present to advise the king how he might manage it best, keeping what is good and avoiding calamities. But for the whole business [of being a monarch], I shall attempt to set out what goals and concerns one should have. [7] Whether the gift I produce will be commensurate with my intentions is initially difficult to see. Many works of poetry and prose produce great expectations while

³ The noun *tyrannos*, lit. "tyrant" but also "monarch" or "absolute ruler," is used throughout this speech with reference to the Cypriot king and, as Andrewes argued (1956: esp. 20–30), may not always have negative resonances, especially when used before the fourth century. Perhaps, the ideal of monarchy that Isocrates espouses in *To Nicocles* is to be regarded as consciously nostalgic.

still being conceived by their authors; but when they were completed and performed to others, they received far less fame than expected. [8] Still it is fine to try to look into a neglected topic and to give advice to rulers. Those who educate private citizens benefit only them, but if someone turns those in charge of the people to virtue, he would benefit both those holding positions of authority and their subjects. He would make the offices of the former secure, and the latter's experience of government milder.

[9] First of all, we must consider what the task of monarchs is. If we are able to give an adequate summary of the whole enterprise, we shall also speak about its parts more effectively with reference to this. I think that everyone would agree that rulers should end a city's misfortune, maintain its prosperity, and make it big if it is small. Other day-to-day matters must be handled with these goals in mind. [10] It is clear that those who will possess this power and must plan matters of such great importance should not be lazy or negligent but must consider how to be more thoughtful than others; for it has been demonstrated that they will have kingdoms that are in keeping with the character of their own thoughts. [11] Accordingly, kings are required to train their souls as no athlete trains his body—for none of the public festivals offers the sort of challenge you (kings) undertake each day.[4]

You must give thought and be attentive to this, that you surpass others in honor only to the extent that you better them in virtue. [12] Do not think that diligence (*epimeleia*) is useful in other matters but has no power to make us better and wiser. Do not presume that humanity's misfortune is so great that while we have discovered the arts of taming the souls of wild beasts to increase their value, we cannot help ourselves become more virtuous. Set your minds instead on the fact that education and diligence have the greatest power to benefit our nature. [13] Associate with the wisest of your advisers, and send for any others you can; and do not think you have the luxury of being ignorant of any of the famous poets or sophists. Listen to the former and study with the latter, and prepare yourself to be a critic of those

---

[4] At 4.45 Isocrates observes that Athens is to be admired for including athletic and cultural contests; cf. also 15.295.

who are inferior and a rival of those who are better. Through these exercises you would in the shortest time develop the qualities I determined you will need to rule correctly and to manage the city as is necessary. [14] You would be encouraged by yourself above all if you thought it a terrible thing for the worse to rule the better, and the ignorant to command the wise. To the extent that you more earnestly despise the stupidity of others, so you should cultivate your own intellect. [15] Those who will perform their obligations must begin from this.

In addition, they must be lovers of the people and the city.[5] For it is not possible to rule a horse, a dog, a man, or any other thing well unless one delights in those for whom one must care. Take thought for the common people, and do everything to rule them in a way that pleases them, [16] knowing that oligarchies and other forms of government which best serve the people (*to plēthos*) last the longest. And you will rule the multitude well if you do not allow them to commit outrage or stand by and let them suffer violence. Rather, make sure that the best people have positions of authority and that others are not wronged: these are the first and greatest principles of the best form of government.

[17] Move and change the established ordinances and activities which are not good, and in particular, either originate what is best, and if not, imitate what works for others. Seek laws that are just in their entirety, beneficial, and consistent with each other, as well as those which produce the fewest ambiguities and the quickest resolutions for the citizens. All these qualities must attend well-enacted laws. [18] Make labor profitable and lawsuits liable to penalty so that the citizens avoid the latter and willingly engage in the former. When there are divergent views on both sides, judge without favoritism and do not contradict yourself, but always be consistent on the same matters. It is fitting and beneficial for the judgment of kings, like well-established laws, to be unchanging on issues of justice. [19] Manage the city just as the home you were born into: make the furnishings splendid and royal, but keep accurate account of expense so that you may earn a good reputation and still have enough. Demonstrate mag-

---

[5] For the adjective *philopolis* ("lover of the city"), see Thuc. 2.60.5.

nificence not in short-lived displays of extravagance but in those I have already mentioned, and in beautiful possessions and favors to friends. All such expenditures remain with you, and you will leave behind to your successors an inheritance worth more than your expenditures.

[20] With regard to the gods, do as your ancestors showed; and regard it the finest sacrifice and the greatest service to show yourself as the best and the most just possible. There is more hope that such men will gain some benefit from the gods than those who discharge many sacrifices. Honor with positions of responsibility the friends who are closest to you and those most kindly disposed to the truth itself. [21] Consider the most secure physical defense to be the virtue of friends, the goodwill of the citizens, and your own wisdom. Through these one would be best able to possess and maintain monarchy. Care for the citizens' homes, thinking both that those who spend their resources are doing so from your possessions and that those who work increase your wealth. For everything which belongs to the city's inhabitants belongs to those who rule well.

[22] Always appear to give pride of place to the truth so that your words are more deserving of trust than the oaths of others. Show the city to be safe for visitors, and make contracts legally binding. Value most highly not the visitors who bear gifts but those who expect to receive something from you, for by honoring the latter you will increase your reputation elsewhere. [23] Free your citizens from many fears, and do not willingly let law-abiding citizens be intimidated. The feelings you place in others toward you will be the same as those you have toward them. Never act in anger, but appear to others to be angry if the occasion requires. Appear to be terrible (*deinos*) by allowing no action to escape your notice, but [seem] gentle by making punishments less than the crimes.

[24] Do not try to exercise authority by harsh or extreme punishments, but by dominating all with your intelligence and by making others think that you plan better than they do for their best interests. Be aggressive in your knowledge and preparations for war, but peaceful in not seeking expansion unjustly. Associate with weaker states just as you would expect stronger ones to associate with you. [25] Do not pick fights in every matter, but only in those you would profit from winning. Do not regard those who gain advantage by yielding infe-

rior, but those who harm themselves by prevailing. Do not consider ambitious those who aim at more than they can manage, but those who seek what is good and are able to accomplish whatever they try. [26] Do not emulate any of those who possess the greatest power but those who use what they have as well as they can, and do not think you will find perfect happiness in ruling all men with fear, danger, and evil but in being the sort of person you should be and acting as you do now, striving for moderate goals and having success in all of them.

[27] Do not become friends with everyone who wishes, but only with those who are worthy of you—not those whose company you enjoy most, but those with whom you will best govern the city. Assess your companions carefully, knowing that all who are not close to you will judge you by your associates. Put men like this in charge of matters which you do not directly manage, because you yourself will be responsible for all they do.[6] [28] Regard as trustworthy not those who praise whatever you say or do, but those who reproach your mistakes. Grant free expression (*parrhēsia*) to those who are sensible so that you may have good advisers to draw on when you are in doubt. See through those who flatter skillfully and those who serve with goodwill so that evil individuals may not gain advantage over good ones. Listen to what people say about each other, and try to discern the characters of both the speakers and those they speak about. [29] Punish those who slander others falsely with the same penalties as those who commit the crimes in question would receive.

Rule yourself no less than others, and realize that it is most kingly if you are enslaved by no pleasure, but rule all your desires better than the citizens. Accept no association randomly or without thinking, but make a habit of enjoying those activities which will improve you and make you appear better to others. [30] Do not appear to be ambitious for such things which even wicked men can also attain, but pride yourself on your virtue, in which the wicked have no share. Consider the truest honors to be not those you receive through fear in public, but the admiration that people express in private for your wisdom more than for your good fortune when they are at home. Don't let

---

[6] The newly discovered Kellis Codex offers the variant reading, "for what they do wrong (*hamartōsi*)."

anyone know if you should happen to enjoy trite things, but show that you are serious about the greatest things.

[31] Do not think that others should live a disciplined life, while kings can live without constraint, but make your moderation an example for others, knowing that the character of the whole state comes to resemble its rulers. Let it be a sign of your good rule if you see your subjects becoming wealthier and more responsible through care. [32] Consider it more valuable to bequeath to your children a good reputation than great wealth. The latter is perishable and the former is immortal; and wealth may be gained through a good reputation, but a good reputation cannot be bought by wealth. Even base men have wealth, but only those who are superior can possess a good reputation. Be extravagant in your dress and in your bodily adornments, but be restrained, as kings should be, in other habits, so that those who judge by your appearance will consider you deserving of power,[7] and those in your company will have the same opinion because of the strength of your soul.

[33] Always monitor your speech and actions so that you make the fewest mistakes possible. It is best to make use of perfect opportunities (*kairoi*), but since these are hard to identify, elect to fall short rather than overstep the mark. Moderation lies in falling short rather than in going too far. [34] Try to be urbane—as befits your social interactions—and dignified—as is appropriate for kingship. This is the hardest command of all, for you will find that in general those who are dignified are cold, and those who wish to be urbane appear base. But you must practice both these qualities and avoid the shortcoming that goes with each. [35] Whenever you seek to have precise knowledge of what kings ought to know, make use of experience (*empeiria*) and study (*philosophia*).[8] Study will show you the path, and practicing the deeds themselves will make you able to act.

Consider current events and their consequences for both private citizens and kings. If you recall the past, you will plan better for the future. [36] Realize that it is terrible that some private citizens are

---

[7] See the discussion of the ruler's dress in Xen., *Cyropaedia* 1.6.22–29, 33; cf. 8.2.10.

[8] See 9.8n.

willing to die in order that they may be praised when they have died, while, in contrast, kings do not dare to engage in activities from which they may gain a good reputation while alive. Prefer to leave behind images (*eikonas*) of your virtue, rather than of your body, as a memorial.[9] Try in particular to maintain your own and the state's security. If you are forced to take risks, choose to die nobly rather than live basely. [37] In all these actions, think of the monarchy and how to do nothing unworthy of this office.

Do not permit your entire being to come to an end at once. Since you have a mortal body, try to leave behind an immortal memory of your soul. [38] Practice speaking about fine pursuits, so that your thoughts may be conditioned to resemble your words. Accomplish in practice whatever seems best when you take thought. Imitate the actions of those whose reputations you envy. You should abide by those precepts which you would teach your own children. [39] Follow my advice or discover something better. Deem wise not those who quarrel over small things, but those who speak well on the most important matters; not those who promise good fortune to others while themselves being in great difficulty, but those who speak modestly about their own situations, are able to deal with people and events, are not thrown into turmoil by life's ups-and-downs, and know how to bear well and moderately both misfortune and good fortune.

[40] Do not be surprised if you already know much of what I say. I am aware of this, and I know that among the enormous multitude of ordinary people and rulers[10] a number have said some of these things, others have heard them, some have seen others doing them, and some have themselves put them into action. [41] One should not look for novelty in these discourses about rules for living, for in them there is no room for paradox, or for what is incredible or unconventional.[11] Instead we should consider most accomplished the man who

---

[9] See 9.73–77, where Isocrates declares virtue and virtuous actions a better testimony to an individual's reputation than statues.

[10] The Kellis Codex has the variant reading "ordinary people, potentates, and other rulers."

[11] Cf. Cleon's warning against the Athenian predilection for rhetorical novelty (Thuc. 3.38.5).

is able to draw together the most ideas held by others and to articulate them most elegantly. [42] For it was apparent to me that while everyone thinks works in prose and poetry which offer advice are the most useful, they do not listen to them with the greatest pleasure but have the same feelings toward them as toward those who admonish them. They praise them but prefer to associate with their fellow wrongdoers rather than with those who dissuade from such errors. [43] As evidence, one could offer the poetry of Hesiod, Theognis, or Phocylides.[12] People say that these give the best advice for people's lives, but even as they say this, they choose to live not according to their precepts but in their own common follies.[13] [44] Furthermore, if one were to select the so-called "sayings" (*gnōmai*) of the leading poets, on which they have expended the greatest effort, people would feel just the same about these. They would enjoy listening to base comedy rather than to what has been so artfully composed. [45] So why should I spend time enumerating each point?

If we wish to consider human nature as a whole, we shall discover that most people do not delight in the healthiest foods, in the finest way of life, in the best actions, or in the most useful creatures; rather, they enjoy pleasures that are in every way opposed to their own advantage, and they consider those who perform their duty long-suffering and diligent. [46] Accordingly, how could someone who advises, teaches, or says anything useful please such people? Besides the reasons I have given, they envy those who have sense, and think that those without sense are simple; accordingly, they flee the truth of the matter to the point of being ignorant of their own interests; they are grieved when they consider their own affairs, but take pleasure in discussing those of others; and they would rather endure bodily hardship than to labor and trouble their soul by examining the necessary facts of life. [47] In their interactions with one another, you would find them

---

[12] Hesiod (seventh century) wrote the didactic text *Precepts of Chiron*, while the *Works and Days* is addressed as moral instruction to his wayward brother Perses; Theognis (sixth century) is the name ascribed to the body of verse known as the *Theognidea*, in which political and moral teachings are addressed to a youth named Cyrnus; Phocylides (mid-sixth century) wrote maxims (*gnōmai*).

[13] The Kellis Codex prefers the reading "faults" (*harmarteias*).

abusing or being abused, and in private, not thinking but making great promises to themselves. I am not criticizing everyone, only those who fit this description.

[48] Clearly those who wish to do or write something to please the masses do not seek the most useful speeches but those that are full of fictions (*mythōdestatoi*).[14] For people delight when they hear such narratives or watch contests and competitions. Thus, one should admire Homer's poetry and the first inventors of tragedy for perceiving human nature for what it is and for using both these forms of pleasure in their poetry. [49] Homer told stories of contests and wars between the demigods, while the tragedians used traditional stories in their contests and actions so that we can both hear and watch stories. Since they have these examples, those who wish to persuade their audiences have been shown that they must steer clear of reprimand and advice and say such things they see will be most delightful to crowds.

[50] I have made these points because I think that you, not being one of the many but ruling over many, should not have the same understanding as others. You should not judge serious matters or sensible men by the criterion of pleasure but should value them for their useful actions, [51] especially since philosophers disagree over the cultivation of the soul, some saying that their pupils will become wiser through eristic discourse, others through political speech, and others through some other speech. Everyone agrees, moreover, that the well-educated individual should clearly be able to offer counsel in each of these areas. [52] Therefore, you should disregard these divisions and test men on the basis of what is agreed by all. Look especially for those who offer counsel at opportune moments, or if not, then, when they speak about affairs in general. Reject those who know nothing that they need to know, for someone not useful in anything clearly would make no one else wise. [53] Value and cherish those who have intelligence and are more insightful than others, for you know that a good counselor is the most useful and most worthy possession for a king.

---

[14] This is a patent echo of Thucydides, who at 1.22.4 concedes that because his own work is not fictional (cf. *to mē mythōdes*) it might appear to be less pleasurable; nonetheless, it has usefulness and is to be an everlasting possession rather than an ephemeral piece for a contest.

Realize those who can most benefit your understanding will make your kingdom the greatest.

[54] I have offered counsel on what I know, and I honor you with the powers I have. As I have said at the beginning, do not wish that others will bring to you the customary gifts, for your debt for these will be greater to those who give them than it would be to those who sell them; but desire instead such gifts as you will not wear out, not even if you use them intensely every day, for these will increase and grow in value when you use them.

3. NICOCLES

INTRODUCTION

Nicocles is the final work in Isocrates' Cyprian trilogy. Speeches 9 and 3 dramatize the instruction of Nicocles in his role as ruler, and in this third work, the former pupil of the rhetorician shows that he has learned his lessons well as he in turn assumes the role of political teacher. He offers a self-justification that draws attention to his virtues in a way that is reminiscent of the rhetorician's instructive encomium of Evagoras (cf. 3.29–46 and the introduction to Isocrates speech 9), and takes it upon himself to instruct his subjects in their duties and obligations. Significant is the extent to which Nicocles' speaking voice resembles that of the author, marking not the failure of, or lack of resourcefulness in, rhetorical characterization but the success of a pedagogical method that aspires to teach the student to be like his teacher.[1]

Nicocles praises monarchy and its virtues at sections 14–25 of the speech. Rather than understand Isocrates to be espousing an absolutist or monarchic ideology, we might see the author as giving voice to a state that has shown itself favorable to Athens' political and military agendas and to Hellenic culture generally. The work's account of Athens' government might also be read as an example of political theorizing on the author's part, perhaps resembling Darius' arguments in favor of monarchy in the constitutional debate in Herodotus (3.82). It might be argued, furthermore, that Isocrates is careful to cultivate the sympathy of Athens for the Cypriot royal family by emphasizing af-

---

[1] See 15.205–206 and Livingstone 1998: 272–280.

finities between the democratic city state and this monarchy. Indeed, Nicocles' particular account of the way in which individual and communal interests are not divergent (48–64; also 2.21) is consistent with the democratic ideology that Thucydides places in the mouth of Pericles (Thuc. 2.60–64), while the famous "hymn to *logos*" (3.5–9), which implicitly constructs Cyprus as a rhetorical community, is one that Isocrates will himself cite verbatim as an aetiology of Athenian greatness as a democratic community at 15.253–257.

3. NICOCLES

[1] Some people are ill disposed toward speeches (*hoi logoi*) and fault philosophers,[2] saying that they engage in such pastimes not for the sake of virtue but for personal advantage (*pleonexia*). I would be happy to learn from those who feel this way why they blame those who wish to speak well but praise those who wish to act well. If personal advantage offends them, I will find that many greater advantages result from actions rather than from words. [2] Moreover, it would be strange if they failed to recognize that we do not show reverence in religious matters, cultivate justice, or practice the other virtues in order to have less than others, but that we enjoy the greatest goods during our lives. Accordingly, we must not criticize the actions through which someone might virtuously gain advantage, but the men whose actions are wrong or whose words are deceitful and unjust.

[3] I am surprised that those who hold this view do not also decry wealth, strength, and courage. If they have problems with public speaking because some men do wrong and lie, they should reasonably blame other good things too, for some people who possess these will clearly do wrong and will use them to harm many. [4] But it is not right to condemn physical strength just because some hit people they meet, or to criticize bravery because some people kill those they should not, or generally to transfer the evil of men to their actions. Instead one should blame individuals who use good things badly and try to harm their fellow citizens using means that could benefit them instead.

---

[2] See 9.8n.

[5] As it stands, those who neglect to make this distinction in each case are ill disposed to all discourse (*logoi*), and they have erred to such an extent that they do not notice that they are opposed to such an activity which, of all the qualities of human nature, is the cause of all the greatest goods. In other respects, we do not differ from other living beings, and we are inferior to many in speed, strength, and other resources. [6] But since we have the ability to persuade one another and to make clear to ourselves what we want, not only do we avoid living like animals, but we have come together, built cities, made laws, and invented arts (*technē*).³ Speech (*logos*) is responsible for nearly all our inventions. [7] It legislated in matters of justice and injustice, and beauty and baseness, and without these laws, we could not live with one another. By it we refute the bad and praise the good; through it we educate the ignorant and recognize the intelligent. We regard speaking well to be the clearest sign of a good mind, which it requires, and truthful, lawful, and just speech we consider the image (*eidolon*) of a good and faithful soul. [8] With speech we fight over contentious matters, and we investigate the unknown. We use the same arguments by which we persuade others in our own deliberations; we call those able to speak in a crowd "rhetorical" (*rhētorikoi*); we regard as sound advisers those who debate with themselves most skillfully about public affairs. [9] If one must summarize the power of discourse, we will discover that nothing done prudently⁴ occurs without speech (*logos*), that speech is the leader of all thoughts and actions, and that the most intelligent people use it most of all. Accordingly, one should hate those who dare to inveigh against educators and philosophers⁵ just as much as those who sin against the gods.

[10] I accept all discourses which have the capacity to benefit us even a little; however, I consider finest, most appropriate to a king, and especially suited to me, those discourses which advise me on my conduct in general and on political matters, and among these, those

---

³ 6–9 is repeated verbatim at 15.253–256. See Gorgias, *Helen* 4, *Palamades* 30–31, and Arist., *Politics* 1.2, for a celebration of the benefits of *logos* for humankind; and also Aeschylus, *Prometheus Bound* 88–127 and 436–516 and Plato, *Protagoras* 322b–d for the innate vulnerability of humankind.

⁴ The Kellis Codex offers the variant reading "lawfully."

⁵ See above, 3.1n.

which teach dynasts how they should treat their people, and the citizens how they should regard their leaders. Through these discourses I see cities becoming most prosperous and greatest.⁶ [11] On the other topic of how one must rule as a king, listen to Isocrates,⁷ but I shall try to outline what a king's subjects must do. This is not in order to outdo him but because it is especially appropriate for me to speak to you about these things. For I could not reasonably be angry at you if you failed to understand my intention (*gnōmē*) when I did not make clear what I want you to do. But if none of my wishes were fulfilled after I had spoken to you beforehand, then I would be justified in finding fault with you if you did not obey.

[12] I think I will best encourage and persuade you above all to remember my advice and obey it if I do not simply enumerate my recommendations and then stop, but if I first show you how the present government deserves your respect, not only because it is necessary since we have it for all time but because it is the finest of governments. [13] Next, I will show that I hold this office not unlawfully or as a usurper, but piously and justly on account of my earliest ancestors, my father, and myself. When these factors have been demonstrated, who would not condemn himself to the severest punishment if he does not obey my counsels and commands?

[14] On the matter of constitutions—for I have taken this as my starting point—I think everyone considers it most terrible for good and evil people to deserve the same reward, and most just for them to be distinguished and not for those who are dissimilar to have the same reward but for each to have the reward and the honor he deserves. [15] Oligarchies and democracies seek equality for those who share in government, and they respect the principle that no one should have more than another—which is advantageous for the wicked. In contrast, monarchies give the most to the best, the second portion to the one after him, and the third and the fourth portions to others following the same reasoning. This may not hold true everywhere, but this

---

⁶ "Nicocles" refers here to *Evagoras* and *To Nicocles*.

⁷ This section of the speech is most explicit about the rhetorician's use of a fictional speaking voice, that of the Cypriot monarch's, and also suggests, perhaps, the way in which education assimilates the student's identity to that of the teacher. See Too 1995: 149–150.

is the intention of this type of government. [16] Everyone would agree that monarchies are better at perceiving people's natures and their activities. So, which sensible man would not prefer to be part of a state in which his good character does not pass unnoticed, rather than to be carried along by the mob, unrecognized for the sort of person he is? I would judge monarchy much gentler in that it is easier to pay attention to the intentions of a single man than to seek to please many different minds. [17] One could demonstrate at length that monarchy is more pleasant, gentler, and more just; however, it is easy to comprehend this from these points.

On the other points, we could consider best how much monarchies differ from other governments with regard to planning and doing what is necessary if we examine the greatest deeds of each compared to others. Now, people who assume public office for only a year become private citizens before they observe any of the state's affairs and gain experience of them.[8] [18] On the other hand, those who always oversee the same matters surpass others in experience even if they have inferior natures. Moreover, the former neglect many things as they look to others to do them, but the latter overlook nothing, knowing that everything must happen through them. In addition, citizens of oligarchies and democracies harm the public good through their rivalries with each other, but people living under monarchies, having nothing to envy, do what is best in everything insofar as this is possible. [19] Furthermore, the former delay action. They spend the greatest part of the time on their own affairs, and when they come to public councils, one would more frequently find them quarreling than deliberating together. But monarchies have neither councils nor times appointed for them, so they do not miss opportunities (*kairoi*) but spend day and night in public business and accomplish each thing as is necessary. [20] Again, the former are ill disposed and would wish those who rule before and after them to rule as badly as possible so that they themselves might receive the greatest praise, whereas monarchs, being in control of public affairs all their lives, are well disposed all the time.

---

[8] There is an implied criticism of the Athenian system of election to office by lot, a process that Isocrates explicitly faults at 7.22 and 12.145–146.

[21] The most significant point is this: the former attend to the commonwealth as if it were someone else's, the latter as if it were their own, and on these matters the former use the most aggressive citizens as advisers, while the latter select the wisest of all. The former honor those who can speak to a crowd; the latter, those who know how to manage affairs. [22] Monarchies not only excel in ordinary, everyday matters but they have also acquired every advantage in war. Monarchies are better able than other governments to prepare their forces, to use these to make the first move unobserved, to persuade some and force or bribe others, and to induce yet others by other means. One might believe this equally from deeds and words.

[23] We all know that the empire of the Persians became so great, not as a result of the subjects' intellect, but because they honored monarchy more than other countries.[9] Dionysius, the tyrant,[10] took over when the rest of Sicily had revolted and not only relieved his own besieged fatherland from its present dangers, but even made it the greatest of the Greek states. [24] Furthermore, the Carthaginians and the Spartans, who governed best of all, are oligarchies at home but become kingships when they go out to war.[11] One might demonstrate as well that the state which particularly detests despotic rule suffers misfortune when it sends out numerous generals and succeeds when it encounters dangers under a single leader. [25] Could someone show more clearly by examples other than these that monarchies are the worthiest governments? States which continue under the rule of a single leader are seen to have the greatest powers, and those which have stable oligarchies appoint either one general or one king to be leader of the armed forces when matters are especially serious, while those who detest tyrannies do not accomplish what they desire when they send out many leaders.

[26] If I must refer to ancient times, then the gods are said to be

---

[9] Isocrates refers to the empires of the Persian kings Cyrus and Darius.

[10] Dionysius was tyrant of Sicily from 405 to 367 BC and is notable for ruling according to democratic principles; see Arist., *Politics* 1305a28. Isocrates addresses *Epistle* 1 to him.

[11] Aristotle also praises the Spartans and Carthaginians at *Politics* 1272b24–38 and describes the Spartan kingship as a "self-authorizing and eternal generalship" (*stratēgia tis autokratōr kai aidios*) at *Politics* 1285a2.

ruled by Zeus. If the account of these matters is true, evidently the gods prefer this state of affairs; but if no one knows for certain but in speculating about these things we suppose it so, this is evidence that we all hold monarchy in high regard. We would never say that the gods have a monarchy if we did not think it far excels other forms of government. [27] Concerning constitutions, it is impossible to discover or to express every aspect in which they differ from one another; but enough has been said on this subject for the present.

The argument that it is appropriate for me to hold power will be much briefer and more readily agreed. [28] Who does not know[12] that Teucer, the founder of our family, collected the ancestors of other citizens, sailed here, founded a city for them, and ruled the territory? That my father, Evagoras, regained the throne after others had lost it, withstood the greatest dangers, and made so great a change that the Phoenicians no longer rule the Salaminians; but that these to whom it initially belonged now have the kingdom?

[29] Of the points I choose to make, it remains to offer an account of myself in order that you may know that your king is the sort of person who not only because of my ancestors but also on my own account would justly be deemed worthy of even greater honor. I think everyone would agree that moderation (*sōphrosynē*) and justice (*dikaiosynē*) are the most esteemed virtues. [30] They not only benefit us in themselves, but if we wish to consider their nature, power, and utility in human affairs, we will discover that those who have no part in these qualities are responsible for great evils, whereas those who demonstrate justice and moderation greatly benefit human life. If some of our forbears were renowned for these virtues, I think that it is appropriate for me to attain the same reputation as they.

[31] You may observe my sense of justice in particular from the fact that, when I came to power, I found the royal treasury empty of wealth and our kingdom impoverished.[13] Matters were full of confu-

---

[12] This history is related at length at 9.29–35.

[13] As there are no other details of the succession, it might be assumed that Cyprus was impoverished due to the burden of conducting war against Persia. Alternatively, Isocrates may be invoking the commonplace of political turmoil attending the handover of an empire in order to emphasize the crucial importance

sion and required a good deal of care and attention and expense. I knew that others in such circumstances get their own affairs in order by every possible means and are forced to do much contrary to their own natures. Nevertheless, I was not corrupted by any such impulse. [32] Instead, I attended to matters piously and nobly, omitting no action which might increase the city and contribute to its prosperity. I behaved toward the citizens with such gentleness that no exile, deaths, loss of wealth, or any other such misfortune occurred during my reign. [33] Although we could not approach Greece because there was war,[14] and we were being plundered on every side, I dealt with most of these [problems]; I paid what was owing to some in full, and to others in part; I asked others to delay, and I reconciled others who had complaints as I was able. In addition, when the inhabitants of the island were ill disposed to me, and the King of Persia was supposedly reconciled but actually hostile, [34] I soothed both parties, readily acting in the service of the latter and presenting myself as fair to the others. I am the last person to want what belongs to someone else. If others have power that is a little greater than their neighbors, they cut off part of their land and seek to gain the advantage (*pleonektein*). I, however, did not think it right to accept the land given to me, but I choose to be just and to possess only what is my own rather than turn evil and possess much more than I now have.

[35] Why should I spend time speaking on each item, particularly when I can reveal myself briefly? It will be clear that I have harmed no one, have benefited many citizens and other Greeks, and have given more gifts to others than all the monarchs before me. Those who have high ideals based on justice and who claim to be superior to many should be able to speak about such noble qualities of themselves.

[36] Indeed, I can speak at even greater length on moderation (*sōphrosynē*). I know that all men value their own children and wives highly and are particularly angry at those who wrong them; that violence toward them is the cause of the greatest evils, and that many private citizens and rulers are now destroyed by this. I avoided these

---

of the training of ruler-in-waiting; see Xen., *Cyropaedia* 8.8.2–26 and Too 1998: 285–288.

[14] Athens and Sparta were at war at sea, while Sparta and Thebes were at war on land.

criticisms to such an extent that, from the time I received the kingdom, I clearly had no physical relation with anyone except my own wife. [37] I realized that those who are just toward the citizens are admired by the majority, even if they seek pleasures from somewhere else. But I wanted to remove myself as far as possible from such suspicions, and at the same time make my character a model for the rest of the citizens, knowing that the common people generally live their lives in the practices in which they see their leaders spending time.

[38] Next, I thought that it was fitting for kings to be better than their subjects to the degree that they have higher positions, and that they behave terribly if they force others to live in an orderly manner, while they themselves are less restrained than those they rule.[15] [39] Furthermore, I saw that, while the majority of people are in control of other parts of their lives, even the best are overpowered by desire for boys and women. Accordingly, I wished to demonstrate my capacity for self-control in matters in which I would excel over not just ordinary people but also those who considered themselves especially virtuous.

[40] As well, I condemned the great vice of men who take wives and share their lives with them but are not satisfied with what they have, and by their own pleasures hurt those whom they think should not cause them any pain, and with regard to other associations present themselves as reasonable, while transgressing in their relations with their wives. They ought to protect these women all the more since they are closer and better than others.[16] [41] In addition, they don't realize that they are creating rivalries and quarrels for themselves in the palace. And yet, those who rule correctly should try to govern in harmony not only the cities which they rule but also their own homes and the places in which they dwell. All these are the deeds of moderation and justice. [42] I also did not share the view of most kings concerning the begetting of children: I did not think that one should have

---

[15] Isocrates stresses the importance of self-control for a leader at 2.31.

[16] It seems to be a utopian ideal in political literature of the classical period to seek the abolition of mistresses; see Pomeroy 1975: 117–118. Pederasty was a feature of classical Athenian education, where an older male (*erastēs*) would take a younger beloved (*erōmenos*) under his care in order to socialize him. Isocrates is extraordinary in rejecting the traditional sexual "double standard."

some children from a baser woman and some from a more noble one, or leave behind some bastards and some legitimate offspring. Rather all my children should have the same origin through both their father and mother—among mortals through my father Evagoras, among demigods through the sons of Aeacus, and among the gods through Zeus: none of my offspring has been deprived of this noble stock.

[43] Although many things urge me to adhere to these practices, the great incentive was seeing that many bad men have a degree of courage, cleverness, and other estimable qualities, but noblemen (*kaloi kagathoi*) have justice and moderation as their special possessions. I thought it would be the finest thing therefore if one could be better than others in these virtues in which the wicked have no share but which are the most legitimate, the strongest, and the most praiseworthy. [44] For these reasons and with this intention, I cultivated moderation to a greater extent than others, and I preferred not to take pleasure in deeds which have no honor, but in those which lead to a reputation based on noble character. One must not judge all virtues according to the same criteria but judge justice among the poor, moderation among those in power, and self-control among the youth. [45] So I have clearly provided a test of my own nature in all these situations. When I was left without wealth, I showed myself just by harming no citizen. When I had gained the opportunity to do whatever I wanted, I became more moderate than private citizens. And I showed self-control in both situations when I was of the age when we find most people going astray in their conduct.

[46] Perhaps, I would have hesitated to say these things to others not because I am embarrassed about what I have done but because my account wouldn't have been credible. But you yourselves are the witnesses to all I have said. It is right to praise and admire men who are orderly by nature, but even more so those who are such because of their ability to reason. [47] Those who are moderate by chance and not by thinking might be persuaded to change, but it is evident that those who are so by nature, and in addition have learned that virtue is the greatest good, will remain moderate throughout their whole lives. For this reason, I have said a lot about myself and about the other matters previously treated, leaving no excuse why you should not willingly and eagerly do whatever I advise and command.

[48] I say that each of you must do what has been appointed to

you carefully and justly. Whenever you are wanting in either of these qualities, you necessarily behave badly in that respect. Do not despise or have contempt for any command because you think that nothing depends on this; but the whole lies in the parts, whether you act well or badly; so take these things seriously. [49] Care for my concerns as much as for your own, and do not think that the honors possessed by those who oversee our affairs well are a small benefit. Keep away from other people's property, so that your own homes will be more secure. You should behave toward others as you think I should behave toward you.

[50] Do not rush to be wealthy before being seen to be good, for you know that the Greeks and barbarians who have the greatest reputations for virtue also are masters of the greatest goods. Understand that the unjust acquisition of property will not make you rich but will put you at risk. Do not think that taking is a profit, and losing is a penalty. Neither of these always has the same effect, but whichever of these should occur at the right moment (*kairos*) and with virtue benefits those who do it.

[51] Do not complain about any of my orders. Whoever of you makes himself most useful to my affairs will most help his own household. May each of you know that whatever he himself is conscious of, I know too, and if I am not there in person, let him think that my consciousness (*dianoia*) is present at what is happening. With this thought, plan more moderately in everything. [52] Do not conceal any of your possessions, your actions, or your intentions, knowing that hidden affairs necessarily bring great fear. Do not seek to conduct your public lives artificially (*technikōs*) or in secret, but do everything transparently and plainly so that it will not be easy for anyone to slander you if he wants to. Examine your actions and regard them as evil when you wish them to escape my notice, and good if I shall think better of you when I learn of them.

[53] Do not be silent if you see people plotting against my rule but denounce them, and realize those who conceal crimes deserve the same punishment as the criminals. Consider fortunate not those who do evil and get away with it, but those who do no wrong. The first group will probably get back what they give, but the latter receive the gratitude they deserve. [54] Do not make associations and affiliations without my knowledge. Such gatherings give you an advantage in

other governments, but in monarchies they are a risk. Abstain not only from wrongdoing, but from practices which necessarily create suspicion. Regard my friendship as particularly secure and firm.

[55] Maintain the present order of things, and do not desire change, knowing that through disturbances states must perish and private households must be overturned. Do not think that it is only their nature that makes rulers harsh or gentle, but also the character of the citizens. Many have been forced to rule more harshly than they intended because of the wickedness of their subjects. [56] Take heart not so much because of my gentleness but because of your own virtue. Regard my safety as your own security; for when my own situation is fine, yours will be in the same state. You should defer to my rule, observe our customs, obey the royal laws, and be conspicuous in your civic liturgies and in the obligations I assign you.[17]

[57] Urge the young to virtue, not only by teaching but also by demonstrating to them how good men should behave. Teach your children to obey, and accustom them to abide by the education (*paideusis*) I have described[18] as much as possible. If they learn to be ruled well, they will be able to rule many. If they are trustworthy and just, they will have a share in our goods; if they are bad men, they will put at risk what they have. [58] Consider that bequeathing my goodwill to your children is the greatest and the most secure wealth you can leave them. Regard as most wretched and unlucky those who violate the trust of others, for such men have no hope, must fear everything, and must live the rest of their lives trusting their friends no more than their enemies. [59] Envy not those who possess the most but those who have nothing bad on their conscience. With such a soul one could live life most happily. Do not think evil can bring more profit than virtue, but only that its name is more unpleasant. And realize

---

[17] Either Nicocles has emulated the Athenian liturgy system or else Isocrates has transferred an Athenian political structure to Salamis in order to assimilate Nicocles' kingdom to Athens. On liturgies, see Series Introduction: xxi.

[18] "I have described" = Greek *eirēmenēn* (in the most reliable manuscript), which has Nicocles' voice assimilated to that of the author and teacher of rhetoric, Isocrates, despite the explicit construction of the former's voice at 3.11. Other manuscripts read *toiautēn,* "of such a kind."

that the name given to each thing is an indication of its qualities (*dynameis*).

[60] Do not envy those who have the highest rank in my government, but emulate them, and by proving yourselves to be good men, try to equal those who excel. Think that you must love and honor those whom the king also does, so that you may receive the same honors from me. In my absence think the same things you would say in my presence. [61] Show your goodwill (*eunoia*) to me in your deeds rather than in your words. Do not treat others in a way that angers you when you are so treated by others. Do not practice in deed acts that you condemn in words. Expect that you will be treated in the same way that you think of treating me. Do not just praise good men but imitate them as well. [62] Take my words to be laws and try to abide by them, knowing that those of you who especially do what I wish will be able to live as they wish most quickly. To sum up what I have to say: be disposed toward my rule as you think your subordinates should be toward you.

[63] If you do this, why must I go on at length about the outcome? If I continue to behave as I have before and you continue to serve me, you will quickly see your lives improve, my rule increase, and the city achieve great prosperity. [64] For the sake of such benefits, you should not neglect anything but must bear whatever toils and dangers may arise. It is possible for you to accomplish all these things without suffering hardship just by being trustworthy and just.

7. AREOPAGITICUS

INTRODUCTION

The *Areopagiticus* is generally thought to have been composed between 358 and 352, either just before, during, or just after the disastrous Social War (357–355) in which Athens was left with a weakened naval empire after her stronger allies, Chios, Cos, Rhodes, and Byzantium, gained their independence from the Confederacy. The positive and confident mood of the work (7.1–3) suggests a date before the war, perhaps 358/7,[1] but the speech also raises issues of particular poignancy for the conflict and its outcome. The speech is one that expresses strong dissatisfaction with the current democracy and espouses a return to the *politeia patrios*, or "ancestral constitution," as a solution to the city's problems and as a guarantee of its supremacy. In particular, Isocrates urges Athens to give back to the Areopagus Court its historical authority to maintain the laws and to supervise the behavior of citizens.

This political program was extremely conservative. The Areopagus Court was founded before Solon as a powerful, aristocratic council of state to ensure the preservation of Athens' laws (cf. Arist., *Ath. Pol.* 3.6, 4.4, 8.4) and to hear and punish cases of homicide. Its membership consisted of all individuals who had held the annual office of archon, of which there were nine each year. The Court may have also included a powerful subgroup of fifty-one citizens, known as the *ephetai*, who heard the legal cases (see Arist., *Politics* 1273b35–1274a7 and Wallace

---

[1] See Jaeger 1940 and Wallace 1986: 77 and notes for summary of the debate.

1985: 12). In 462/1 BC Ephialtes reformed the Court in response to its mismanagement of the city's affairs. It seems that he took away the special privileges of its members and gave to the people the guardianship of the laws.[2] In the fourth century, the Court dealt with cases of homicide, wounding, arson, and various religious offenses.[3]

Toward the end of the fifth century, the Areopagus became a focus for conservative, and even oligarchical, ideology as espoused by individuals such as Theramenes, Xenophon, Plato, and Timotheus. Isocrates' articulation of Areopagus ideology in this work is somewhat idiosyncratic, for it presents a pedagogical ideal both distinct from and complementary to that offered in his other paideutic works, *Against the Sophists* (speech 13) and *Antidosis* (speech 15). If these two works portray the rhetorician as a teacher of the youth of Athens and the larger Greek-speaking world in "philosophy" (i.e., rhetoric[4]) in opposition to the contemporary sophists, the *Areopagiticus* concerns itself above all with the moral instruction to the city as a whole. According to Isocrates, in Solon's time, the Areopagus guarded the laws, educated the young, and oversaw the maintenance of Athens as a democratic state (7.37–38), preventing what the rhetorician caricatures as the corruptions and excesses of the populist democracy. Isocrates now presses for the restoration of the Court as the only institution with the authority and capacity to rehabilitate Athens from the moral decadence that has resulted from the education of the sophists and from the culture of litigation produced by it.

7. AREOPAGITICUS

[1] I suppose many of you are wondering what my intention is in coming forward to speak about our security as if Athens were in danger, or its affairs were in a perilous state, or it did not possess more than two hundred triremes, enjoy peace in its territory, and rule the sea. [2] Indeed, our city has many allies who will readily help, if the

---

[2] The founding of the Areopagus Court to hear the case of Orestes in Aeschylus' *Eumenides* pays tribute to the reforms.

[3] Wallace 1985: 106–110.

[4] On the meaning of "philosophy," see the Introduction to Isocrates.

need arises, and many more paying contributions and carrying out its orders. In this situation, one might say that it would be reasonable for us to have confidence that we are far from danger and that our enemies should be afraid and take thought for their own security. [3] You,⁵ as I know, accept this argument and despise my address, for you expect to rule all Greece by this power.

Yet I fear for just these reasons. I see cities that think their circumstances are best making the worst decisions, and those which are particularly confident soon finding themselves in the greatest dangers. [4] The reason for this is that no good or evil comes to mankind of its own accord; wealth and power produce and are accompanied by senselessness (*anoia*) and lack of restraint (*akolasia*), while poverty and humble circumstances bring moderation and restraint.

[5] Accordingly, it is difficult to determine which of these circumstances one would prefer to leave to his children. We would find that affairs generally improve when they appear to be bad, but when they seem better they generally change for the worse. [6] I can produce the greatest number of examples from the situations of private citizens, which undergo changes most frequently; but more important and better known to my audience is what happened to us and to the Spartans. We became the leaders of Greece after Athens had been overtaken by the barbarians because of our fear for the future and our attention to our affairs,⁶ but when we thought we had invincible power, we were nearly enslaved.⁷ [7] The Spartans rose long ago from base and humble cities,⁸ and controlled the Peloponnesus because they lived moderately and in a military state, but after this, they were more

---

⁵Readers of the *Areopagiticus* would have understood "you" as a reference to the Assembly of Athens, in keeping with the fictional setting of the speech.

⁶In the Persian War, the Athenians abandoned their city during the battle of Salamis, when Xerxes destroyed Athens. After the war, Athens assumed leadership of the Delian Confederacy; see 4.71–72 and 6.42–43.

⁷Following the end of the Peloponnesian War, a weakened Athens was nearly destroyed and her citizens reduced to slavery by Sparta's allies. Sparta, however, did not permit Athens to be enslaved due to her service to Hellas; see 8.78 and 105, 15.319, and Xen., *Hellenica* 2.2.19–20.

⁸See 4.61 and 12.253.

arrogant than necessary and when they had gained control of land and sea, they then encountered the same dangers as we.⁹

[8] Anyone who knows that such changes have happened and that such great powers are quickly destroyed and who still trusts present circumstances is extremely foolish, especially as our city is far less prosperous now than at that time, since the Greek's hatred and the Persian king's enmity, which then overcame us, has again been renewed. [9] I don't know whether to suspect that you are not concerned about public affairs, or that you care about them but are so unperceptive that you fail to see the great confusion that has overcome Athens. You certainly seem to be in this condition, for you have lost all the cities in Thrace, have wasted more than a thousand talents to no avail on foreigners,¹⁰ [10] have earned the scorn of the Greeks and the enmity of the barbarians,¹¹ and moreover, were forced to save the friends of the Thebans, while you lost your own allies.¹² In such conditions, we have twice made sacrifices celebrating the arrival of good news, but when we discuss these matters in the Assembly, we are less serious than men who have achieved all they want.

[11] It makes sense that we act in this way and suffer this result. Nothing can turn out well for those who do not plan well about all aspects of government, but if they have success in some actions, whether through good fortune or through some man's virtue, they soon slip up a little and again find themselves in the same uncertainty (*aporiai*). Anyone could learn this from our own experience, [12] for when all of Greece was in our control after Conon's naval battle and Timotheus' campaign,¹³ we were unable to keep our good fortune for

---

⁹The Spartan hegemony began in 404 and lasted until the state's defeat at the battle of Leuctra in 371. During this period Athens enjoyed a second naval empire in 387.

¹⁰During the Social War Athens hired mercenary soldiers; see 8.44–47 and Dem. 4.20.

¹¹By "barbarians" Isocrates most probably refers to the Messenians, whom the Thebans had liberated from the Spartans. Dem. 16.9.

¹²Isocrates refers to the city's loss of allies, Chios, Cos, Rhodes, and Byzantium, following the Social War, which ended in 355.

¹³For Timotheus' military successes, see 15.107–126; Timotheus' campaigns took place between 375 and 364.

any time, but we rapidly squandered it away. For we neither have nor do we really seek a government that correctly deals with public affairs.

[13] And yet, we all know that prosperity visits and remains not with those who have cast the finest and largest walls around themselves, nor with those who have gathered together with the largest number of people in the same place, but with those who manage their city in the best and most moderate manner. [14] The soul (*psychē*) of the city is nothing other than its constitution, since it has as much power as the intellect does in the body. For it is this that deliberates in all matters, preserves what is good, and avoids misfortune. Laws, public speakers, and private citizens all necessarily resemble it, and the fortunes of each citizen are determined by the form of constitution they possess. [15] But we think nothing of it when it has been destroyed, nor do we consider how to correct it. Sitting in our shops, we criticize the current situation, and complain that we've never had a worse government under the democracy, but in our actions and thoughts we are fonder of it than of the democracy left by our ancestors.

This ancestral (democracy) is the subject on which I am about to speak and have registered this address. [16] For I find that this would be the only means of averting future dangers and escaping from current evils, if we are willing to restore the democracy which Solon, who was the most democratic ruler, established by legislation, and Cleisthenes, who expelled the tyrants and returned the people to power, originally founded.[14] [17] We would not find a constitution more democratic or more beneficial for the state.[15] The greatest proof is this:

---

[14] As archon (594/3), Solon established the city's laws, creating the basis for the democratic constitution. In 507 BC Cleisthenes established a constitution that Aristotle says was similar to Solon's (*Ath. Pol.* 29.3; cf. 41.2), and he subsequently received the unofficial designation "leader of the people" (*Ath. Pol.* 28.4). Where Isocrates makes Cleisthenes directly responsible for the expulsion of the tyrants (Dem. 21.144), Aristotle simply refers to his leadership as coming after the dissolution of the tyrants (*Ath. Pol.* 28.7 and 41.2); also see 15.231–232. Ober (1996: 32–52) argues that the origins of the Athenian democracy lay with the common people rather than the aristocratic leaders like Cleisthenes, whose constitution framed the popular revolution.

[15] See 15.232 for praise of the historical, conservative democracies with which Isocrates allies himself.

those who lived under it, when they had accomplished many fine deeds, won fame from all men, and received the command (*hēgemonia*) from the Greeks, with their consent.[16] In contrast, those who prefer the present constitution are hated by all, have suffered many terrible things, and were just short of undergoing the ultimate disaster.[17] [18] How can one praise and be fond of this constitution, which has been the cause of so many previous evils and each year goes from bad to worse? Must one not fear that if such a progression continues, we shall in the end run aground on much harsher circumstances than those we faced then.

[19] In order that you do not listen only to summary points but have detailed information when you evaluate these constitutions and make your choice, it is your duty to pay attention to what I say, while I shall try to explain both to you as concisely as possible. [20] Those who governed the city in those days did not establish a constitution which only in name was the most populist and the most gentle, while proving to be quite the opposite to those who experienced it, nor one which educated the citizens to regard license (*akolasia*) as democracy, lawlessness (*paranomia*) as freedom, free speech (*parrhēsia*) as equality under the law (*isonomia*), or freedom to do what you want (*exousia*) as happiness (*eudaimonia*),[18] but rather by hating and punishing such men, it made all the citizens better and more moderate.

[21] But the greatest contribution to governing Athens well was that, of the two recognized kinds of equality—one which allots the same to everyone and the other which gives each what is appropriate—they were not unaware which was more beneficial. They thought it wrong to regard good and bad citizens as deserving the same, [22] and they preferred that equality which honors and punishes each according to what he deserved. Through this they governed the state; they did not allot political offices to all, but chose the citizens who were best and

---

[16] For similar statements regarding Athens' deserved hegemony, see, e.g., 4.72, 12.67, 15.233, 294.

[17] After the disastrous battle of Aegospotami in 405, Athens surrendered and came under the tyranny of the Thirty (404/3).

[18] For similar characterizations of fourth-century Athenian democracy, see 15.283 and Plato, *Republic* 560d–561a.

most capable for each task. They expected that others would mirror those who were in charge of public affairs.

[23] Moreover, they considered this constitution to be more populist (*dēmotikōteros*) than that which is based on the casting of lots. In the latter, fortune governs, and often those who desire oligarchy are appointed to receive the offices, while in one based on the selection of the best, the people have the authority to choose those who are most devoted to the current constitution. [24] The reason why the majority accepted this and why offices were not hotly contested was that people had learned to work hard and to be thrifty, and not to neglect their own affairs while having designs on others, nor to manage their own affairs from the public purse, but to help the common interest from one's own resources if the need ever arose. Furthermore, they did not know the incomes from public offices in greater detail than the income from their own affairs. [25] Indeed they so strongly refrained from civic affairs, that it was more difficult at that time to find people willing to undertake public office than it is now to find people not seeking office. They regarded the care of the common interests not as a business, but as a public service;[19] and they did not from the first day watch to see if those who previously held office had omitted any income,[20] but much rather, if they had neglected any matter urgently requiring resolution.

[26] To summarize, they recognized that the people, just like a monarch, must appoint public officials, punish transgressors, and judge disputes and that those who had leisure and possessed adequate means should take care of common interests, as if they were servants; [27] that they should be praised for being just and be pleased with this honor; while those who govern badly should not be excused but should receive the harshest penalties. So how could anyone find a de-

---

[19] For "liturgy" (*lēitourgia*), see the Glossary. Here, and elsewhere in speech 15, Isocrates broadens the understanding of a liturgy to encompass any service, including the teaching of rhetoric, performed for the overall benefit of the community; see 15.158, 224–226; and Lys. 21.19 for the idea that the best liturgy is good citizenship; also Too 1995: 109–110.

[20] Following his term of office, a magistrate could be called to account in a procedure known as a *euthyna*, particularly over the spending of public money, although generals could be called to account for their actions at any time in their office. Harrison 1971: 14–15, 208–211.

mocracy more secure or more just than this, one which puts the most
able people in charge of public matters and makes the people sover-
eign over these.

[28] Such was the structure of their constitution. It is easy to see
from this that they always carried out daily affairs justly and lawfully,
for those who made such fine principles for the whole state must necessarily manage smaller matters in the same manner. [29] First of all,
as for matters regarding the gods—for it is right to begin with this—
they did not worship or perform the celebrations inconsistently or
erratically. They did not dispatch three hundred oxen whenever they
felt like it,[21] nor did they arbitrarily omit the ancestral sacrifices.[22]
They did not sumptuously conduct foreign festivals at which there
was feasting, while making the sacrifices required by the holiest of rites
on the basis of the lowest contracted price. [30] They made certain of
only one thing, that they did not destroy any ancestral custom, or add
anything beyond what was customary. They did not think that piety
was a matter of great expense, but rather of not changing anything
their ancestors had handed down to them. Moreover, they received
gifts from the gods not unsteadily or randomly, but at the right moment for working the land and harvesting the crops.

[31] They pursued relationships among themselves in the same
manner as this. Not only did they agree about both public affairs and
their private lives, but they had as much thought for each other as is
necessary for people who are sensible and have a common interest in
the fatherland.

Poorer citizens refrained from envying those who had more to the
extent [32] that their concern for large households was the same as for
their own, for they thought that the prosperity of these entailed their
own wealth. Those who possessed property did not look down on
those who lived less well, but considered the citizens' poverty as a
disgrace to themselves, and assisted them in their distress. They provided farmland at moderate rent to some, sent out some to engage
in trade, and presented to others the capital for other enterprises.
[33] They did not fear either of two results: losing their whole invest-

---

[21] Animal sacrifices were made at public festivals, such as the Great Panathenaia, where Athens' allies and colonies were required to make a contribution.
The sacrifice would result in a public feast (see Aristoph., *Clouds* 386).

[22] Cf. 2.20.

ment, or after much trouble, reaping only a part of what they had ventured; but they were as confident about what they had given out as of what they had retained. For they saw that people on trial for breach of contract did not plead for equity[23] but adhered to the laws; [34] that in the trials of others, they did not provide themselves with license to do wrong[24] but were more outraged at thieves than at their victims since they thought that the poor were more greatly harmed than the rich by those who made contracts untrustworthy. This is because if the [rich] stop lending, they will lose only a small amount of income, whereas if the poor are deprived of this half, they find themselves in dire straits. [35] Because of this way of thinking, no one hid his wealth or hesitated to contribute; indeed, they derived greater pleasure from seeing men borrow than paying back the loan. As sensible men should wish, they had both of the following results: they benefited the citizens and put their own wealth to work. This is the essence of good relations among men: the ownership of property was secure for those to whom it rightly belonged, but it was enjoyed in common by all the citizens who needed it.

[36] Perhaps, one might criticize what I've said, because in praising actions which happened at that time, I do not discuss the reason relations among citizens and the management of the state were so good. I think I have said some such thing,[25] but despite this, I shall try to speak more clearly about this matter.

[37] Our ancestors did not put many people in charge of their education (*paideia*) or allow citizens to do what they want once they were inscribed as an adult.[26] Instead, they paid more attention to them at

---

[23] Litigants were generally expected to adhere strictly to the laws, but other considerations often entered into their pleadings. Isocrates is here criticizing the litigious culture of contemporary Athens; cf., e.g., 15.42–43. For "equity" (*epieikeia*), see Arist., *Rhetoric* 1372b18, 1374a27, and 1375a31–32.

[24] See 15.142–143.

[25] See above, 20–27.

[26] Upon his eighteenth birthday, a youth underwent a *dokimasia* or scrutiny to ensure that he was of age and therefore eligible to participate in public life; see Arist., *Ath. Pol.* 42.1–2 and MacDowell 1978: 58 and 205–206. Individuals who were to hold public office were also required to undergo *dokimasia* before taking up their office.

that time than when they were children. Our ancestors placed such a premium on moderation (*sōphrosynē*) that they established the Areopagus Council to oversee public order, and only those who were well born and gave evidence of particular virtue and moderation in their lives belonged to it.[27] As a result, it naturally took precedence over the other councils in Greece. [38] One could use what happens today as evidence for the institution in those days. Even now when everything connected with the selection and examination *(dokimasia)*[28] of magistrates is neglected, we can see those who are insufferable in other matters hesitate to show their true nature when they enter the Areopagus and abide by its laws rather than by their own wickedness, so great was the fear our ancestors aroused in the wicked, and such was the memorial to their own virtue and moderation that they left in this place.

[39] As I said, such was the institution they put in charge of overseeing public order. This Council considered it simple ignorance if someone thought that the best men are found in cities with the most precise laws. In that case nothing would prevent all the Greeks from being alike, since written laws are easily borrowed from each other. [40] But progress in virtue comes not from these but from everyday activities: most people turn out to conduct themselves according to the habits in which they were educated. Second, a large number of specific laws is a sign that a city is badly governed, for in erecting these obstacles to crime, people are forced to make many laws. [41] Those who are properly governed do not need to fill the stoas with written [laws][29] but to have justice in their souls. Cities are well governed not

---

[27] For the history of the Areopagus Council, see the Introduction.

[28] See above, 37n.

[29] The laws of Athens were written on stone slabs set up in different places, especially Stoa Basileios. Written laws were deemed to ensure justice; cf. Gorgias, *Palamedes* 30; Solon Fr. 36 W = Arist., *Ath. Pol.* 12.4; Euripides, *Suppliants* 433–437; Harris 1989: 75; and Thomas 1989: 32; also Thomas 1995: 74, which argues that the monumental inscription of law served not only to fix it publicly but also to accord it the impressiveness and respect accorded to oral law. Unwritten law was deemed to govern the ideals and conventions of social life, such as respect for the old, so that *nomos* continued to signify both "law" and "convention"; see Thomas 1989: 31. According to Plutarch, Lycurgus refused to put Sparta's laws

by legislation but by customs, and those who have been badly brought up will venture to transgress even meticulously written laws, whereas those who have been well educated will be willing to obey even simple laws. [42] This was the understanding of our ancestors when they considered in the first place not how to punish the disorderly but how to produce citizens who would not commit crimes meriting punishment. They regarded this as their main task and thought eagerness for punishment was appropriately left to people's enemies. [43] They were concerned about all the citizens, but especially the younger ones. They saw that people of such an age are most undisciplined and full of many desires and that their souls require taming through the cultivation of the finest practices and pleasant tasks. These alone hold the attention of men who have been raised as free citizens and are accustomed to noble thoughts. [44] It was not possible to prepare everyone for the same occupations since their circumstances were different; so instead, they gave each an occupation that fit his economic situation. Those who had fewer means, they directed to farming and trade, knowing that poverty stems from idleness, and crime, from poverty. [45] By removing the origin of wickedness, they thought they would also remove the other crimes which attend it. Those who had sufficient means were forced to occupy themselves with horse training, gymnastics, hunting, and philosophy, seeing that some people achieve preeminence through these pursuits and others refrain from the majority of vices.[30]

[46] After enacting these ordinances, they did not spend the rest of their time idly, but after dividing the city into districts, and the country into demes, they watched over the life of each person[31] and brought those who violated public order before the Council. The

---

into writing because he deemed it better to have the laws fixed *within* the citizens by education; for Sparta's legislator, education was the greatest and noblest task (*Lycurgus* 13.1–14.1; also Plut., *Moralia* 780C).

[30] For the idea that different sorts of education preparing for different "careers" are suited to different classes of citizen, where class is determined by wealth, see also 15.304. For the apportioning of employment as a feature of conservative ideology, see Wallace 1985: 148–152.

[31] Aristotle (*Ath. Pol.* 42) informs us that each district appointed guardians to supervise the young even later on.

Council reprimanded some, threatened others, and punished some as was fitting. They knew that there are two ways, both to encourage injustice and to restrain wrongdoing. [47] Where no vigilance has been established over such things and judgments are not strict, even those with honest natures are corrupted, but where it is not easy for wrongdoers to escape notice or to be pardoned when they are caught, there corrupt natures are destroyed. Our ancestors knew these things and kept the citizens in check by both means, by punishments and by watchful discipline. Not only were those who had done wrong inevitably detected, but they even saw ahead of time who was likely to do something wrong.

[48] Therefore, the young did not spend time in the gambling houses, or with flute girls,[32] or in such gatherings as those in which they now spend their days.[33] Instead, they spent all their time in activities that were assigned to them, admiring and competing with the best in these pursuits. They so strenuously avoided the *agora,* that even when they were forced to pass through it, they clearly did so with great embarrassment and modesty. [49] They thought it more shocking to talk back to their elders, or to abuse them verbally, than it is now to wrong one's parents. No one, not even an honest slave, dared to eat or drink in a tavern. They took life seriously, and did not make it a joke. Our ancestors regarded those who were witty and had a facility for jesting, whom people now call "gifted" (*euphyeis*), as unfortunate.[34]

[50] No one should think that I have something against young people. I do not hold them responsible for what's happening, and I am aware that most of them are not at all pleased with this state of

---

[32] Respectable girls and women remained indoors in sections of houses specifically reserved for them; flute girls were entertainers at male gatherings, such as symposia, and provided sexual services.

[33] Cf. 15.286–287.

[34] Cf. the description of the moral climate at Athens with 15.283 and 286, and see 8.14 for criticisms of comic excess. Aristotle speaks of the buffoon as being inferior to the comic (*geloios*) (*NE* 1128a33–34). Buffoons exceed the limits of comedy, are base, boorish, and rough (1128a5–9) and are to be aligned with those who are slavish in nature and uncultured; they are also defined by distinction from the free, the reasonable (*epieikēs*), and the cultured citizen (1128a18–22; also 1128a30–31).

affairs, which permits them to spend time in these excesses. It would not be reasonable to criticize them, but it would be fairer to blame those who managed the state a little before our time. [51] These were the ones who encouraged them to these acts of contempt and undid the power of the Areopagus. As long as it had authority, Athens was not filled with lawsuits, accusations, taxes (*eisphorai*), poverty, or wars, but the people lived at ease with one another and maintained peace with all others. They earned the trust of the Greeks and the fear of the barbarians, [52] for they had saved the former and had punished the latter so severely that they were pleased if they suffered no further harm.

For these reasons, our ancestors lived so securely that their homes and other buildings in the country were finer and more splendid than those inside the city walls, and many of the citizens did not come to the city for the festivals but elected to stay at home and enjoy their private blessings rather than share in public benefits.[35] [53] For they did not conduct festivals extravagantly or conspicuously, which would induce them to visit, but sensibly. They judged happiness (*eudaimonia*) not by processions, or competitiveness in the financing of choruses,[36] or such acts of ostentation, but by sober government, by the conduct of daily life, and by the elimination of need. By these standards one must judge those who are truly fortunate and do not live vulgarly. [54] These days what sensible individual would not be upset at what is happening when he sees many citizens drawing lots at the entrance of the courts to see whether they will have the necessities of life or not,[37] while they agree to support other Greeks who are willing

---

[35] Classical authors celebrate Athens for the number and quality of its festivals; see Thuc. 2.38 (for festivals as a relief from labor); Isoc. 4.43–46; Pseudo-Xen., *Ath. Pol.* 3.8.

[36] The financing of choruses (*chorēgia*) was one of the liturgic obligations undertaken by the wealthier members of the Athenian community. Litigants often attested to their good citizenship by citing past liturgic undertakings; e.g., Lys. 7.31, 12.20, 19.57–56, 21.1–11; cf. 19, 25.12, 26.3.

[37] Upon Pericles' completion of the Ephialtean reforms, which ensured wider participation in political process, jurors earned two obols a day (later increased by three by Cleon)—a living wage—for jury service. See 8.130, 15.152, and Aristoph., *Wasps* 303–306, for the negative consequences of jury pay.

to row ships; dancers on stage in golden cloaks, even as they spend the winter in unspeakable garments, and [to tolerate] other such contradictions in the management of the city which bring great shame upon Athens?

[55] None of this happened under that Council [i.e., the Areopagus]. For it relieved the poor from their poverty by providing work and benefits from the rich; it relieved the young from unruliness by giving them occupations and keeping watch over them; it relieved those engaged in government from seeking profit by setting penalties and not allowing wrongdoers to go unnoticed; it relieved the old from despair by granting them public honors and ensuring that the young took care of them. How could a constitution be more worthy than this one which watched over everything so well?

[56] We have discussed most of the basic features of that government. From what has been said it is easy to comprehend what I omitted, because it is of the same kind. But while some people who have already heard me describe this constitution have praised it to the limits and have congratulated our ancestors for governing Athens in this manner, [57] they did not think, however, that you would be persuaded to adopt it but would prefer through force of habit to suffer misfortune under your current government than to lead a better life with a more discriminating constitution. They said that although I gave the best counsel, I was in danger of appearing to be an antipopulist and of seeking to turn Athens into an oligarchy. [58] If I were speaking about matters unfamiliar and not of common understanding, and urged you to select a committee (*synedros*) or commissioners (*syngraphoi*) on these matters—bodies which had previously destroyed the democracy—[38] this criticism would be fair. But in fact, I have said no such thing. I have discussed a government that is not hidden but open to all, [59] which you all know was our fatherland and was responsible for the greatest goods for Athens and for the rest of Greece. In addition, it was established and its laws written by men

---

[38] Isocrates refers to the crisis of 411, when the Four Hundred established a commission to establish a definitive constitution (see *Ath. Pol.* 29.2–30.9), and 404, when a commission of thirty men, who would become the Thirty tyrants, were selected to make the constitution conform to tradition, i.e., more conservative (see Xen., *Hellenica* 2.3.2 and 11).

whom everyone would agree to be the most democratic of the citizens. Hence it would be a terrible wrong if by introducing such a constitution, I should appear to desire revolution.[39] [60] Furthermore, it is easy to recognize my intentions from this. In most of my previous speeches, I clearly condemn oligarchy and political advantage (*pleonexia*), and praise equality (*isotētas*) and democracy—not all democracies randomly, but giving just and sensible praise to those which are well established. [61] I know that under this constitution our ancestors far excelled others and that the Spartans are best governed because they are most democratic. For in the selection of public offices, in their daily life, and in their other practices, we would see that fairness (*isotēs*) and uniformity (*homoiotēs*)[40] have greater priority among them than among others. Oligarchies are hostile to these principles, but those who have well-ordered democracies continue to employ them. [62] If we want to examine the most renowned and greatest of other states, we will find that democracy provides more benefits than oligarchy. For if we compare our constitution (which all criticize) not to the one I've described but to the one established by the Thirty, there is no one who would not think it divinely inspired. [63] And even if some people say that I am straying from my theme, I want to show and explain how greatly this government surpasses that one (of the Thirty), so that no one will think that I am scrutinizing the mistakes of this democracy while omitting any of its fine or noble achievements. My account will not be long or without benefit for my listeners.

[64] When we lost our ships near the Hellespont and Athens experienced those disasters,[41] which of the older men among us does not know that the so-called "populists" (*dēmotikoi*) were ready to go to

---

[39] The phrase *neōterōn . . . pragmatōn* (lit. "new matters") denotes revolutionary events; see, e.g., Herod. 5.19.2, 5.35.4; Xen., *Hellenica* 5.2.9. It reflects a familiar classical Athenian anxiety about what is unprecedented or novel in political circumstances; cf., e.g., 15.159–161 and 317.

[40] At Sparta, the *homoioi* or "peers" were the citizens who had the right to hold state offices (Xen., *Hellenica* 3.3.5 and Arist., *Ath. Pol.* 1306b30). With his praise of Sparta, Isocrates aligns himself with a more conservative, because selective, government.

[41] Isocrates uses a common euphemism to refer to the devastating defeat by the Spartans at Aegospotami in 405 at the end of the Peloponnesian War.

any length to avoid doing what the enemy ordered and thought it would be terrible if anyone should see the city which had ruled Greece now subject to others, while those who desired oligarchy were ready to destroy the city walls and endure slavery?[42] [65] Or that when the people controlled the government, we guarded the acropolises of other cities, but when the Thirty took over the government, the enemy controlled ours?[43] Or that at that time the Spartans were our masters, but when the exiles returned and dared to fight for freedom, and Conon gained his naval victory, ambassadors came from Sparta and gave Athens mastery of the sea?

[66] Furthermore, who of my own contemporaries does not remember that the democracy so adorned Athens with temples and public buildings that even now those who visit think it deserves to rule not only Greece but also all others,[44] but that the Thirty neglected the buildings, plundered the temples, and gave away the dockyards to be destroyed for three talents, although the city spent no less than a thousand talents on them? [67] And no one would justly praise the mildness of the Thirty as opposed to that of the people. When they took control of Athens by a vote, they put to death fifteen hundred citizens without a trial, and they forced more than five thousand to flee to Piraeus.[45] But when the exiles took power and returned with arms, they put to death only the most guilty criminals and governed the others so well and lawfully that those who had toppled the democracy owned no less than those who returned from exile.[46]

---

[42] The Spartan leader Lysander wanted the "long walls" that connected Athens to Piraeus destroyed as a term of peace.

[43] The Spartans stationed a garrison on the Acropolis of Athens in 404 (Xen., *Hellenica* 2.4.10–23).

[44] For similar statements reflecting a hegemonic ideology, see 15.234 and 294, 4.57.

[45] The Thirty ordained death for anyone who remained in Athens with the exception of a small number of citizens known as the Three Thousand; see Lys. 12.95, 13.47, 25.22; Xen., *Hellenica* 4.1. Piraeus, the port of Athens, became a rallying point for the opposition forces.

[46] In 403 a political and economic amnesty was declared so that immunity was granted to citizens (except for the Thirty themselves) who had otherwise committed crimes against the democracy during the oligarchy; see And. 1.20–21 and Plato, *Menexenus* 243e. Aristotle confirms the amicable relations between the parties involved; see *Ath. Pol.* 40.3 and also Dem. 20.11–12.

[68] But the finest and greatest testimony of all to the fairness of the people is that those who remained in the city had borrowed a hundred talents from the Spartans for besieging those who held Piraeus under siege, and that during a meeting of the Assembly concerning the return of the money, many said that those who had borrowed the money, not those who had been besieged, should pay it back. Yet the people decided to use common funds for the repayment. [69] With this decision they fostered such harmony among us and led the city to make such progress that the Spartans, who gave us orders nearly every day under the oligarchy, came as suppliants under the democracy, asking [us] not to sit by and let them be driven from their homes. Such was the essence of the attitudes of each party: the oligarchs wanted to rule the citizens and be slaves to the enemy, whereas the populists wanted to rule others and give equality to the citizens.

[70] I have related these events for two reasons. First, I want to show that I am not a supporter of oligarchies or of their special privileges, but that I desire a just and orderly constitution; second, that badly instituted democracies cause less misfortune (than oligarchies), whereas well-governed ones have the advantage of being more just, more equitable, and more enjoyable for those who live in them. [71] Perhaps, someone might wonder why I seek to persuade you to change from a constitution which has accomplished so many fine things to another, and why, having praised democracy so highly, I change again at whim and criticize and condemn the current order. [72] Well, I blame private citizens if they do a few things right while doing many wrongs, and I consider them worse than they should be; moreover, I reprimand those who come from noble stock and are only a little more decent than the exceptionally wicked and much worse than their fathers, and I would advise them too to stop such conduct. [73] I have the same view of public matters. I think that we must not pride ourselves, or be content if we have been more law-abiding than wretched and insane men, but rather that we should be upset and discontent if we are worse than our ancestors. We must compete with their virtue, not with the evil of the Thirty, especially as it is appropriate for us to be the best of all men.

[74] This is not the first time I have made this argument, but I have already done so many times, before many people. I know that in other places there are fruits, trees, and animals particular to each place that

are far better than those of other lands, and that our land gives birth to and nourishes men who not only have a natural gift for crafts, for politics, or for speaking but also excel others in courage and virtue. [75] It is fair to cite the evidence of the ancient battles they fought against the Amazons, the Thracians, and all the Peloponnesians, and the Persian peril, in which both alone and with the Peloponnesians, fighting on foot and on the sea, they defeated the barbarians and won distinction for their valor.[47] They would have achieved none of these things if they were not naturally superior.

[76] Let no one think that my eulogy is appropriate for our current government; just the opposite. Such speeches praise those who prove themselves deserving of our ancestors' virtue and condemn those who disgrace their good birth by their laziness and cowardice. And this is what I am doing, for the truth will be spoken. Although we have such a nature, we have not preserved it but have fallen into folly, confusion, and desire for evil. [77] But if I continue attacking and condemning those aspects of our current state of affairs, I fear I will stray far from my theme. I have previously spoken about these things,[48] and will do so again, if I do not persuade you to stop making these mistakes.

But for now, I will say a few words on the topic I proposed at the outset, and then, shall give way to those who still wish to offer more advice. [78] If we continue to govern the city as we do now, it is inevitable that we shall take counsel, make war, live, suffer, and do nearly everything just as we now do in the present as in the past. But if we change the constitution, it is clear that by the same logic our situation will become the same as our ancestors'. For the same form of government will necessarily lead to identical or similar political outcomes. [79] We must compare the most important of these outcomes and consider which we should choose.

First, let us consider how the Greeks and barbarians feel about that constitution, and how they now feel toward us. These peoples contribute much to our happiness, when they are well disposed toward us. [80] Now the Greeks had such confidence in those who governed

---

[47] This list of Athens' military successes against the Amazons, the Peloponnesians, and the barbarians is a commonplace, especially in the Athenian funeral oration; see, e.g., Lys. 2.4–16 and Plato, *Menexenus* 239b–241c.

[48] At 8.49–56.

at that time that most of them willingly entrusted themselves to our city; and the barbarians were so far from having designs on Greek affairs that they did not sail their long ships on this side of Phaselis,[49] nor did they march their armies beyond the Halys river,[50] but they remained very quiet. [81] Now it has come to the point that the Greeks hate Athens, and the barbarians despise us. You have heard our generals themselves report on the hatred of the Greeks, and the King's feelings are apparent from the letters he has sent.[51]

[82] In addition to these things, under that former discipline the citizens were taught such a degree of virtue that they did not harm each other but fought and defeated all who invaded our land. We are the opposite. Every day we injure each other, and military affairs are so neglected that we do not even dare to participate in the military reviews unless we are paid. [83] But the most important point is that at that time no citizen went without life's necessities, and no one shamed the city begging from passersby, whereas now the needy outnumber those with means. And we can hardly blame them if they disregard public affairs and consider only how to get through each day.

[84] Thus, thinking that, if we imitate our ancestors, we shall be freed from these troubles and become the saviors not only of Athens but also of all Greece, I have therefore come before you and made this speech. You should consider everything I have said, and vote for what you think will be best for Athens.

---

[49] According to the agreement known as the Treaty of Callias made in 448, Persia agreed not to venture west of Phaselis, which at the time was the principal commercial port on the East coast of Lycia (in southern Turkey).

[50] The river Halys in Anatolia (modern Turkey) runs north into the Black Sea; today it is known as Kizihrmak.

[51] The Persians sent threatening letters to Athens as Chares had supported the rebel satrap Artabazus; see 10n and Diodorus Siculus 16.22.

15. ANTIDOSIS

INTRODUCTION

In classical Athens, the wealthiest citizens were liable to perform liturgies, a form of taxation that required them to finance various public concerns. These might relate to a festival, such as the training of a chorus (*chorēgeia*), or the fleet, such as the command and maintenance of a ship in the fleet (*triērarchia*). More rarely, the liturgy might entail the advance payment of a tax, known as *proeisphora*. The liturgy system was one which ensured that rich citizens expended some of their resources in the interests of the community as a whole, and while it was burdensome (e.g., Xen., *Oeconomicus* 2.5–6), litigants in trials often attested their civic pride by citing their past undertaking of liturgic obligations, and citizens occasionally spent much more than they were required to in order to win popular favor. In 356, a wealthy citizen Megacleides was summoned to undertake the funding of a trireme. Instead of discharging the obligation, he went to trial, claiming that the rhetorician Isocrates should be liable for the trierarchy since he was the wealthier of the two (cf. Pseudo-Plut., *Isocrates* 18). Now an old man, Isocrates lost the case and had to assume the liturgy, or public service.

This historical trial becomes the pretext for the *Antidosis,* a fictional legal defense, which the author wrote when he was eighty-two (354–353), as Plutarch's life of Isocrates informs us (838A). The title of the speech refers to the *antidosis* ("exchange") procedure, according to which a citizen who unsuccessfully challenged another supposedly wealthier citizen to undertake a liturgy in his place was obliged to exchange properties with the latter.[1] Isocrates invents a prosecutor named Lysimachus, who is portrayed as a sykophant or habitual litigant. Lysimachus drags the now eighty-two-year-old rhetorician into court to defend himself against the charges that he corrupted the young of Athens through his teaching and has taught them how to argue unjustly (15.8)

In speech 15, this legal fiction is a vehicle for the rhetorician's self-presentation: the speech is described as an image (*eikōn*) of Isocrates' life, thought, and character (15.7). Furthermore, self-representation has its conventions and commonplaces, even if these are to be subverted or assimilated to different contexts. The charges brought against the rhetorician are the same ones with which Socrates was charged in 399, and the rhetorician explicitly reworks portions of Plato's *Apology*.[2] Like Socrates, Isocrates is an individual who engages in "philosophy."[3] By "philosophy," however, the rhetorician means the use of language to maintain order where an individual's home, the city state, and Athens' larger political interests are concerned; if *logos* is the basis of the political community, then "philosophy" helps to create and maintain this community as such (see 15.285). For him, the philosopher is the true "sophist" (*sophistēs*), who is not to be understood as the contemporary teacher motivated by greed and fame but as the true political wise man (*sophos*), for whom the paradigm is Athens' great legislator Solon (15.235 and 313).

Such self-representation is necessary in a world where rhetoric is of supreme importance, and "reality" is thus to be regarded as any set of images put into circulation by oneself and one's supporters, and by one's detractors, rivals, and enemies, whom Isocrates depicts as belonging to the contemporary rhetorical establishment. (The embedded, posthumous apology that Isocrates creates for the general Timotheus [15.101–139], one of his former students, demonstrates forcefully the destructive potential of the rhetoric of blame at Athens.) The self-

---

[1] Some scholars doubt whether an actual exchange of property was ever the outcome of such a legal proceeding, although indisputable evidence for the procedure comes from, e.g., Lys. 4.1.

[2] See Momigliano 1971: 59.

[3] For references to philosophy in the *Antidosis*, see sections 10, 41, 49, 50, 147, 162, 167–187, 205, 209, 215, 243, 247, 270, 285, 292, 304, and 313.

characterization that the speech offers is that of the "quiet Athenian," the citizen who advocates political aloofness as responsible behavior in an Athens troubled by the activities of sykophants and popular orators. But quietism itself is a politics of marginality, which marks out the aristocratic and oligarchical members of the democratic community to each other and to their fellow citizens.

Isocrates declares himself and his discourse unlike anyone and anything else in the contemporary city, despite the fact that distinguishing oneself from one's audience runs against rhetorical instinct (cf. 143). He is "like no other citizen" (144); has stood apart from all public matters (145); and importantly, is unlike both contemporary sophists and lay people (148). Moreover, the *Antidosis* is itself an atypical speech in light of fourth-century speech genres. The defense begins with the author claiming that the current speech does not resemble any conventional lawcourt speech or any epideixis. It is novel and different, opening the rhetorician to the charge of being "out of place," "strange," "unconventional," which are all conveyed by the adjective *atopos* (1; cf. 150). It is atypical because it deals with philosophy, that is, with rhetoric and its several cultures. Later, at section 179 Isocrates draws attention to the idiosyncratic and extraordinary nature of his defense, for he is after all dealing with a situation that is unlike any other. These statements are in keeping with, and insist on, the idea that the activities of philosophy, its teachers, and practitioners are distinct from those of all other arts (cf. section 263) and therefore should be judged on their own terms.

Through this speech Isocrates offers a characterization of rhetoric that is distinct from the perception of it held by many contemporary Athenians. For him, rhetoric is philosophy, that is, the ability to speak, to reason, and to act. It is not an abstract and impractical activity such as Isocrates judges the verbal quibblings of the Presocratic thinkers to be. Rhetoric/philosophy does not rely on a fixed body of knowledge (*epistēmē*) but on ability to guess and conjecture (*doxa*) at the right opportunities. These skills allow the orator or the politician to say and do what is necessary in any particular situation. *Logos* and the arts associated with it are responsible for the advantages that human beings have over other animals, for those that the Greeks have over the barbarians, and most importantly, for those that the Athenians have over the rest of the Greeks. Rhetoric/philosophy has been the basis for the

military and cultural hegemony that Athens historically enjoyed because its historical leaders—Solon, Themistocles, and Pericles—were
men endowed with skill in *logos;* it remains the basis for Athenian
superiority, provided the city recognizes its importance to what it has
been and could be.

Isocrates seeks to show that, as a teacher of rhetoric, he has been
concerned with the overall welfare of Athens and its interests and has
given far more to Athens than he has taken from it. This is the concern of the true sophist and not of the corrupt individual who goes
by that title in fourth-century Athens. Isocrates is thus the individual
who shows that the label "sophist" may be rehabilitated for the fourth
century, once the public understands that the true sophist, like Solon,
Cleisthenes, or Pericles, is one who works for the best interests of the
democratic city. The *Antidosis* is the celebration of an overall intellectual and literary career that has made a genuine contribution to the
political community. The rhetorician is the individual who claims to
have taught the most important figures of the civilized world, justify-
ing the boast of Athens to be the teacher of the Greek world.[4]

Modern readers have not generally understood that Isocrates' eccentric self-fashioning does not by any means call into question the
author's identity as a significant figure in the history of rhetoric.[5] After
all, writers in antiquity and in the Renaissance deemed Isocrates the
preeminent rhetorician of classical Athens. The Roman historian Velleius Paterculus goes so far as to call him the sole figure of note in the
whole history of rhetoric, for in his view, before Isocrates and after his
pupils there is nothing of note as far as the art of public speech was
concerned: *Quid ante Isocratem, quid post eius auditores eorumque dis-
cipulos clarum in oratoribus fuit?* (*Historia Romana* 1.16.5). This flattering portrait may owe something to Cicero's presentation of Isocrates
as a "great orator and accomplished teacher" (*magnus orator et perfectus
magister*), whose home virtually became a school and speech workshop (*officina dicendi*) for the whole of Greece (*Brutus* 8.30). Quintil-

---

[4] Cf. Pericles' description of the entire city of Athens as the "teacher of Greece"
(Thuc. 2.41.1).

[5] In the twentieth century Isocrates has become a secondary figure in the historical and social (re)construction of Athens, perhaps precisely because he was
Athens' foremost speech artist. See, for instance, the less than flattering comments
of Marrou 1956: 131 and de Romilly 1958: 101.

ian describes the rhetorician as "the most distinguished student of Gorgias," notwithstanding disagreements between the two individuals (cf. *Institutio Oratoria* 3.1.13).

Lawcourt speeches were limited in length to what could be delivered in the space of one day. The *Antidosis* is an extraordinarily long speech and must have strained the fiction of the forensic setting. The structure of the work may be laid out as follows:

1–13	first (nonfictional) prooemium
14–28	second prooemium
29–51	the charge (*graphē*)
52–83	defense with citation of (witness) speeches
84–101	defense of rhetorical education
102–139	defense of the general Timotheus
140–166	interlude with reported speech by an associate and historical reflection
167–214	encomium of philosophy (i.e., rhetoric)
215–242	what is a sophist?
243–269	encomium of philosophy continued
270–309	discussion of philosophy and its education
310–323	closing remarks

15. ANTIDOSIS

[1] If the speech I am about to read resembled speeches composed for the lawcourts or for display, I don't think I would make any prefatory remarks about it. But because it is new and different, I must first declare the reasons why I chose to compose a speech so unlike the others; for if I do not make this clear, it may perhaps appear eccentric (*atopos*) to many.

[2] I am aware that some sophists speak ill of my occupation. They say that it is concerned with forensic oratory, and they act much as if someone were to dare to label Phidias,[6] who made the statue of

---

[6] Phidias was the renowned sculptor (ca. 490–432), who is particularly celebrated for making the ivory and gold statue of Athena on the Parthenon (Pliny, *NH* 34.54 and Plut., *Pericles* 31). Because of his close association with Pericles, Phidias became the target of two lawsuits, the first, an unsuccessful one for embezzling gold from the Parthenon statue of Athena and a second one, for impiety

Athena, a "doll maker," or were to say that Zeuxis and Parrhasius[7] possess the same skill as scribes.[8] I never defended myself against these petty attacks, [3] since I did not think their babblings had any authority, and I thought I had made everyone aware that I chose both to speak and to write not about private disputes but about public matters of such great importance that no one else would attempt them, apart from those who had spent time with me[9] or wanted to imitate these. [4] So until this point in my life, I thought that because of this choice and my general noninvolvement in political affairs (*apragmosynē*), I was well regarded as far as all private citizens were concerned. Now at the end of my career, I am subject to an exchange (*antidosis*) over the matter of funding a trierarchy and to a trial in connection with it, and I sense that some people were not disposed to me as I hoped but were for the most part deceived about my affairs and were inclined to believe those who utter prejudicial things. Others, who know perfectly well how I spend my time, were jealous and experienced the same feelings as the sophists, and they delighted in those holding a false impression of me. [5] They have shown their disposition in this way: when my opponent spoke completely unjustly on the matters under judgment, slandered the power of my speeches, and exaggerated my wealth and the number of my students, they judged the liturgy to be my responsibility. Thus I bore this expense, as is fitting for those who are not too put out by such affairs and are not in any way wasteful or heedless where money is concerned.

[6] Perceiving, as I said, that more people than I had thought were mistaken about me, I turned my thoughts to how I could reveal to them and others in the future my nature, my life, and the education

---

for representing himself and Pericles on the Parthenon. As a result of this second trial, the sculptor was cast into prison, where he fell ill and died.

[7] Zeuxis of Heraclea (late fifth century) and Parrhasius of Ephesus (ca. 400) were famous painters. Pliny relates how in a contest Zeuxis painted grapes that were so realistic that the birds came to peck at them, while Parrhasius so effectively painted a curtain that the former asked him to draw it back. Parrhasius won the contest (for this story, see *NH* 35.36.65–72).

[8] Lit., "those who inscribe votive tablets," which were set up in temples to thank the gods for recovery from illness or other deliverance.

[9] I.e., as my students.

(*paideia*) that is my preoccupation so that I do not allow myself to be condemned without a trial on these matters, at the mercy of those who habitually slander me, as is now the case. [7] I considered these things and found that my only course of action was to write a speech that would be (as it were) an image (*eikōn*) of my thoughts and my life as a whole. I hoped that this would be the best way to make the facts about me known and to leave this behind as a memorial, much finer than bronze statues. [8] I saw that, if I were to attempt a eulogy of myself, I would not be able to include everything I chose to cover or speak in an acceptable manner without arousing envy. But I saw that I could treat all the topics I wanted if I invented a lawsuit that threatened me, a sykophant who had brought this charge to cause me problems and who had invoked the slanders employed in the exchange suit, and then composed my arguments after the fashion of a legal defense.

[9] With this in mind, I wrote this speech not at the prime of my life but when I had turned eighty-two. For this reason it is necessary to make allowances if it appears to be less vigorous than those I previously published, as it has not been easy or simple but laborious. [10] Some of what I have written is suited to delivery in the lawcourt, and some is not fitted for such disputes but is a wide-ranging discussion and exposition about philosophy[10] and its power. This is the sort of thing which would benefit the young to hear as they embark upon their studies and education. Moreover, much of what I wrote a long time ago is combined with what I have recently said not in an illogical or untimely fashion but as suits the present topic.

[11] It was by no means a small matter to have in view such a large topic, synthesize and draw together so many different types of discourse, make later passages fit with earlier ones, and make them all agree with one another.[11] Although I was of an advanced age, I did not shrink from completing this speech, which was composed most truthfully; as for its other qualities, let those who hear it decide. [12] Those who read it should realize that they are listening to a mixed discourse, encompassing all these different subjects, and they should pay greater attention to what will be said than to what came before.

---

[10] On "philosophy," see Introduction to this volume and the Glossary.
[11] Cf. Plato, *Phaedrus* 264c2–5.

In addition, they must not attempt to go through it all the first time but only as much as will not tire the audience.[12] If you abide by these guidelines, you will be better able to see if I say anything worthy of my reputation.

[13] That was a necessary preface. Now read my defense, which purports to have been written for a trial, and seeks to make clear the truth about myself, and to make those who are ignorant aware and those who are envious pained even more by this disease—for I could not get revenge on them by any better means.

[14] I think[13] that individuals who dare to blame others for the things they themselves are guilty of are the most wicked and deserve the harshest penalties. This is just what Lysimachus has done. For in his composition (*syngegrammena*), he spoke more about my compositions than about all other matters, acting as someone who prosecutes another for theft from a temple but is seen with the gods' property in his own hands. [15] I would have valued it if he really thought I was clever (*deinon*), as he told you, for then he would never have tried to cause me trouble. But in fact, although he says I am able to "make weaker speeches stronger,"[14] he despised me to such an extent that he expects to defeat me easily by telling lies when I speak the truth. [16] Everything has gone against me: while others refute slanders through speech, Lysimachus has slandered precisely my speeches so that if I appear to speak successfully, I will stand convicted of the accusations he has made against my cleverness (*deinotēs*). Yet if I speak less adequately than he has led you to expect, you will think less well of my conduct. [17] I ask you, thus, to withhold belief or disbelief from what he has said until you hear fully my side of the story. Bear in mind that there would be no need to allow the accused to make a defense if

---

[12] Isocrates has in mind an audience that listens to the text being read out. Cf. 12.86 and possibly 12.200 for the rhetorician speaking of reading out speeches to a group of pupils. For silent reading, see Knox 1968.

[13] Isocrates now begins the fictional speech with a second, fictional prologue (14–28).

[14] The exercise of making "weaker speeches stronger" may have begun with Protagoras. It was one of the stock charges leveled against rhetoricians and sophists; see Arist., *Rhetoric* 1402a24–28; Aristoph., *Clouds* 112, 883–884; Plato, *Apology* 18b8–9 (of which this is a direct echo).

it were possible to decide justly from the accuser's words alone. At this point everyone present could tell if he spoke well or badly, but the jurors cannot easily know from the first speech alone whether he uttered the truth: rather, they would be satisfied if they could determine the just case from hearing both sides of the argument.

[18] I am not surprised that people spend more time on the accusations produced by deceitful individuals than on their own defenses or say that slander is the greatest harm. What could do more harm than this? It makes liars appear respectable, the innocent seem to do wrong, and jurors violate their oaths.[15] All in all, it destroys the truth, gives the audience false opinions, and unjustly destroys any citizen it comes upon. [19] You must guard against such a thing happening to you, so that you do not fall into the conduct which you reproach in others. I think you are not unaware that the city has frequently regretted judgments based on anger rather than on proof, so that shortly afterwards it wanted to punish its deceivers and would have gladly seen those who were slandered emerge better off than before.[16] [20] You must remember this and must not believe rashly the words of accusers nor listen to the defense case in a disorderly and prejudicial manner. It is shameful that although in other matters we are agreed to be the most merciful and gentle of all the Greeks, our behavior in court cases here patently contradicts this reputation.

[21] Elsewhere, when men judge a capital crime, a portion of the votes is set aside for the defendant,[17] but with us the defendants are not even on equal footing with the sykophants.[18] Each year we swear

---

[15] Isocrates refers to the Heliastic Oath, which, ever since the time of Solon (Dem. 19.6), the 6,000 registered voters of the popular courts swore at the beginning of each year. The jurors vowed to uphold the democracy, to vote according to the laws and their conscience, and to give both prosecuting and defending parties a fair hearing when it was their turn to speak. Reference to the oath is also made at Dem. 19.17, 24.151, 39.1.40, 57.63; Hyperides 3.40; Aristoph., *Wasps* 725 and 919; also cf. Isoc. 8.11.

[16] The most notorious example of such a judgment concerns the condemnation to death of the generals after the battle of Arginusae; see Xen., *Hellenica* 1.7.35 and Plato, *Apology* 32.

[17] We know nothing else about the practice to which Isocrates refers.

[18] This is another echo of Plato's *Apology* (37a–b).

to listen to accusers and accused alike,[19] [22] but we compromise to
such an extent that we accept whatever the accuser says, and we sometimes refuse to hear the voice of the defendant who tries to refute
them.[20] Furthermore, we think that states in which citizens are put to
death without a trial are uninhabitable, without recognizing that those
who do not give equal consideration to both litigants do exactly this.
[23] Most terrible of all is when someone on trial complains about
those who slander him but does not have the same view of the matter when he judges another. Yet, reasonable men must be the sort of
judges of others whom they would hope to have for themselves, for
they realize that because people dare to bring false cases it is unclear
who will stand trial and be forced to speak as I now do to those who
are going to vote on him.

[24] Living an orderly life does not mean one can expect to live in
Athens without fear. Those who choose to neglect their own affairs
and concern themselves with those of others do not refrain from attacking those who manage their affairs soberly and bring only those
who do wrong before you. Instead, they display their power by prosecuting the innocent and thus earn more money from those who have
clearly done wrong. [25] Lysimachus understood this and put me on
trial, thinking that the trial against me would earn him money from
other sources. He expected that if he won against me, who he says is
a teacher of others, his power would seem unassailable to everyone.
[26] He hopes to do this easily, as he sees that you are too quick to
accept charges and slanders and that I shall not be able to mount a
defense equal to my reputation because of my old age and my inex-
perience in such contests. [27] I lived my past life without anyone
accusing me of violence or injustice during either the oligarchy or the
democracy; and it is clear that no one has sat as an arbitrator or juror
concerning my affairs. I know not to harm anyone myself and not to
seek revenge in court when I am wronged but to resolve our differences with the help of my opponent's friends.[21] [28] None of this

---

[19] See above, 18n. Athenian legal procedure was notable for permitting anyone
who wished (*ho boulomenos*) to initiate a prosecution, providing favorable circumstances for sykophants and a theme for a common aristocratic complaint.

[20] Dem. 45.6 provides one, admittedly rare, example of a prosecutor speaking
so convincingly that the defendant was not listened to.

[21] I.e., by informal arbitration.

helped me, but even though I have lived to such a great age free from reproach, I now find myself in just as much danger as if I had wronged everyone.

I am not at all disheartened by the magnitude of the potential penalty, but if you are willing to listen with goodwill, I am optimistic that those who have been misled about my activities and those who were persuaded by those who wished to slander me will quickly change their minds about these matters, while those who consider me the sort of person I really am will be more firmly convinced.

[29] As I do not want to burden [you] with a lengthy preface to my argument, I shall leave off here, and instead I shall attempt to instruct (*didaskein*[22]) you in the things about which you will vote.

Now read the charge (*graphē*)....[23]

[30] On this charge the prosecutor tries to accuse me falsely of corrupting the young by teaching them to speak well and of gaining the upper hand in the lawcourts contrary to the interests of justice. In the rest of his speech he makes me out to be unlike anyone who has ever frequented the lawcourts or spent time in philosophy. Moreover, he says that my students were not only laypersons but also public speakers, generals, kings, and tyrants, that I took great sums of money from them, and that I continue to do so even now. [31] This is the sort of accusation he makes, for he thinks that his exaggerated claims about me, my wealth, and the number of my students will stir envy among his audience and that my legal activity will stir you to anger and hatred. When a jury experiences these emotions, they give litigants a very hard time. But on the first charge he has gone too far, and on the others I think I can easily show that he tells complete lies. [32] I think you should pay no attention to the speeches that you earlier heard from individuals who want to slander and slur me. Do not believe

---

[22] Litigants often used didactic language to describe the legal discourse and process, presenting themselves as teachers instructing their jury-pupils. This terminology is particularly poignant, given the speaker's defense of himself as a teacher. Isocrates presents himself as instructing the city state in the role and value of the teacher of rhetoric (also 58, 89, 197), and the jury-audience as learning from him (cf. 40, 178).

[23] The actual text of the charge, which in real cases was read by the court clerk, and of all other literary evidence in the trial, is omitted from the speech. In some, especially later, legal speeches these texts are preserved.

what was said without proof and judgment or give credence to opinions which these men have unjustly implanted in you. Rather, consider me such as I am on the basis of the present accusation and defense alone. If you make your decision in this way, you will appear to judge well and lawfully, and I will be completely vindicated.

[33] I think the danger in which I currently find myself is the best evidence that no citizen of Athens has been harmed by my cleverness or by my compositions. If anyone has been wronged and even if he kept quiet about it all this time, he would not let the present occasion pass without being here either to accuse me or to testify against me. Since someone who has never heard a negative word from me has put me in such grave danger, surely those who have suffered wrong would try to get back at me. [34] It is neither plausible nor possible that I have wronged many and that those who have fallen on hard times because of me should keep quiet, should not dare to accuse me, and in fact should be gentler when I am in danger than those who have suffered no injustice, when they only need to show what they have suffered to obtain the greatest revenge from me. [35] And yet no one before or now will be seen to have brought such a charge against me.

Accordingly, if I were to agree with the prosecutor and admit that I am the cleverest of all men and a writer of harmful prose such as no other has been, I would deserve a reputation for honesty rather than punishment. [36] One might plausibly credit good fortune when someone is better at speaking or acting than others, but everyone ought rightly to praise my character for using my natural ability well and with restraint.[24] Even if I can speak like this about myself, I shall never be seen to have concerned myself with those [lawcourt] speeches. [37] You will recognize this from my activities, from which you can better learn the truth than from my detractors. I think everyone knows that all men generally spend time where they have chosen to make their living. [38] Thus you would see men who make a living off your contracts and the lawsuits connected with them virtually living in the lawcourts, whereas no one has ever seen me at the Council-

---

[24] Isocrates here as elsewhere recognizes the dual importance of nature and nurture where oratorical and other political ability is concerned: see 15.199–214 and 13.14–15 (repeated at 15.186–188); also Shorey 1909 for the topos of "nature, nurture, knowledge" in educational discourse of the period.

board (*synedrios*),²⁵ in preliminary hearings, at the courts, or before the arbitrators. I keep utterly away from all this, more than any other citizen. [39] Second, you would find that these men can earn money only in your city, for if they were to sail anywhere else, they would be deprived of their livelihood. I, in contrast, have means—exaggerated by that man—which come entirely from outside Athens.²⁶ Moreover, those who are themselves in difficult circumstances or want to create trouble for others associate with these men, whereas my associates are the more leisured of the Greeks.

[40] You have heard my accuser say that I received many valuable gifts from the king of Salamis, Nicocles. And could any of you believe that Nicocles gave me these so that he might learn forensic oratory, when as ruler, he judged the disputes of others?²⁷ From what my accuser has himself said, you will easily understand that I do not concern myself with litigation over contracts. [41] Indeed, that those who compose speeches for others who have cases in the lawcourts are legion is apparent to everyone. Yet as many as there are, none of them have ever been seen to deserve students, while I have received more, as my accuser says, than all those who devote their time to philosophy. So how could it be plausible that those whose daily business is so different are thought to be involved in the same activities?

[42] Although I can point out many differences between my life and that of people who concern themselves with lawsuits, I think that I would most quickly dispel the view that I resemble them if someone were to demonstrate that my students do not engage in the activities which my accuser has spoken of, and that I am not terribly accomplished (*deinos*) in contract suits. [43] Now that the former charge against me has been refuted,²⁸ I think that you are looking to change

---

²⁵ The *synhedrion* was the board made up of the six junior archons, or Thesmothetae, who fixed the dates of trials and assigned courts to the magistrates (cf. *Ath. Pol.* 59; Dem. 21.47). These archons were originally selected to write down the regulations (*thesmia*) for deciding disputes, probably before the time of Draco; see Arist., *Ath. Pol.* 3.4 and Gagarin 1981: 71.

²⁶ According to Pseudo-Plutarch, Isocrates did not charge his Athenian students fees (*Isocrates* 838–839).

²⁷ See 2.1–4.

²⁸ I.e., that Isocrates engages in litigation and forensic rhetoric.

your minds and want to hear what other kinds of speech I have been concerned with that have given me such a great reputation. I do not know if it will help my case to declare the truth: for it is difficult to assess your attitude. Still, I shall speak frankly to you. [44] After all, since I have often said that I would have all the citizens know about my life and my discourses, I would be embarrassed in front of my associates if I now did not display them to you but was found to be concealing them. So pay attention, as you are about to hear the truth.

[45] You must first learn (*mathein*) that there are as many kinds (*tropoi*) of prose as of verse.[29] Some authors have spent their lives investigating the genealogies of the demigods; others have interpreted the poets; others sought to compose histories of wars, while still others, whom they call antilogicians (*antilogikous*), devote themselves to question and answer. [46] It would be no small task for someone to count all the forms (*ideai*) of prose. So I shall pass over the others and mention only the one which is my concern.

Some people experienced in the forms I have mentioned did not choose to write speeches for private contract suits but ones of a political character pertaining to Hellas to be delivered in panegyric assemblies.[30] Everyone would agree that these are more like musical and rhythmical compositions than those uttered in the lawcourts. [47] They set out events with a more poetic and complex style and seek to employ grander and more original enthymemes,[31] and in addition, they dress up the whole speech with many other eye-catching figures of speech (*ideai*). The whole audience enjoys when they hear these as much as poetic compositions, and many wish to study them, for they think that those who are at the forefront of this kind of com-

---

[29] Lit. "compositions with meter"; see 9.10n.

[30] I.e., the sort of speech to be delivered before a panhellenic assembly at Olympia. Examples include Isocrates' *Panegyricus* (4) and the funeral orations of Gorgias and Lysias.

[31] In general literary usage, the enthymeme is a piece of reasoning or an argument (see, e.g., 9.10; also Sophocles, *Oedipus at Colonus* 292, 1199); for Aristotle, the enthymeme is a rhetorical syllogism constructed on the basis of probabilities (see, e.g., Arist., *Rhetoric* 1354a10–16; 55a6–10; 57a13 and 16; 1394a27 and 32; 1395b21).

position are much wiser and better and can be more useful than those who are eloquent in legal matters. [48] They recognize that the latter have gained their experience in legal contests through political meddling, but the former have developed their skill in the speeches which I just described through philosophy. Moreover, those who appear to be skilled in juridical speech are tolerated only on the day they happen to be pleading, whereas the others are well regarded and highly respected in all public gatherings all the time. [49] In addition, if the former are seen twice or three times in the lawcourts, they are hated and criticized, whereas the latter are more admired the more often they appear and the more people hear them. Finally, those who are skilled (*deinoi*) at legal speeches have no ability for those other speeches, while the others, if they wished, could quickly pick up forensic pleading. [50] When they consider these things and realize that this is by far the better choice, they wish to share in this culture with which I have associated myself and which has given me a much finer reputation. You have heard the whole truth about my "power," or my "philosophy," or my "pastime," however you wish to label it.

[51] But I also wish to set out a more demanding standard for myself than for others and to utter a bolder speech than suits my age. If my speech is harmful, I expect to receive no mercy from you, and if it is not superior to everyone else's, to receive the gravest punishment. And I would not have made such a daring promise unless I were about to demonstrate this to you and make your verdict easy.

[52] This is how it is. I think the best and most just defense is one which instructs the jurors as best it can about the matters on which they vote, so that they do not wander in their purpose or doubt who speaks the truth. [53] Now, were I being tried for some crimes I had committed, I would not be able to offer them to you to see; you would have to conjecture on the basis of the arguments in order to decide what happened as well as you could. But since I am accused for my speeches, I think I will better be able to show you the truth. [54] I shall present to you the very speeches I have spoken and written so that you will not conjecture but will know clearly what they are like when you vote on them. I could not declare them all from beginning to end, since the time allotted to me is short. But, like fruits, I shall try to offer a sample of each. When you have heard a small portion of

them, you will easily recognize my character, and you will learn the power of all my speeches.

[55] I ask those of you who have often read what I am now about to say not to seek new speeches from me at this time nor to think me tedious if I utter what has long been in circulation among you. If I spoke them to make a display (*epideixis*), I would reasonably be guilty of this; but as I am now under judgment and in peril, I am forced to use them in this way. [56] I would be most ridiculous if, when my accuser charges me with writing the sort of speeches that harm the city and corrupt the young, I defend myself through other means, when by presenting the speeches themselves I can absolve myself of the slanders spoken against me. For this reason I ask you to make allowances and be my allies. For the sake of others [i.e., those who are not familiar with his speeches], I shall proceed by offering a brief preface so that they may follow the argument more easily.

[57] The first speech I shall present to you[32] was written at the time when the Spartans ruled Greece and we [Athenians] were in a wretched state. It summons the Greeks to a campaign against the barbarians, and it challenges the Spartans for the leadership. [58] Having this as my theme, I show that Athens was responsible for all the good things which the Greeks have. After I have rounded off the narrative of these benefactions in order to show even more clearly that leadership of Greece belongs to Athens, I try to teach (*didaskein*) that it is much more fitting for the city to be honored for the dangers it endured in war than for its other benefactions. [59] I thought I could relate these things myself, but now old age impedes me and causes me to cut short my account. In order not to be utterly exhausted while I still have much to say, begin from the place marked and read the discussion of the leadership of Athens:[33]

---

[32] The *Panegyricus*. In this and other works, Isocrates declares a panhellenic program, which urges the Greeks to unite in a military campaign against the barbarian. For the idea that the general Timotheus enacted a panhellenic ideal, see below, 15.107–134; see also the encomium of Agamemnon at 12.74–87 for the Trojan War as a forerunner to a contemporary panhellenic campaign. See Too 1995: 130–148.

[33] In keeping with the forensic fiction, Isocrates instructs the clerk to read the speech.

[AN EXCERPT FROM *Panegyricus:* 4.51–99][34]

[60] One can easily learn (*katamathein*) from what has been read that the leadership rightly belongs to this city. Consider among yourselves, if you think I corrupt the young by my words rather than persuade them to be virtuous and undertake dangers on behalf of the city. Should I be justly punished for what I have said? Or shouldn't I instead receive your deepest thanks? [61] I have praised the city, its ancestors, and the dangers of that period, and as a result, those who previously wrote on this theme destroyed all their speeches, embarrassed by what they had produced, and those who are now supposed to be skilled (*deinoi*) no longer dare to speak about these things but instead find fault with their own ability. [62] Nevertheless, as matters stand, some of those who cannot compose or say anything of note will be found to be practiced at criticizing and disparaging the texts of others. They will say that these things have been said "in a pleasing manner"—they are not generous enough to say "well"—but that speeches which denounce our current mistakes are much more useful and more powerful than those which eulogize our past deeds, and likewise, those which advise what we must do are better than those which narrate our history.

[63] To prevent such comments, I shall cease defending what I have written[35] and shall present to you a passage from another speech as long as the previous excerpt, from which it will be clear that I have devoted great care to all these issues. The beginning of the speech is concerned with the peace of the Chians, Rhodians, and the Byzantines. [64] After I demonstrated that it benefited Athens to end the

---

[34] A translation of *Panegyricus* is found in this series in Isocrates, Volume Two. This portion of the speech celebrates Athens' ancestors as the benefactors of others from long ago (54), helping among others the sons of Heracles against Thebes (58–61). Athens was superior to all, including Argos, Thebes, and Sparta (64). It celebrated victories over the barbarians (Scythians, Thracians, Amazons, and Persians, 66–70); it fought and won in the Persian War (71). Its soldiers deserve the highest praise (75). Rivalry between Sparta and Athens guaranteed the Greeks victory over Persia (85–98). Athens should have the leading role in a war against the barbarian.

[35] The idea that one's speeches require help, ideally from their author, is found also at Plato, *Phaedrus* 275d–e.

war, I criticized our control over the Greeks and our naval supremacy, showing that it did not differ from tyranny in its actions or outcomes; and I recalled what happened to the Spartans and all the others as a result of it. [65] After these topics, I lamented the fortunes of Greece and advised Athens not to allow this situation to continue. Finally, I summoned the city to justice, reproached its errors, and counseled it on the future.

Begin where I discuss these matters, and read this section to the audience:

[66] [Excerpt from *On the Peace*, 8.25–56 and 132–145, is read.] [36]

[67] You have now heard two speeches. I wish also to read a brief selection from a third, so that it may become even clearer to you that all my speeches pertain to virtue and justice. The one I am going to present is for the Cyprian Nicocles, who was king at that time, and it advises him how he should rule his citizens. It is not written in the same manner as those that have been read. [68] In the others, the preceding and following parts always agree and are linked together, but in this one, the opposite occurs: by keeping parts discrete and separate, as if I had made different headings, so to speak, I try to express each piece of advice succinctly. [69] I made this my subject because I thought that by informing his thinking I would benefit him, and I would also make my principles clear in the quickest way. Also on this occasion I have chosen to present this work to you for the same reason not because it is my best composition but because it will make clear how I normally deal with both ordinary citizens and rulers. [70] It will be evident that I have spoken to Nicocles as suits a free citizen and an Athenian and have not deferred to his wealth or power.

---

[36] A translation of *On the Peace* is found in this series in Isocrates, Volume Two. These passages argue for peace and an end to the Social War (which concluded 355) with the former allies who now want their independence (25). The speaker observes the injustice of Athens taking what rightfully belongs to others (34) and cites the city's ancestors as a model of good political behavior. The first portion from the speech concludes with a critique of the contemporary sykophants (52–56). The second portion (132–145) urges the city to select good leaders to replace the sykophants (133). The speaker reminds his audience that the fate of Athens is also the fate of all Greece (136). He repudiates tyranny in closing (142).

In fact, I defended his citizens and urged him, as far as I could, to create a government as mild as possible for them. And if whenever I speak with a king, I do so on behalf of his subjects, I would surely exhort those who live under democracy to consider the interests of the people.

[71] In the preface and opening words, I censure monarchs, because, although they ought to cultivate practical understanding (*phronēsis*) more than others, they are less well educated than ordinary citizens. After discussing these points, I urge Nicocles not to be lazy, not to regard taking up the kingship as if it were a priesthood,[37] but to disregard pleasure and pay attention to public affairs. [72] I also try to persuade him to treat it as a terrible matter if he sees worse men ruling the better classes, and the foolish giving orders to the more sensible. And I add that, insofar as he disparages others' stupidity more vigorously, so much more so should he cultivate his own understanding.

So start where I have stopped, and read the remaining section of this speech to the jury.

[73] [Excerpt from *To Nicocles,* 2.14–39, is read.][38]

[74] These speeches are enough citation at length, although I won't refrain from citing small sections of my earlier writings but will quote something if I consider it appropriate to the present occasion. It would be curious if, when I see others using my words, I alone were to avoid using my speeches, especially now when for your benefit I have chosen to cite not only brief portions but whole sections. I shall do as circumstances require.

[75] Before these texts were read out, I said that if I were to employ

---

[37] I.e., not to treat kingship as a casual undertaking; most priesthoods required only occasional ritual duties.

[38] This passage from *To Nicocles* (2) is translated above. It begins with the idea that the best people in the state should be rulers (14–15). It proceeds to argue that subjects should be well treated (15–16), and that to ensure that the king does the best for his nation, he must write laws, change them, or borrow them from other nations (19). The selection goes on to describe the king's relations with and obligations to the gods (20), to friends (21), to foreigners (22), and to other states (24–25). It warns him to be wary about friendships (27), to govern himself well (29–32), and to assume kingly behavior (33–39).

harmful words, I would deserve to be punished and that if I did not speak better than anyone else, I would merit the harshest penalty. If some of you thought my words were boastful and exaggerated, I trust they would no longer justifiably hold this opinion. I think that I have fulfilled my promise, and the speeches that were read to you are as I promised at the beginning. [76] But I want to plead briefly on behalf of each of them, and make it even clearer that I spoke then, and now continue to speak the truth about them.

First, is any speech more moral or more just than one which praises our ancestors in a manner worthy of their virtue and their deeds? [77] Second, is any speech more public-minded and more suited to Athens than one which demonstrates that, because of our benefactions and the risks we have undertaken, the hegemony should be ours, rather than the Spartans'? Third, what speech could be about finer and greater deeds than one which exhorts the Greeks to a campaign against the barbarians and counsels us to have a united purpose?

[78] I have discussed these things in the first speech; in the later ones, I treat matters that are less important but no less valuable or beneficial to Athens. You will know the power of these speeches if you set them beside others by authors who are well respected and considered useful. [79] I think everyone would agree that the laws are responsible for the most and greatest goods in human life, although their use can only benefit public affairs and personal contracts. If you were to be persuaded by my words, you would govern the whole of Greece well and justly and in the best interests of Athens. [80] Sensible men must be concerned about both Athens and Greece, but of the two, they should prefer the greater and worthier. Second, they should recognize that countless Greeks and non-Greeks are able to write laws, but few have the ability to speak about what is beneficial in a manner that Athens and Greece deserve. [81] For these reasons, we should value those who make it their business to write speeches of this kind more than those who legislate and inscribe laws, insomuch as their products are rarer, more difficult to create, and require a more acute mind, especially at the present time.

[82] When humankind began to exist and settle in cities, it was natural that people had similar goals. Now that we have progressed to the point that speeches that are delivered and laws that are established are innumerable, and the oldest laws and the most novel speeches are

praised, the task requires a different approach. [83] Those who choose
to legislate have at hand a multitude of established laws; they have no
need to seek others, but they need only to gather together those that
are well regarded elsewhere—which anyone who wishes could easily
do. Those engaging in oratory have a very different experience, since
most [topics] have been taken up. If they say the same things as their
predecessors, they will appear to be shameless babblers, but those who
seek novel topics have great difficulty finding something to say. For
this reason I say that both should be praised but especially those who
can accomplish the more difficult task.

[84] It should be evident that I am more truthful and useful than
those who claim to turn people toward self-restraint and justice. For
they exhort people to a virtue and to a wisdom unrecognized by others and debated over by themselves, whereas I exhort them to one
acknowledged by everyone. [85] They are pleased with themselves
if they can attract pupils into their company by their reputations,
whereas I shall never be seen inviting anyone to follow me; instead, I
try to persuade the whole city to undertake activities which will lead
to their own happiness and will free the rest of the Greeks from their
present evils. [86] How is it reasonable that an individual who exhorts
all citizens to better and more just leadership of Greece could corrupt
his students? Would anyone with the ability to compose such discourses try to invent wicked speeches about wicked matters, especially
when he has benefited from his discourse, as I have? [87] When my
speeches were written and published, I achieved a good reputation
among many and gained many students, and none of them would
have remained with me if they had found me to be other than they
had expected. In fact I have had many pupils, some of them spending three or four years with me. None of these will be found to have
faulted their experiences with me, [88] but at the end, when they were
about to sail back to their parents and friends, they so valued the time
spent with me that we parted with regret and tears.

Should you believe those who know well my speeches and my character? Or someone who knows nothing about me and has elected to
bring a false accusation against me? [89] That man has reached such a
degree of evil and daring that he has charged me with teaching people
to speak in ways that will give them an unfair edge, though he produces no evidence of this. He persists in saying that it is terrible to

corrupt the young, as if anyone disputed this, or as if he had to prove what everyone acknowledges rather than simply showing (lit. "teaching," *didaskein*) that I have committed this crime. [90] If someone were to arrest him as a slave trader, a thief, or mugger, and did not show that he had done any of these things but merely related how terrible each of these crimes is, he would say that his accuser is mad and raves, and he thinks you will not notice that he himself uses such arguments. [91] But I think that even the most ignorant know that for accusations to be credible and authoritative, they must be applicable only to those who have committed crimes and not to those who are innocent. But he has disregarded this point, delivering a speech that has no relevance to the accusation. [92] For he ought to show the speeches by which I corrupt my students, and name the students who have become worse through association with me. As it is, he has done none of these things; instead, having omitted the most valid means of accusation, he has tried to deceive you.

In contrast, I shall make my defense on grounds that are relevant and just. [93] A little while ago I read my speeches to you. Now I shall identify those who spent time with me from my youth to old age, and from those of you who are my contemporaries, I shall produce witnesses to what I say. Eunomos, Lysitheides, and Callippus were among the first to study with me; after them, Onetor, Antikles, Philonides, Philomelos, and Charmantides.[39] [94] Athens has crowned all these with gold crowns not because they were greedy for other people's belongings but because they were good men and spent much of their own wealth on the city.

Make what you will of my relations with these men. For what concerns us, things are all in my favor. [95] If you regard me as their

---

[39] Some of the pupils Isocrates mentions in this section are prominent enough to be mentioned by other writers of the period. For Eunomos, see Lys. 19.19, where he is named as a guest and friend of Dionysius of Syracuse; for Onetor, one of the richest Athenians, see Dem. 30.10; for Philomelus, an associate of Meidias, see Dem. 21.174 and MacDowell 1990: 391–392, Lys. 19.15, and Davies 1971: 549; for Lysitheides, son of the banker Pasion, see Davies 1971: 356–357 and MacDowell 1990: 377 (and also for Callippus); for Antikles, son of Memnon, see Davies 1971: 309; for Philonides, the brother of Onetor, see Davies 1971: 423; and for Charmantides, who was victorious as choregus in dithyramb at the Thargelia before 366, see Davies 1971: 573.

adviser and teacher, you ought to be more grateful to me than to those you feed in the Prytaneum for their achievements.[40] Each of these has proven himself to be a fine citizen, whereas I have provided the large group I mentioned a moment ago. [96] If I was responsible for none of their accomplishments but they were simply my friends and associates, I think even this is an adequate defense against the charge I face. For if I pleased those who have received gifts for their achievements, and have a different opinion (*gnōmē*) from this sykophant, how could I reasonably be judged to be corrupting those in my company? [97] I would be the most unfortunate of all if I alone did not receive the same assessment as others who are judged better or worse on the basis of their activities and associations but instead were to have the same reputation as those who are discredited for their activities and associations, even though I spent my life with men like these and have conducted myself beyond reproach until this point in my life. I would like to know what fate I would have suffered if one of my associates had been a man like my accuser. Although I hate all such people and am hated by them, I nonetheless find myself in this predicament.

[98] Nor would that argument justifiably harm me, which some of those who are completely prejudiced against me would perhaps dare to state, that I have kept company with those whom I mentioned only to be seen talking with them, and that I have many other meddlesome students whom I am hiding from you. Yet I have an argument which will refute and absolve me of all these slanders. [99] If some of those who have associated with me have behaved well toward Athens, toward their friends, and toward their own households, I ask you to praise them and not give thanks to me; however, if they turned out to be wicked and the sort of men who denounce (*phainein*) others, indict (*graphesthai*) them, lay charges, and desire their goods,[41] then punish me. [100] What offer could be less invidious or more fair than

---

[40] Cf. Socrates' request to be fed in the Prytaneum, or public mess hall (Plato, *Apology* 36d7), where Olympic victors, distinguished generals, and certain families, such as the descendants of the tyrannicides Harmodius and Aristogeiton, were fed at public expense. Socrates is in turn citing Xenophanes (early 5th century), who laments the honoring of athletes above those who benefit the community through their wisdom (poem 2 West).

[41] Denunciation (*phasis*) and indictment (*graphē*) were two types of legal action.

this one, which does not argue about good citizens but volunteers to pay the penalty if some have turned out to be wicked? I do not speak these words emptily, but I yield the floor to my accuser or to anyone else who wishes, if he has something to say in this regard—not that there aren't some individuals who would gladly perjure themselves against me, but since they would immediately be revealed to you, the penalty would be theirs, not mine. [101] I do not know how I could make my point more clearly on the charge against which I defend myself and on the issue of not corrupting my associates.

Lysimachus mentioned my friendship with Timotheus, and he tried to discredit both of us.[42] He was not ashamed of speaking slanderous and completely scandalous words about a man who had died and had been responsible for many good things for Athens.[43] [102] I thought that even if I had been clearly proven to have done wrong, I would be saved by my association with him, but since Lysimachus tries to use this association to harm me when it rightly should help me, I am obliged to speak about these matters. Because Timotheus' accomplishments are of quite a different order, I did not mention him at the same time as my other companions. [103] My accuser did not dare say anything incriminating about the others, but he devoted more energy to the case against Timotheus than to the one against me.[44] Moreover, my other students were in charge of a few things,

---

[42] Isocrates offers a favorably biased characterization of his former student, the statesman and general Timotheus (cf. 7.120); a very different picture is given in Dem. 49. Born ca. 414, he was elected general in 378 and served with great success in the war against Sparta. In 374, while preparing an expedition for Corcyra, he was deposed and prosecuted for betraying the city's ally (Dem. 49.9, 13; Lys. Fr. 228). He then served as a mercenary, commanding Persian forces in Egypt, but returned to Athenian service in 366. His aggressive actions led Athens' allies to revolt in the Social War (357–355). After a disastrous naval battle, he was impeached and fined an enormous sum. He went into exile in Calchis, where he died before 352.

[43] There were constraints against speaking ill of the dead. Hyperides informs us that the penalty for slander (*kakēgoria*) against the dead is 1,000 drachmas; also cf. Isoc. 20.3; Lys. 10.2; Dem. 21.88, 40.49; and MacDowell 1978: 127–128. Demosthenes (20.104) attributes this piece of legislation to Solon (cf. Plut., *Solon* 21).

[44] See 15.129 and note for the trial of Timotheus.

although they managed what had been entrusted to each of them so
well that they acquired the honor of which I spoke a little while ago;
he, on the other hand, was in charge of many great affairs over a long
time. Accordingly, it would not be fitting to speak about Timotheus
together with the others, but it is necessary to separate the two subjects
and arrange them in this manner.

[104] You must not regard this portion of the speech about Timotheus as irrelevant to the present situation or think that I digress from
the case. When ordinary citizens have spoken as they should in defense of their actions, they sit down to avoid seeming to overdo it; but
those deemed to be political advisers and teachers must defend their
associates, just like themselves, especially if they are being tried on this
charge [i.e., liturgy evasion], as in my case. [105] Thus it might be
enough for someone else to state that it is unjust if he shares the blame
for any wrong Timotheus may have committed when he acted, since
he did not share in the gifts and honors voted to him, and no speaker
proposed that he deserved praise for being Timotheus' adviser. Justice
requires that he have a part in his rewards or that he not share in his
misfortune. [106] I, however, would be ashamed to say this; instead, I
make the same proposal about him as about the others: if Timotheus
was a bad man and committed many wrongs against you, I ask to be
party to this, to be punished, and to suffer just like the guilty. But if
he is shown to be a good citizen and a general unlike any other we
know of, then I think you should praise him and thank him, but with
regard to this case, you should judge my actions as you think just.

[107] I can say this in general about Timotheus, considering all
his actions, that he captured by military force more cities than any
general ever has, either from Athens or from the rest of Greece; and
when some of the cities were captured, the whole adjoining area was
forced to join the side of Athens, so great was the power of each city.
[108] Who does not know about Corcyra lying in the most strategic
and fairest spot among the cities near the Peloponnesus, about Samos
among the Ionian cities, about Sestus and Crithotes among those in
the area of the Hellespont, and about Potidaea and Torene among
those in Thrace? He gained possession of all these and gave them to
you without great expense, without mistreating our existing allies, and
without forcing you to pay heavy taxes. [109] Instead, for the sea expedition around the Peloponnesus the city gave him only thirteen tal-

ents and fifty triremes, and with these he took Corycra, a city which
had eighty triremes. At about the same time he defeated the Spartans
at sea and forced them to make a peace, which brought such a change
to each of the cities [110] that from that day we commemorate it each
year with a sacrifice because no other peace has so benefited Athens.⁴⁵
After that time no one has seen a Spartan vessel on this side of Malea,
or a land army passing through the Isthmus, and one can see that this
is the reason for their disaster at Leuctra.

[111] After these achievements, he marched to Samos, which
Pericles, a man with the greatest reputation for wisdom, justice, and
moderation, had seized with two hundred ships and a thousand tal-
ents.⁴⁶ Timotheus captured it without any additional help from you
or the allies. He besieged it for ten months with eight thousand light
shield bearers and thirty triremes, and he paid for all these from the
war spoils. [112] If you know of anyone else who has accomplished
such a deed, I will admit that I am foolish to try to give exceptional
praise to someone who has done nothing that surpasses the achievements of others. After he left Samos, he captured Sestus and Crithotes
and forced you to pay attention to the Chersonesus, which you had
previously neglected. [113] Lastly, he captured Potidaea, on which
Athens had previously spent two thousand four hundred talents, using
the wealth that he himself together with Thrace's contribution provided. And in addition he defeated all the Chalcideans. If I must speak
not on each individual point but in summary, he made you masters
(kyrioi) of twenty-four cities, and he spent less than our ancestors did
on the siege of Melos.⁴⁷ [114] Just as it was easy to enumerate his
accomplishments, so I wish to describe briefly the circumstances in
which each of them was carried out, the state of Athens' affairs, and

---

⁴⁵A reference to the Peace of Callias (371), which all but gave Athens control
of the sea and limited Sparta to land.

⁴⁶Timotheus captured Samos in 366 with a force of some 8,000 peltasts and
thirty triremes in an operation that lasted just under a year. The comparison between Timotheus and Pericles, a subject of praise at 16.28, emphasizes the greatness of the former's achievements. For Pericles' campaign against Samos, see
Thuc. 1.116–117.

⁴⁷For an account of the events leading up to the siege and the siege itself, see
Thuc. 5.84–116.

the power of the enemy. The benefits you received and his reputation among you would thus be much greater. Yet because it is such a large topic, I shall omit this.

[115] I think you would like to hear why some of the men among you who are well regarded and are thought to possess military ability were not able to capture even a village, whereas Timotheus, who had no great physical strength and no experience in military campaigns around the world but was simply a citizen among you, accomplished such important things. The account of these things incurs resentment but is worth presenting. [116] Timotheus surpassed the others in that he did not hold the same views as you about the affairs of the Greeks and their allies and how they should be managed. You vote for generals who are physically strongest and who have had considerable experience on foreign campaigns, thinking that these qualities will allow them to do what is necessary. But Timotheus used men like this as his company leaders and brigade commanders, some of whom became famous and served the city well as a result of accompanying him on campaign.[48] [117] But he himself was astute in the matters which a good general must know about.

What are these things, and what power do they have? About this I must not oversimplify, but I need to give a clear account. First, to be able to determine against whom war must be waged and whom one should have as allies. This is the first principle of generalship, and if one errs in this matter, the war will necessarily be unsuccessful, difficult, and a waste of effort. [118] With regard to these kinds of decisions, not only has there been no person like him but no one has even been close. And one can readily recognize this from his achievements. Although he undertook the majority of his wars without Athens' support, he won all of them, and he seemed to all the Greeks to have done so justly. Could anyone provide a clearer or better demonstration of his strategic thinking than this?

[119] What is the second requirement of a good general? He must bring together an army suited to the current enemy, organize it, and use it advantageously. His actions themselves have shown that he knew

---

[48] "some of whom . . . on campaign"; the Budé text contains this clause, which the Loeb edition omits, following the authority of the traditionally most reliable manuscript.

how to employ an army effectively. He surpassed all others in providing magnificent and worthy equipment—and none of the enemy would dare say otherwise. [120] Moreover, for enduring the hardships and deprivations of campaign and finding adequate resources, who of his fellow soldiers would not judge that Timotheus excelled in both these respects? For they are aware that he found himself in dire straits at the beginning of the war as a result of not receiving anything from the city; however, he was able to reverse this situation, by being victorious in the war and paying full wages to his men.

[121] Now, although these matters were important and urgent, someone might praise him even more—and deservedly—for what followed. While he saw that you have regard only for men who threaten and terrify other city states and continually cause revolts among the allies, he did not follow your views; he did not want to win a reputation at the expense of the city. Instead, he reflected (*ephilosophei*) and then acted so that no Greek city would fear him, but all would feel secure except those which acted unjustly. [122] He knew that those who are afraid hate those who make them feel this way and that Athens became the most prosperous and the greatest city through its friendships with others, whereas through hate, it came close to falling into the worst disaster. Perceiving this, he routed the enemy with the power of Athens and then by his own character gained the goodwill of others; he believed that this strategy was greater and finer than the destruction of many enemies and numerous victories in battle.

[123] He made certain that no city should have the slightest suspicion that he was plotting against them. Accordingly, whenever he was about to sail past any which had not given its contributions,[49] he sent word ahead to the leaders, so that when he was suddenly seen outside their harbor, he would not throw them into fear and confusion. [124] If he happened to weigh anchor in their territory, he did not allow his men to loot, or steal, or pillage homes but took the same care that no such thing should happen as do masters of property. He was concerned not that he would have a good reputation among his men but that Athens would have one among the Hellenes.

---

[49] The contribution was paid into the Allied Treasury, to be distributed at the discretion of the Council of allied states; see 7.2; Xen., *Hellenica* 6.2.9; and Dem. 49.49. In the fourth century, "contribution" (*syntaxis*) replaced "tribute" (*phoros*) and its negative associations with the past empire of Athens.

[125] Moreover, he treated captured cities more gently and lawfully than any other ally had done, thinking that by showing himself such toward the enemy, he had given the greatest proof that he would never venture to wrong the others. [126] Because of the reputation he gained from these actions, many cities that were badly disposed toward you received him with their gates thrown wide open. He created no distress among them, but when he departed, he left them just as he had found them governed when he went in.

[127] In summary, although many terrible things regularly afflicted the Greeks at others times, under his generalship no one could find any cities that suffered revolutions, or changes in their constitutions, or slaughters, or exiles, or any other intolerable evil. During that time such disasters abated to such a degree that of all those we can remember, he alone made this city blameless among the Greeks. [128] It is truly necessary to regard him a good, even the best, general and not someone, like Lysander, who achieved similar success by an act of good fortune because no one else happened to have the opportunity,[50] but as someone who always acted correctly and showed good sense in many various and difficult matters. That was the way things turned out for Timotheus.

[129] I think that many of you are surprised at what I have said and regard my praise of him as a condemnation of Athens, since he captured so many cities but did not destroy a single one and was put on trial for treason.[51] And again, when he submitted his accounts (*euthynai*), and Iphicrates assumed responsibility for the actions, and

---

[50] During the battle of Aegospotami (405) Lysander captured 171 Athenian ships and executed all Athenian prisoners, who totaled about 3,000 men, and liberated other prisoners: see 4.119, 18.59; *Ath. Pol.* 34.1; Xen., *Hellenica* 2.1.1–29; Diodorus Siculus 13.104–106. He then swept across the Aegean, and his fleet blockaded Piraeus.

[51] Timotheus, Iphicrates, Menestheus (Iphicrates' son), and Chares were commanders in the campaign against Byzantium in 357. At the battle of Embata, probably in the winter of 356/5, Chares continued an attack that the other generals abandoned because of a severe storm. He was defeated, and on his return to Athens charged the others with treason and acceptance of a bribe from the Chians and Rhodians; cf. Dinarchus 1.14 and 16–17; Diodorus Siculus 16.21.4; Nepos, *Timotheus* 3.4–5. The trial instigated by Chares is thought to have been motivated by political rivalry to remove Timotheus and his more careful approach. See, e.g., Moysey 1987.

Menestheus submitted the account of expenses, the city acquitted them, but it fined Timotheus a sum of unprecedented magnitude. [130] That's how it was.

Still I want to say a word on behalf of Athens. If, looking to justice itself, you take thought in these matters, what happened to Timotheus must seem to everyone terrible and harsh. But if you factor in the ignorance that all men have, and the envy that arises in us, as well as the confusion and the disorder in which we live, you will find that none of these things occurs unreasonably or lies outside of human nature; and Timotheus contributed some part to being improperly understood in these things. [131] He did not hate the common people, nor was he a misanthrope, or arrogant, and he did not have any other such vice. But because of his greatness of mind, which was suited to generalship but inappropriate to day-to-day demands, everyone thought he was guilty of all the faults I have mentioned, for he was as unsuited by nature to the cultivation of other men as he was talented in his management of public affairs.

[132] Often he heard me say such things as:[52] "those who wish to engage in public life and be well liked must choose the best and most useful deeds, and the truest and most just words; in addition, however, they must consider carefully how they can be seen by others to say and do everything graciously and benevolently, for those who give little thought to these matters appear to their fellow citizens to be rather difficult and intolerable. [133] You see how the mob (hoi polloi) is by nature disposed toward pleasure and that they love those who attend to their pleasures rather than those who do the right thing and those who cheat them with a smile and friendliness rather than those who benefit them with gravity and dignity. You have never concerned yourself with these things, since you think that if you deal with matters outside Athens fairly, the citizens here will be well disposed toward you. [134] This is not the case, but the opposite generally happens. If you gratify the people, they judge everything you do not according to how things actually are but in whatever way helps your cause; they will

---

[52] Isocrates dramatizes his instruction of Timotheus as he purports to recall a lecture he delivered to his former pupil on the topic of goodwill. Compare this reported conversation with 15.142–149 below, where the rhetorician cites teaching by an associate, and 12.234–263, a reported conversation with a former pupil.

overlook mistakes and will exalt your success to the heavens. Goodwill (*eunoia*) makes everyone behave in this fashion.⁵³ [135] You seek to acquire by every means the goodwill of other cities toward Athens, and you think it the greatest good, but you do not realize that you must secure it from Athens for yourself. You are responsible for most of our good fortune, but you have a lower standing than those who have done nothing worthy of note. [136] That makes sense, for they cultivate public speakers and those who are able to speak well in private gatherings and those who pretend to know everything. You, on the other hand, not only neglect these men but also declare war on those of them who at any time have the greatest success. Do you stop to think how many men have fallen upon misfortune or have lost their civic rights because of these men's lies? How many of our ancestors are without name, although they were more virtuous and noteworthy than those who are the subjects of poems and tragedies? [137] The latter, I think, had poets and speechwriters to sing their praises, but the former had no one. If you trust me and have any sense, you will not despise such men, whom the common people generally trust in matters concerning both citizens and overall affairs of state. Rather, you will make them your concern and cultivate them so that you will have a good reputation with regard to both your deeds and their words."

[138] When Timotheus heard this, he said that I was right, but he was unable to change his nature. He was a gentleman (*kalos kagathos*) worthy of both Athens and Greece, but he could not adapt himself to such men who are hostile to those who are superior by nature. As a result, the orators have assumed the task of inventing many false accusations against him, and the people that of accepting what they say. [139] If I had the opportunity, I would gladly offer a defense against them, for I think that when you have heard me, you would hate those who persuade Athens to be angry at Timotheus as well as those who dare to criticize him. As it stands, I shall leave these things and return to speaking about myself and the current situation.

[140] I am uncertain how to arrange the rest of my speech,⁵⁴ what sort of thing to mention first and what second; I have lost my ability

---

⁵³ See de Romilly 1958.

⁵⁴ Isocrates feigns rhetorical ineptitude in keeping with self-representation as someone who does not frequent the lawcourts, e.g., 15.4; also cf. 15.153 and 310.

to organize my words. Perhaps, I must speak about matters as they happen to come up. Thus the topic that occurs to me is one I thought I should clarify for you; however, I will not conceal from you that someone else advised me not to mention it. [141] When Lysimachus brought this charge against me, I thought about these very issues, as each of you might, and I examined my life and my accomplishments, spending the most time on what I thought I ought to receive praise for. When one of my associates heard me, he had the courage to say the harshest thing of all, that, although the things I mentioned deserved recognition, he himself particularly feared that they might irritate the majority of those who heard them.

[142] "Some people," he said, "turn so savage and hostile because of envy and lack of resources that they make war not against evil, but against good deeds. They hate not only the most reasonable men but also the best activities; and in addition to their other vices, they congregate with other criminals and show them sympathy, while destroying those they envy if they can. [143] They do these things not because they are ignorant of the issues on which they vote; rather, they hope to do injustice and do not expect to be caught. They think that by saving those who are like themselves they are helping themselves. I have said these things to you so that forewarned you might handle the situation more effectively and use more secure arguments before the jurors. But now what decision can you expect such men to take if you describe to them a life and deeds that are not in the least like theirs but are such as you are trying to describe to me? [144] You prove that the speeches you composed do not deserve blame but the greatest gratitude, that some of those who had been close to you committed no crime or misdemeanor, but others were crowned by Athens for their virtue, and that you yourself have lived from day to day such a decorous and orderly life as no other citizen I know of, and moreover, that you brought no suit against anyone nor were you brought to trial except in the matter of the exchange, and that you were never party to trial or served as witness for anyone else. Indeed, you have not done a single one of the things that all those in public life do.

[145] "In addition to these personal eccentricities, you say that you avoided positions of authority along with the benefits these bring, and all other public matters, but you numbered not only yourself but your son too among the twelve hundred taxpayers and liturgists. Three times already you have funded a trierarchy, and you discharged

other liturgies more splendidly and lavishly than the laws require. [146] Don't you realize that those who hear this account but themselves do just the opposite will be irritated and will think you are arguing that their lives are not respectable? If they saw that the resources to support the liturgies and the rest of your affairs came through hard work and struggle, they would not think about it in the same way; but they think that the income you receive from foreigners is much greater than what is actually paid, [147] and they believe that you live more comfortably than others, even those who engage in philosophy and in the same profession as you. They perceive that most of these—except those who have a passion for your way of life—produce rhetorical displays (*epideixeis*) for the public assemblies and private gatherings, where they compete with one another, make exaggerated promises, argue, and find fault with one other, omitting no abuse. [148] But they trouble only themselves, and they let their listeners laugh at their speeches, or occasionally praise them, but most often hate them or feel however they wish about them. You have no part in all this but live differently from the sophists and from private citizens, whether rich or poor. [149] Reasonable and sensible people might perhaps admire you for this, but others who are less talented and who generally are more upset at the honest success of others than at their own misfortune, can only be annoyed and resentful. Since this is how they feel, consider what you should say and what you should omit."

[150] As he was making this speech, I thought, and even now think, that those who are irritated by hearing me present myself to Athens as a liturgist who does what is ordered are the strangest and most difficult of all people. I do not need to enter my lot for public office,[55] receive the benefits Athens gives to others, or, for that matter, defend and prosecute cases. [151] I have organized my life not for the sake of wealth or out of arrogance, and I do not look down on those who do not live as I do myself. I loved peace and the quiet life (*apragmosynē*),[56]

---

[55] Nearly all Athenian magistrates were chosen by lot from a group of applications; cf. 7.25.

[56] *Apragmosynē*, which characterizes the lifestyle of the fourth-century "quiet Athenian," serves as an aristocratic code, standing in opposition to *polypragmosynē*, which most often denotes the meddling of sykophants and ambitious public figures. Note that for Thucydides' Pericles, speaking before the rise of the "new politicians," to be "undoing" is the same as being useless (cf. Thuc. 2.40. 1).

and in particular I saw men who live this kind of life enjoying a good reputation both here and elsewhere. I thought that such a life was sweeter than the life of those who are always occupied and was, moreover, more suited to the activities in which I initially engaged. [152] For this reason I chose this way of life. I did not accept benefits from the city, for I thought it would be terrible if I got in the way of someone else who was forced to support himself in that way and through my presence someone was deprived of life's necessities when I could maintain myself on my own private means. For these reasons, I deserve your praise rather than criticism. [153] Now I really do not know where to turn or what I could do to please such people. If I always made it my task not to wrong, or bother, or trouble anyone and by these same actions I trouble some people, how could I satisfy them? What course remains except that I will appear unfortunate, and such men will seem ignorant and ill disposed toward their fellow citizens? [154] It is silly to try to defend myself against men who think completely differently from others and are harder on those who do no wrong than on those who do. Evidently the more respectable one shows himself to be, the less effectively he argues his case among these men.

But to the others, I must speak about Lysimachus' slander that I possessed great wealth; otherwise his account will be believed and will land me in more and larger liturgies than I could undertake. [155] As a rule, you will find that none of the so-called sophists has earned much money. Some live their lives meagerly, others very modestly. The one who earned the most was Gorgias of Leontini.[57] He spent

---

[57] Other contemporary and later texts insist on the great material success and wealth of Gorgias: e.g., Plato, *Hip. Maj.* 282b4–9; Diodorus Siculus 12.53.1 (= Diels-Kranz 82 A 4) reports that Gorgias earned 100 minas from his pupils; cf. *Suda* g 388. Athenaeus (505d–e) recounts an anecdote in which Plato remarks upon seeing the sophist that "the handsome and golden Gorgias comes" when he sees the sophist, making it apparent that with Gorgias, the importance and wealth of the teacher have displaced the value of his teaching. Gorgias was the author of works including *Encomium of Helen, Palamedes,* and *On Not Being.* Ancient sources depict Gorgias as the teacher of Isocrates (see Introduction to Isocrates), but this later linking of the two rhetoricians as teacher and pupil respectively is

time in Thessaly, when the Thessalians were the most prosperous of the Greeks; he lived a long time and was concerned with making money. [156] Since he had no fixed residence in any city, he had no public expenditure and did not have to pay taxes; moreover, he never married and had no children, and thus was not subject to this unrelenting and costly liturgy.[58] Yet even with such an advantage in saving more than others, he left behind only a thousand staters.[59] [157] So where the wealth of others is concerned, you must not believe those who criticize at random, or think that the incomes of sophists and actors[60] are equal, but rather compare those in the same profession with one another, and assume that those of the same ability in each area will have similar wealth. [158] Thus, if you compare me with the one who earned the most, and set me against him, you clearly will not be making an unreasonable conjecture about such matters; nor will you find that I have managed my public and personal affairs badly, since my living expenses were less than I paid out for liturgies. Those who are thriftier in their personal lives than in their public expenditure rightly deserve praise.

[159] As I speak, I realize to what extent the city has changed and that people in public life now regard these matters quite differently than people in the past. When I was a child, having wealth was thought to make one so secure and dignified that nearly everyone claimed to have more money than they really had, for they wanted the prestige of wealth. [160] But now one must carefully prepare a defense against being rich as if it were one of the worst crimes, if one wants to remain secure. Those who appear to be prosperous are considered

---

due largely, if not wholly, to biographical convention: see Too 1995: 235–236. Isocrates mentions the older sophist on two other occasions (15.268 and 10.3) and in each case is critical or dismissive.

[58] Isocrates extends the language of liturgy to a broader context of commitment or benefit to the city. This extended use of the liturgy vocabulary is important in helping him to highlight his own rhetorical career as a form of public service.

[59] A stater was a gold coin worth about twenty-eight drachmas.

[60] For payment to dramatic actors, who could also receive prizes from public funds, see von Reden 1995: 146–147.

much worse than those openly doing wrong, for the latter are either let off or pay small fines, while the former are totally ruined. And we would find that many more have been stripped of their wealth than punished for their crimes.

[161] Why must I speak about public matters? I myself suffered no small setback in my own affairs as a result of this transformation [of Athens]. At that time I was beginning to recover my own wealth, since in the war against the Spartans, the entire family fortune was lost, which my father had used to support his own service to the city and to educate me with such care that I became more prominent and better known among my fellow students and comrades than I am now among my fellow citizens. [162] When, as I mentioned, I began to attract some students, I thought that if I could acquire and pre-serve more wealth than those who had embarked on the same career, I would acquire a distinguished reputation for philosophy and for greater orderliness in my own life. But things have turned out just the opposite. [163] For if I had been worthless and had preserved nothing, no one would bother me, and if I had openly done wrong, I would have lived safely, at least from the sykophants. Now instead of the reputation I anticipated, contests, dangers, envy, and slanders be-siege me.

[164] At present Athens takes such pleasure in oppressing and deni-grating respectable people, allowing the wicked to speak and act as they want, that Lysimachus, who has chosen to make his living from sykophancy and from doing harm to some citizen each day, has come before you to accuse me. But I, who have never done anyone any wrong, have kept away from sykophancy, and have instead benefited from foreigners, who think they have been treated well, find myself in this great peril, as if I have done something terrible. [165] Those who have any sense should pray to the gods that most of our citizens could have this ability to take money from foreigners and with it make themselves useful to the city, as I have done. Among the great absurd-ities in my situation, the worst would be if those who had given me money were to be so grateful that even now they continue to watch out for me, whereas you, on whom I have spent my resources, were to punish me. [166] It would be even more terrible if our ancestors hon-ored the poet Pindar for just a single expression in which he named Athens "the bulwark of Greece," gave him the title "friend of the city"

(*proxenos*), and granted him a gift of ten thousand drachmas,[61] while I, on the other hand, who have praised the city and our ancestors much more finely, should be unable to live the rest of my life safely.

[167] I think that I have said enough in my defense about this and the other accusations.[62] But I shall not hesitate to tell you truthfully how I feel about my present predicament, and how I initially felt about it. At first I was very hopeful that I could defend my personal activities successfully. [168] I had confidence in my past life and deeds, and I thought that I had many valid arguments about them. But when I saw not only that those who are customarily hostile to everyone were upset by the culture of discourse but also that many other citizens were opposed to it, I feared that my personal situation would be overlooked and that I might incur some harm from the popular prejudice against the sophists. [169] After a while, as I began to deliberate and consider what I should do in this situation, I stopped being afraid and upset; this was not unreasonable, since I took account of the probable outcome and comforted myself. [170] I knew that those of you who are fair, to whom I would direct my remarks, would not be satisfied with opinions that arose unjustly but would follow the truth and be persuaded by those whose words were just. And I believed I could show by many arguments that philosophy had been unjustly slandered and that it should more rightly be cherished than hated. Even now I continue to hold this view. [171] It is not surprising if certain fine pursuits have been overlooked and unrecognized, or some people have been deceived about them. In fact, we could find the same situation holding true for ourselves and for countless other matters. For our city is responsible for many of the benefits enjoyed by its citizens and by other Greeks, both at present and in the past, and it abounds in many delightful pleasures. Yet

---

[61] Pindar, born ca. 518 at Thebes and died ca. 446, was a professional poet who wrote victory poems for the athletic competitions. The line cited is preserved as Pindar Fr. 76. Pindar was rewarded with the role of *proxenos,* or public guest-friend, who in his own city welcomes and helps visitors from the appointing city, in this case Athens.

[62] Isocrates now moves from the specific charges to the issue of his teaching. From here to 214 he discusses what rhetorical education consists of, explaining what is required for someone to become a good orator and in the process, showing why the promises of the professional teachers are misleading.

it has this serious problem. [172] Because of its size and the number of inhabitants, it is not readily understood as a whole or in detail, but like a swollen river, it carries along whoever or whatever it picks up, and it gives to some people a reputation that is completely inappropriate. That is what has happened to this form of education (*paideia*).

[173] You must bear these things in mind and not judge any matter without discussion, and when you are jurors, you must not behave as you do in personal matters, but you must be precise on each point and seek the truth. Remember the oaths and laws under which you have assembled to pass judgment. The discussion and the judgment in which we are engaged concern not small matters but the most important ones; and you will cast your vote not only about me, but about a career that attracts many of the young. [174] I think you must know that older citizens hand down the affairs of the city to the young, their successors. Since this cycle always continues, the condition of the city necessarily depends on how the young are educated. Thus sykophants cannot be in charge of such an important matter, and those who refuse to give them money must not be punished, nor should those who give them money be allowed to do whatever they want. [175] If philosophy does in fact have the power to corrupt the young, you must not only punish whomever any sykophant brings into court on a charge, but also get rid of all those who spend time in this pursuit. If the opposite is true, however, and it benefits and improves those who study it and makes them more valuable, then you must stop those who spread slanders about philosophy; you must deprive the sykophants of their civic rights;[63] and you must advise the young to engage in this activity rather than other pastimes.

[176] If it was my fate to face this charge, I would have much preferred to find myself in this predicament at the height of my abilities. Then I would not be discouraged but would have been better able to defend myself against the prosecutor and to advocate the cause of philosophy. But now although philosophy has enabled me to speak rea-

---

[63] Isocrates suggests that sykophants should be punished with *atimia*, which was otherwise automatically incurred for such offenses as mistreating one's parents, failing in military duties, certain sexual offenses, and squandering one's patrimony. This penalty entailed loss of the right to address the Assembly and Council, entry to holy places, and participation in public rites.

sonably well about other matters, I fear that I have not discussed philosophy itself as well as other matters that were less important to me. [177] And yet, I would be content—I must speak the truth even if my words sound foolish—to end my life once I had spoken as the subject deserves and had persuaded you to realize what the pursuit of discourse (*hoi logoi*) actually is. I would prefer that to living a great deal longer and seeing it treated by you as it is now. [178] I am aware that I shall speak far less well than I would like; nevertheless, I shall try as far as I can to give an account of its [philosophy's] nature and power, how it is similar to other arts, how it benefits those who pursue it, and what kinds of claims we make for it. When you learn the truth, I believe you will more readily deliberate and decide about it. [179] If I seem to be giving a speech quite unlike those customarily uttered among you, I ask you not to be annoyed and to make allowances. Understand that those who advocate a case that is unlike any other must speak about it with words that are equally unusual. So having tolerated my manner of speech and my outspokenness and having allowed me to use up the time allotted for my defense, then cast your votes as seems just and lawful to each of you.

[180] Like the genealogists, I wish to speak first about the culture of discourse (*hē tōn logōn paideia*). It is agreed that our nature is composed of body and soul. No one would deny that of these two, the soul is superior and more valuable, for its task is to deliberate about matters private and public, while the body's is to serve the soul in carrying out its decisions. [181] In light of this, some of our ancestors long ago saw that although many arts existed for other matters, none had been established for the body and soul, and when they had invented two disciplines, they handed them down to us: physical training for the body, of which gymnastic is a part, and philosophy for the soul, which I shall be discussing. [182] These two disciplines are complementary, interconnected, and consistent with each other, and through them those who have mastered them make the soul more intelligent and the body more useful. They do not separate these two kinds of education but use similar methods of instruction, exercise, and other kinds of practice.

[183] When they take on pupils, physical trainers instruct their students in the positions that have been discovered for competitions, and those whose concern is philosophy pass on to their pupils all the

structures which speech (*logos*) employs.[64] [184] When they have given them experience and detailed knowledge of these, they again exercise the students and make them accustomed to hard work, and then force them to synthesize everything they have learned in order that they may have a more secure understanding and their views (*doxai*) may be better adapted to the right moments (*kairoi*).[65] It is not possible to learn this through study, since in all activities, these opportune moments elude exact knowledge (*epistēmē*), but in general those who are particularly attentive and can understand the consequences most often apprehend them. [185] Watching over their pupils and educating them in this way, both kinds of teachers can lead them to become better and more capable, whether in their intellect or their physical conditions. But neither has that knowledge by which he could make anyone he wished an adequate athlete or orator. He may contribute some share, but as a rule, real ability is found only in those who excel both in native talent and in training.

[186] Now that you have a brief sketch of philosophy, I think you would learn its power better if I rehearse the claims I make to those who wish to study with me. [187] I tell them that those who are going to excel in oratory, or public affairs, or any other profession must first have a natural talent for what they have chosen to do; then, they must be educated and gain knowledge of that particular subject; and third, they must practice and become familiar with its use and its implemen-

---

[64] The language of gymnastics had been used to describe the art of rhetoric as early as Aeschylus, whose Furies refer to each rhetorical point they score in the trial of Orestes as a wrestling "fall" (*Eumenides* 589, 600); for the analogy with wrestling, see also Protagoras' work entitled *Kataballontes [Logoi]* (= *Overthrowing [Arguments]*) and the Hippocratic work *On the Nature of Humans* 2 (in Gagarin and Woodruff 1995: 166), and in the fourth century, Plato, *Gorgias* 464b–c, *Republic* 410b–c3. In the following sections Isocrates explores similarities of training, practice and discipline; in particular, just as the gymnastic teacher instructs in bodily forms (*schēmata*), so the teacher of rhetoric instructs in verbal forms (here *ideai*, but commonly in the language of rhetoric, *schēmata*).

[65] The orator requires *doxa*, often translated as "opinion," rather than a fixed body of knowledge (*epistēmē*), in order to be able to respond to the discursive situation and his audience; cf. also 13.8, 13.17, 15.271; Plato, *Gorgias* 463a7. For discussion of rhetorical *doxa*, see Cooper 1985.

tation (*empeiria*). After this, whatever the profession, they will become accomplished and far outstrip others. [188] Both teachers and students have their own parts to play: in particular, the pupils' responsibility is to bring the requisite natural ability, and the teachers', to be able to educate these kinds of students, but common to both is practical experience (*empeiria*). Teachers must meticulously oversee their students; students must resolutely follow what they have been taught.

[189] That is what I have to say about every art. If someone, leaving aside the other arts, should ask me which of these plays the greatest role in education in speaking, I would respond that nature (*physis*) is paramount and stands far ahead of everything else. Someone must have a mind capable of inventing, learning, working hard, and memorizing; a voice and clarity of speech that has the capacity to persuade audiences not only by what he says but also by his harmonious diction; [190] and furthermore, courage that does not signify shamelessness but prepares the soul with moderation (*sōphrosynē*) so that it has as much confidence in addressing all the citizens as in deliberating with himself. Doesn't everyone know that even if such a person does not acquire a thorough education but only a general education that is common to all, he would be such an orator that in my view no Greek could equal him?

[191] Furthermore, we know that if men whose natures are inferior to these apply themselves to practice and training, they become better, not just than they were but also than those who are naturally talented but are too complacent about themselves. Each of these [i.e., nature and training] would make one gifted at speaking (*legein*) and at acting (*prattein*), and both in the same person would make him unsurpassable by others. [192] I know this about nature and experience; however, I cannot deliver such a discourse about education (*paideia*), for its power is not equal or similar to theirs. If someone should hear everything about oratory and he were to have more precise knowledge of it than others, he would be a more pleasing composer of speeches than most, but when facing a crowd, if he did not have this one thing—daring—he would be unable to speak.

[193] Let no one think that before you I moderate my claims but that when I converse with those who wish to spend time in my company, I claim all power for it. To defend myself against such a charge, when I embarked on this profession, I published a speech I had writ-

ten in which I clearly criticized those who make exaggerated promises, revealing my own views. [194] I shall omit my accusations of others, for they are too much for the present occasion, but I shall repeat for you what I said about my own view. I begin here:

[AN EXCERPT FROM *Against the Sophists*, 13.14–18, IS READ.][66]

[195] The style of this passage is more elegant than what I read before, but its intention is to make the same point as those passages, and this should be the greatest proof for you of my honesty. Clearly I did not boast or make exaggerated claims when I was younger, and now that I am older and have benefited from the profession, I make philosophy a modest activity. I have used the same words in my prime and in my retirement, both when I was confident and when I am in danger, both to those who wish to be my students and to those who are to cast their votes on me. I don't know how anyone could prove himself more true or just on the subject of philosophy. [196] Let this passage then be added to what I have said before. I am aware that I have not yet said enough to change the minds of those hostile to me, and many more arguments of all sorts are still needed for them to change the view they now have of me. [197] So I must continue to teach and speak until one of two things happens, either I change their views or I prove that the slanders and accusations against me are false.

The charges are of two types. Some say that the activities of sophists are all foolishness and trickery, since no such education has been invented through which a person might become more skilled (*deinos*) at speaking or more adept at public affairs, but that those who ex-

---

[66] *Against the Sophists* is translated in this series in Isocrates, Volume One. In this section of the treatise Isocrates articulates his own views as to what is required for rhetorical/philosophical education to succeed. Natural ability explains why some people have rhetorical skill despite lack of formal training (14); training, however, makes them even better. Without natural ability, there is no hope (15). The student must find a responsible teacher, who must be able to offer instruction on invention, disposition, and adornment of the speech (16). The student requires great diligence and a tenacious and imaginative mind to learn the different types of speech; the teacher must expound his teachings as precisely as he can and offer himself as an example (17–18). This passage has been interpreted as offering a theory of imitation or *mimēsis;* cf. Shorey 1909 and Russell 1979.

cel in these areas are naturally superior to others. [198] Other critics agree that those who undergo this training are more skilled but maintain that they are also corrupted and become worse, for when they gain this power, they begin plotting to get the property of others. I am quite confident that I can make it apparent to everyone that neither group speaks soundly or truthfully.

[199] First, notice that those who say this education is nonsense very patently themselves make no sense. They disparage it as deception and trickery that can offer no benefit, but they think that the moment students arrive to spend time with me they should be better than before, [200] that when they have spent a few days with me, they should be clearly better and wiser with regard to discourse than those who are older and more experienced, that when they have spent only a year with me, they should all be good and accomplished orators, that the lazy should be no worse than the diligent, and that those without natural talent should be as good as those who have robust minds. [201] They expect this, though they have not heard me make such claims, nor have they seen any of these results in other areas of training or education. We acquire knowledge through hard work, and we each put into practice what we learn in our own way. From every school only two or three become competitors, while the rest go off to be private citizens.

[202] How could we not conclude that people are stupid if they dare to demand from this pursuit—which they deny is an art—powers not present in the recognized arts and think that greater benefits should come from an art they do not believe in than from those that seem to have been precisely founded? [203] Sensible people should not have conflicting judgments about similar matters, or reject an education which accomplishes the same things as most arts. Who among you does not know that many who have been under the influence of the sophists have not been deceived or affected, as these say? [204] Didn't some of them turn out to be competent competitors, while others were able to teach, and those who wished to live as private citizens were more gracious in their interactions than previously and became more acute judges and advisers than most? How then could we despise an activity which has the capacity to turn those who engage in it into men like these? [205] Everyone should agree that as far as all arts and crafts are concerned, we think that the most skilled are those

who turn out students who work as much as possible in the same way. This will also prove to be the case with philosophy. [206] All those who have had a true and intelligent leader would be found to have so similar an ability in discourse (*hoi logoi*) that it becomes obvious to everyone that they received the same education. If they had no common character or basic technical training instilled in them, they could not have achieved such a similarity.[67]

[207] All of you here could name many of your classmates who seemed extremely stupid when they were children, but when they became older, excelled in intellect and speech to a greater degree than they fell short as children. From this especially, one could recognize the great power of practice (*epimeleia*), for it is clear that in childhood, all of them used the mental capacities they had from birth, but when they became men, they surpassed their contemporaries and transformed their intellects, because while others lived lazily without purpose, they devoted their attention to their affairs and to themselves. [208] Wherever some men became better through their own effort, how could they not far surpass themselves and others if they have taken on an older and more experienced mentor, who has learned some things from others and found out other things himself?

[209] In addition to these, there are other reasons why everyone would naturally be surprised at the ignorance of those who so casually dare to despise philosophy. First, although they know that all pursuits and arts are acquired by practice and hard work, they think that these have no power where the training of intellect is concerned. [210] Then, although they agree that no body is so weak that it cannot be improved by exercise and labor, they do not think the soul, by nature superior to the body, can become finer as a result of education and the proper training. [211] Furthermore, although they see that some individuals are skilled at making horses, dogs, and most other animals braver, or gentler, or cleverer, they think that no such education (*paideia*) has been discovered to develop these same qualities in human beings. [212] Instead, they condemn us all to such misfortune that they would agree that every other being becomes better and more useful through our intellect, but they dare to declare that we who have

---

[67] Cf. Cicero, *De Oratore* 2.94.

this intellect by which we make everything else more valuable could not help each other at all to become better.

[213] The most terrible thing of all is that every year in spectacles they see lions being more gentle toward their trainers than some men are toward their benefactors; and bears rolling around, wrestling, and imitating our knowledge. [214] Yet they cannot ascertain from these examples how much power education and training have, or that these would improve our natures much more rapidly than those of animals. Consequently, I do not know which should properly astonish us, the gentleness in the most aggressive wild beasts or the savagery present in the souls of such men.

[215] One might say more about these things, but I fear that if I go on too long about matters on which most people agree, you will think that I have nothing to say on the issues in dispute. So having stopped here, I shall turn to these others, who do not simply despise philosophy but criticize it much more bitterly and transfer the evils of those who claim to be sophists but who really do something quite distinct from those whose activity is not at all the same. [216] I am speaking not for all those who claim to be able to educate, but only for those who justly have this reputation. If you are willing to hear me to the end, I think I shall clearly demonstrate that those who accuse me have fallen far short of the truth.

[217] First, I must identify the needs and the motives that lead people to do wrong. If we define these well, you will better understand whether the charges against me are true or false. Thus I assert that everyone does everything for pleasure, profit, or honor. For I do not see that people desire anything apart from these things. [218] If this is the case, it remains only to consider which of these I could acquire by corrupting the young. Do I derive pleasure at seeing or learning that they are evil, or have the reputation of being evil among the other citizens? Who is so insensitive that he would not be hurt to hear such criticism of himself? [219] I would certainly not be admired or have such a high reputation if I turned out such students; instead, people would despise and hate me more than those who are guilty of other wicked crimes. Even if I should ignore this, I would not maximize my profits, by directing education in this way. [220] I think everyone must know that the sophist's fee is the finest and greatest when some of his pupils become intelligent gentlemen (*kaloi kagathoi*) and are

honored by the citizens. Such students inspire in many the desire to
share their education with them, whereas the wicked repel even those
who previously were intending to study with their teacher. So who
could fail to know the better course, when these situations are so far
apart?

[221] Someone might perhaps venture to respond to this, that
through their lack of discipline (*akrasia*) many men do not follow
their reason, but neglecting what is beneficial, they rush toward pleasure. I agree that many people, including the self-styled "sophists,"
have such a nature. [222] Nonetheless,[68] no such person is so undisciplined as to admit students of this kind. He would not be able to
share in the pleasures which he would get from their lack of discipline
(*akrasia*),[69] and he would receive as his reward the greatest part of the
notoriety that results from their evil. Next, we should ask whom they
would corrupt and what sort of people they would get as their students? This is an issue worth examining. [223] Are they already corrupt and wicked? But who would try to learn from someone else what
he knows by his own nature? Or are they respectable and eager to do
useful things? No such person would venture to converse with those
who utter or do evil. [224] I would like to learn from those who are
angry at me what they think of those who sail here from Sicily, Pontus,
and other places to be educated? Do they think these students travel
here because they lack evil men at home? Yet one could find an abundance of men everywhere who want to conspire in evil and wrong-

---

[68] Some manuscripts present a very different text for sections 222–224, and
one, the *Laurentianus* Codex, contains an expanded text, which is translated at
the end of this speech. Scholars are divided as to whether to regard the expanded
text as revision by the author himself (so, e.g., the Budé editors, pp. 157–158)
or as an attempt by subsequent commentators to elaborate Isocrates' own argument. Where a revision, or a change of mind, has occurred in the composition
of the speech, the rhetorician is inclined either to dramatize or to acknowledge
this (see 15.243; cf. 12.232–233 and Too 1995: 124–125); in my view, therefore, the
text translated here is the original, and the longer, alternate version is a later
composition.

[69] The Budé text follows the manuscript reading *akroasin*, lit. "hearing." But
the original text probably had *akrasian* (adopted by Norlin), for in this passage
pleasure is to be regarded as the consequence of lack of self-control, just as ill
repute is the result of wickedness.

doing. [225] Or do they pay a lot of money to become criminals and
sykophants? Yet those with this intention would prefer to take other
people's money than to pay any of their own to others. Furthermore,
who would waste money for the sake of evil, when they can do evil
whenever they want without paying anything? No one needs to learn
such deeds; he only has to do them.

[226] It is evident that people travel by ship, pay money, and go to
all sorts of trouble because they think they will become better and that
their educators here will be more intelligent than those at home. All
Athenians should be proud of this and value those who are responsible
for the city's reputation in this. [227] Still, some people are very unreasonable; they know that the visitors who come here and those who
supervise their education do nothing wrong but are among the most
politically uninvolved (*apragmonestatoi*) [70] in Athens; they keep themselves apart, are concerned only with themselves, and interact with
one another. [228] Furthermore, they live their daily lives in the sim-
plest and most orderly manner, they do not study speeches concerning
private contract disputes or those that attack others, but only those
that men everywhere respect. Nevertheless, knowing all this, those
men dare to slander them and say that they undergo their training in
order to profit unjustly from legal disputes. [229] Which individual
would want to live a more moderate life than others if he cultivated
injustice and wrongdoing? Have those who say these things ever seen
anyone delaying and storing up wickedness rather than immediately
exercising their natural inclinations? [230] These things apart, if dexterity in speech makes for having designs on other people's property,
then everyone who is a capable speaker should be a meddler and
sykophant, for the same cause generally produces the same result in
everyone.

[231] As it is, you will find that among those who are currently in
public life or just recently deceased, the ones who are most concerned
with speech (*logoi*) are the best of those who step up to the speaker's
platform. Among our ancestors, moreover, beginning from Solon,
the best and most renowned orators were responsible for the greatest
goods in Athens.[71] [232] When Solon was in charge of the people, he

[70] See above, 151n.
[71] For Solon and Cleisthenes, see 7.16n.

enacted legislation, arranged public affairs, and ordered the state so well that even now the constitution organized by him is revered. Later, Cleisthenes persuaded the citizens of Amphictyon to lend him the god's money when he had been driven from Athens by the tyrants.[72] He led the people back to power, drove out the tyrants, and established that democracy, which has produced the greatest goods for the Greeks. [233] After him, Themistocles became the leader in the Persian War and advised our ancestors to leave Athens.[73] Who could persuade them to do that without extraordinary skill in speech? He advanced the affairs of the city to such a degree that after being homeless for a few days, they became rulers of the Greeks for a long time. [234] Finally, Pericles, a fine popular leader and the best orator,[74] so enriched the city with temples, monuments, and every other such adornment that even now visitors think Athens deserves to rule not only the Greeks but everyone else too. In addition, he brought to the Acropolis no less than ten thousand talents. [235] Not one of these men who had done such great things neglected speech (*logoi*); rather, they paid much more attention to it than to other things. As a result, Solon was included among the Seven Sophists and thus had the label "sophist," which is now dishonored and placed on trial before you.[75] And Pericles was a student of two of these sophists, Anaxagoras of Clazomenae and Damon,[76] who was considered the wisest citizen of his time.

---

[72] The money came from the treasury of Apollo.

[73] Themistocles commanded the Athenian navy at the battle of Salamis, during which the Athenians abandoned the city after dedicating it to Athena: see 4.96, 6.43; Lys. 2.33–43; Plut., *Themistocles* 10.2–3.

[74] Thucydides (1.139.4) characterizes the Athenian general and leader Pericles as an extraordinary and preeminent Athenian orator: see 2.65.1 and Aes. 1.25. After the defeat of Persia Pericles oversaw a civic building program that saw among other things the construction of the definitive temple of Athena, the Parthenon, in 438; see, e.g., 8.126 and Plut., *Pericles* 13.

[75] Here the Seven Sophists is the name given to the "Seven Sages," a group of sixth- and fifth-century thinkers generally including Solon, who are mentioned in literary sources from the fifth century onwards; see, e.g., Herod. 1.27. See Momigliano 1971 : 27–28.

[76] Anaxagoras was credited with teaching that the sun is a stone, and the moon earth (cf. Plato, *Apology* 26d and Diogenes Laertius 1.16). As a result of his materialistic doctrines, he was prosecuted for impiety by Cleon, fined, and exiled (cf.

[236] Could there be a clearer demonstration than this that the power of speech does not turn men into criminals? No, it is those who have my accuser's nature who, I think, continually engage in evil words and actions. [237] I can even show you where anyone who wishes may see the names of meddlers and others who are guilty of the charges my accusers bring against the sophists. They must appear on the tablets[77] erected by the magistrates: sykophants and others who wrong Athens appear on those put up by the Thesmothetae; common criminals and their instigators appear on those put up by the Eleven; those who commit private crimes and bring unlawful charges appear on those put up by the Forty. [238] On many of these you will find the names of Lysimachus and his friends inscribed, but you will not find me or those who engage in the same activity as I on any of them. We keep to our own affairs in order to avoid suits in our court. [239] Isn't it more fitting to praise rather than put on trial men who do not get involved in such matters, and who do not live without discipline, or engage in any other shameful activity? It is clear that we educate our students into the same sort of activities as occupy us.

[240] You will learn even more clearly from what I am about to say how far I am from corrupting the youth. If I were doing this, it is not Lysimachus or those of his ilk who would be upset on their behalf, but instead you would see the fathers and the relations of the students all upset, bringing charges, and seeking to punish me. [241] Instead, they bring me their sons, pay my fees, and rejoice when they see them spending the day with me, while the sykophants slander us and give us trouble. Who would be happier than these to see many of the citizens corrupted and depraved? They know that among people like that they have power, but they are ruined by gentlemen of intelligence, when they are caught. [242] Thus it makes sense for them to seek to root out all such activities which they think will make people better and less tolerant of their evils and sykophancies. But it is right for you to do just the opposite, and treat those activities to which they are most hostile as the finest of all.

Diogenes Laertius 2.7). Damon, who served as Pericles' adviser, was known as one of the founders of ancient Greek music and had other fields of expertise: see Plato, *Laches* 180d.

[77] Boards were set up in the marketplace on which public notices, and particularly the charges for a trial, were published for public knowledge.

[243] Something extraordinary has happened to me. I will be honest even if some say I change positions too easily. A little before, I said that many gentlemen (*kaloi kagathoi*) were deceived about philosophy and were highly critical of it. Now I have assumed that the arguments I made are so clear and apparent to everyone that I do not think anyone is unaware of its power, or condemns me for corrupting my students, or feels as I accused them of feeling a little while ago. [244] If I must speak the truth and say what is in my mind, I think all who envy me want to be able to think and speak well themselves, but they neglect these things, some through laziness, others because they downplay their own natural ability, and still others for various other reasons (and there are many). [245] But toward those who apply themselves diligently and wish to acquire the things they themselves desire, they are irritated and jealous, they are upset, and they go through the same sort of experience as lovers. What more fitting explanation could one offer for their behavior than this? [246] They praise and envy those who can speak well, but they fault young people who wish to achieve this honor, although there is no one who would not pray to the gods to be able to speak well himself, and if not himself, then his children and relatives. [247] They claim that those who accomplish this through labor and philosophy—which they want to get for themselves from the gods[78]—are neglecting their duty. Sometimes they pretend to mock them as being deceived and cheated, but then when they feel like it, they change and speak of them as able to profit from their expertise. [248] When some danger befalls the city, they listen to their advisers who are best at speaking on public matters and they do whatever such men advise. Yet they think they should slander those who take the trouble to present themselves to be useful to the city at such times. They find fault with the ignorance of the Thebans and of other enemies, but they continually criticize those who seek to do everything they can to escape this disease.

[249] This is a sign not only of their confusion, but also of their disrespect for the gods. They regard Persuasion (*Peithō*) as a god, and they see Athens sacrificing to her every year, but they claim that those who wish to share in the power that the goddess has are being corrupted by desire for something evil. [250] Worst of all, although they

---

[78] I.e., without working for it.

assume the soul is more important than the body, despite knowing this, they welcome those who engage in gymnastics more than those who engage in philosophy. Surely it is irrational to praise those who engage in a lesser activity rather than a higher activity. Everyone knows that Athens never accomplished the remarkable deeds for which it is renowned through physical training, but that it became the most blessed and greatest of all the Hellenic city states through man's intellect.

[251] Someone younger than I without the anxieties of this occasion might bring together many more of their contradictions. For instance, on the same subject one could say that if some people inherited a vast sum of money from their ancestors and did not serve the city's interests but instead abused their fellow citizens and dishonored their wives and children, would anyone dare to blame those who were responsible for the wealth and not demand that the offenders themselves be punished? [252] What if others who have learned armed combat do not use their knowledge against the enemy but cause an uprising and kill many fellow citizens, or receive the best possible training in boxing and the pankration,⁷⁹ but then instead of entering athletic contests, they hit everyone they meet? Who would not praise their teachers and then put to death those who made bad use of what they learned?

[253] Thus we should have the same understanding of speaking (*hoi logoi*) as we do of other matters, and not judge similar cases in the opposite way, or show hostility toward this facility, which of all human capabilities is responsible for the greatest goods. For in our other facilities, as I said earlier,⁸⁰ we do not differ from other living beings, and in fact we are inferior to many in speed, strength, and other resources. [254] But since we have the ability to persuade one another and to make clear to ourselves what we want, not only do we avoid living like animals, but we have come together, built cities, made laws, and invented arts (*technē*). Speech (*logos*) is responsible for nearly all our inventions. [255] It legislated in matters of justice and injustice and beauty and baseness, and without these laws, we could not live with one another. By it we refute the bad and praise the good; through it, we educate the ignorant and recognize the intelligent. We regard speaking well to be the clearest sign of a good mind, which it requires,

---

⁷⁹ Lit. "a complete contest"; an exercise involving both boxing and wrestling.
⁸⁰ Sections 253–257 are cited verbatim from 3.5–9.

and truthful, lawful, and just speech we consider the image (*eidolon*) of a good and faithful soul. [256] With speech we fight over contentious matters, and we investigate the unknown. We use the same arguments by which we persuade others in our own deliberations; we call those able to speak in a crowd "rhetorical" (*rhētorikoi*); we regard as sound advisers those who debate with themselves most skillfully about public affairs. [257] If one must summarize the power of discourse, we will discover that nothing done prudently occurs without speech (*logos*), that speech is the leader of all thoughts and actions, and that the most intelligent people use it most of all.

Because Lysimachus perceived none of this, he dared to prosecute those who had their hearts set on an activity responsible for so many important benefits. [258] Why should we be surprised at him, when even some of those who are experts in argumentation bring similar charges against beneficial public speeches as those brought by the basest men? They are not ignorant of the speeches' power, or of the speed with which they benefit those who employ them, but they expect that by slandering their discourse they will increase the honor of their own profession. [259] Perhaps, I could speak much more bitterly about them than they do about me, but I do not think I should either be like those who are destroyed by envy or blame those who do no harm to their pupils but are also less able to benefit others. Still, I shall say a few things about them, primarily because they have done so about me, but also so that you may better understand their power and may treat each of us fairly, [260] in addition to making clear that although I am concerned with political discourse (*hoi politikoi logoi*), which they say is quarrelsome, I am much gentler than they are.

If they always disparage me, I am not inclined to do the same but will speak the truth about them. [261] I think the leaders in eristic and those who teach astrology, geometry, and other branches of learning do not harm but rather benefit their students, less than they promise but more than others think. [262] Most men regard such studies as babbling and hairsplitting, since none of them is useful in personal or public life. Students do not remember them for very long because they do not have a bearing on our lives, or help with our activities, but are in every respect nonessential. [263] On this matter my view is not the same nor is it so different: I think that those who consider this education irrelevant to public affairs are correct, and those who praise it also utter the truth. I have stated contradictory views on this issue because by their nature these subjects are not at all like the other ones we teach. [264] Other subjects naturally help us when we gain an understanding of them. But these do not benefit us even if we become specialists in them (unless we choose to earn our living from them), but they do benefit us when we learn them. [265] When we spend time in the detail and precision of astrology and geometry, we are forced to put our minds to matters that are hard to learn, and moreover, we get used to working persistently hard at[81] what has been said and demonstrated to us, and we cannot let our minds wander. When we are exercised and sharpened in these matters, we are able to receive and learn more important and significant material more quickly and easily. [266] I don't think we should call what does not at present benefit our ability to speak or act "philosophy." Instead, I call such activity a "mental gymnastics" and a "preparation for philosophy" — a more mature subject than what children learn in schools but for the most part similar. [267] When children have worked hard at grammar, music, and the rest of education, they have not yet made progress in speaking better or in deliberating on public affairs, although they have become better prepared to learn the greater and more serious subjects. [268] I would advise the young to spend some time in these subjects but not to allow their natures to become withered up by them or stranded in the discourses of the older sophists,[82] of whom one said the number of elements is infinite;[83] Empedocles, that it is four, among which are strife and love;[84] Ion, that it is not more than

---

[81] The majority of manuscripts read "we get used to speaking (*legein*) and working on . . ."

[82] "The older sophists" are the Presocratics and not the great political leaders, like Solon, Cleisthenes, and Themistocles, mentioned in 232–235. By using "sophist" in connection with these thinkers, Isocrates is attempting to give the noun a more positive connotation than it often has at this time.

[83] The reference is to Anaxagoras of Clazomenae (ca. 500–428). In his work *On Nature*, he declared that all things were infinite with respect to their number and size.

[84] Empedocles of Acragas (ca. 495–435) wrote a poem in two books entitled *On Nature* in which he taught that there were four elements, fire, water, earth, and air, which came together through love and were divided by strife.

three;[85] Alcmaeon, that it is only two;[86] Parmenides and Melissus, that it is one;[87] and Gorgias, [that it is] nothing at all.[88] [269] I think that such quibblings resemble wonder-workings, which provide no benefit but attract crowds of the ignorant. Those wishing to do something useful must rid all their activities of pointless discourse and irrelevant action.

[270] I have presented a sufficient account and advice on these matters. Concerning wisdom (*sophia*) and philosophy (*philosophia*), it would not be fitting for someone pleading about other issues to speak about these terms, since they have nothing to do with all other activities, but since I am on trial for just such matters and am claiming that what some people call "philosophy" is not really that at all, it is appropriate for me to define it and to show you what it is, when rightly understood.

[271] I understand it quite simply. Since human nature cannot attain knowledge that would enable us to know what we must say or do, after this I think that the wise (*sophoi*) are those who have the ability to reach the best opinions (*doxai*) most of the time, and philosophers are those who spend time acquiring such an intelligence as quickly as possible. [272] I can reveal which activities have such power, but I hesitate to do so because they are so very unexpected and so far removed from other people's ideas. I fear that as soon as you hear them you will fill the whole courtroom with shouting and protest. But despite these feelings, I shall try to discuss them. I am embarrassed if I

---

[85] Ion of Chios (fifth century) is credited with the idea that everything is made up of three things. Some of them are always at war, but when they come together, they produce offspring.

[86] Alcmeon of Croton (fifth century) proposed that human affairs generally occur in opposing pairs; health was a balance—or not—of these opposites.

[87] In his poem *Truth,* Parmenides of Elea wrote of what *is* as being all together, one and continuous. He is said to have come with Zeno to Athens, where he met the young Socrates. Melissus, the pupil of Parmenides, wrote a work entitled *On Nature or on What Exists.* Paraphrases are preserved in the Pseudo-Aristotelian *On Melissus, Xenophanes, and Gorgias.*

[88] Gorgias, introduced as the successful but also irresponsible teacher of rhetoric at section 155, now appears a nihilist. This aspect of his thinking is represented by his work *On Not Being;* cf. 10.3.

appear to some to be afraid of betraying the truth because of my old age and the short life I have left. [273] I ask that you do not decide ahead of time that I am so mad that being in peril I would choose to utter words contrary to your view, unless I considered them consistent with what I have already said and thought that I had true and evident proofs of them.

[274] I think that an art that can produce self-control (*sōphrosynē*) and justice (*dikaiosynē*) in those who are by nature badly disposed to virtue (*aretē*) has never existed and does not now exist, and that those who previously made promises to this effect will cease speaking and stop uttering nonsense before such an education (*paideia*) is discovered. [275] In my view, people improve and become worthier if they are interested in speaking well, have a passion for being able to persuade their audience, and also desire advantage (*pleonexia*)—not what foolish people think it is but that which truly has this power. [276] I think I can quickly show that this is so.

In the first place, someone who chooses to speak and write speeches worthy of praise and honor will not possibly select topics that are unjust or insignificant or that deal with private arguments but those public issues which are important and noble and promote human welfare. If he does not discover any such topics, he will accomplish nothing. [277] Then from the evidence relevant to his topic, he will select the most appropriate and advantageous. Someone who is accustomed to examine and evaluate such topics will have this same facility not only for the speech at hand but also for other affairs. As a result, those who are philosophical and ambitious in their devotion to speaking (*logoi*) will at the same time speak well and think intelligently. [278] Moreover, anyone who wishes to persuade others will not neglect virtue but will devote even more attention to ensuring that he achieves a most honorable reputation among his fellow citizens. Who could fail to know that speeches seem truer when spoken by those of good name than by the disreputable, and that arguments acquire more authority when they come from one's life than from mere words. The more ardently someone wants to persuade his audience, the more he will strive to be a gentleman (*kalos kagathos*) and to have a good reputation among the citizens.

[279] Let none of you think that everyone else knows how it supports the cause of persuasion if one can please the jury, and that phi-

losophers alone are ignorant of the power of goodwill. They know this far more acutely than others. [280] In addition, they know that plausibility (*to eikos*), and inference, and all forms of proof contribute only that part of the speech in which each of them is uttered, whereas the reputation of being a gentleman not only makes the speech more persuasive but also makes the actions of one who has such a reputation more honorable. Intelligent men must covet this more than anything else.

[281] This brings me to the subject of advantage (*pleonexia*), which is the most problematic of the issues I have mentioned. If someone assumes that people gain advantages by stealing, misrepresenting, or doing something evil, he is under the wrong impression. No one is more disadvantaged in his entire life than such men; no one lives in greater poverty or in greater disrepute; and no one is more thoroughly wretched. [282] You should now realize that those who are most righteous and most devoted in service to the gods receive and will continue to receive more advantages from the gods, just as those who are most devoted to the interests of their family and fellow citizens and have the best reputation among them will gain more advantages from other human beings. [283] This is the truth, but it is, furthermore, helpful to speak in this way on the subject, since Athens is in such a state of confusion and chaos that some people no longer use words naturally but transfer them from the finest deeds to the basest activities.[89] [284] They call buffoons and those who can mock and imitate others "talented" (*euphyeis*), when this term rightly applies to those who are most virtuous by nature.[90] And they think that those who rely on a wicked nature and evil deeds to gain a little profit while acquiring an evil reputation are at an advantage, not those who are most righteous and just, who profit from good and not evil. [285] And they declare that those who neglect the necessities of life and admire the logical tricks of the ancient sophists do "philosophy," having disregarded those who learn and practice what allows them to manage

---

[89] Isocrates may have in mind Thuc. 3.82. Aristotle (*Topics* 112a32) treats the misassignments of words as a form of verbal attack.

[90] Cf. 7.49. Note that at 7.74 Isocrates says that he will cite less extensive passages from his prior works.

well their own homes and the city's commonwealth⁹¹—for which one must work hard, engage in philosophy, and do everything necessary.

Because you accept the arguments of those who slander this kind of education (*paideia*), you have been driving the young away from such activities. [286] You have led the most promising of them to spend their youth in drink, social gatherings, amusements, and games, while neglecting the serious business of self-improvement, and those with baser natures to pass the day in the sort of undisciplined behavior that no honest slave would have previously dared.⁹² [287] Some of them chill wine in the Nine Fountains;⁹³ others drink in the taverns, while others play dice in the gambling dens; and many hang out in the schools for flute girls.⁹⁴ And none of those who claim to be concerned about these youths has ever brought those who encourage such behavior before this jury of yours. Instead, they harass me, although if anything, I deserve thanks for turning my students away from such activities.

[288] The race of sykophants is so hostile to everyone that far from reproaching those who spend twenty or thirty minas to obtain women who will consume the rest of their household, instead they rejoice at their lavishness; but if someone spends anything on his own education (*paideia*), the sykophants say they are being corrupted. Who could bring a more unjust charge than this against my pupils? [289] Although they are in the prime of their lives, they disregarded the pleasures that most men of the same age desire, and although they had the option of taking life easy and spending nothing, they chose to pay out money and work. As soon as they left childhood, they knew what many older people do not, [290] that in order to supervise this age correctly and properly and to start life in a favorable way, a person must tend to himself before attending to his affairs, must not hurry or

---

⁹¹ Protagoras had claimed to teach *euboulia*, i.e., good management of one's household (*oikos*) and the city (*polis*); see Plato, *Protagoras* 318e–319a.

⁹² Cf. 7.48 on the pastimes of contemporary youth.

⁹³ The Nine Fountains were most likely situated between the Acropolis and the Pnyx; see Thuc. 2.15.5.

⁹⁴ See Plato, *Symposium* 212c–d, for the association of flute girls with a dissipated lifestyle. Flute girls may have also doubled as prostitutes for young men.

seek to rule others before finding someone to oversee his intellect, must not rejoice in or pride himself on other good things as much as on those that the soul produces as a result of education. Surely one should not blame but rather praise those who use such logic, and regard them as the best and most prudent of their contemporaries.

[291] I am amazed that those who congratulate naturally able speakers for the fine talent they have been endowed with nonetheless still find fault with those who wish to become like these and accuse them of desiring an unjust and bad education. Does anything that is noble turn out shameful or wicked if one works to attain it? We will not find any such thing, and everywhere else we praise those who can acquire some benefit by their own effort, more than those who inherit it from their ancestors. [292] This is reasonable. It is better in all other matters and especially in speaking to gain repute not by good luck but by practice. Those who become skilled speakers by nature and luck do not aspire for what is best but are accustomed to use words as they come. On the other hand, those who acquire this ability by means of philosophy and reasoning do not speak thoughtlessly and are less careless in their affairs.

[293] As a result, it is appropriate for everyone, especially you jurors, to want many to become skilled speakers through education. For you excel and are superior to others not because of your attention to military matters, or because you have the best constitution, or are the most effective guardians of the laws your ancestors left to you, but because of that feature which makes human nature superior to that of other living creatures and the Greek race superior to the barbarians, [294] namely, a superior education in intellect and speech. Accordingly, it would be a most terrible outcome if you vote to condemn those who wish to surpass their contemporaries in the very things in which you surpass everyone else, and pile misfortune on those who obtain the kind of education in which you are the leaders. [295] You must not ignore the fact that our city is thought to be the teacher of all those who are skilled in speaking and teaching.[95] And this is reasonable, for people see that the city makes available the greatest rewards for those who have this ability and provides the greatest number and

---

[95] For the motif of Athens as the teacher of Greece, see Thuc. 2.41.1, 7.63, and Plut., *Moralia* 784b; cf. Plut., *Lycurgus* 30, for Sparta as the teacher of Greece.

variety of opportunities for exercising them for those who choose to compete and wish to engage in such activities. [296] Furthermore, everyone here acquires experience, which most of all produces the ability to speak. In addition, they think that our common dialect, and its moderation,[96] our flexibility, and our love of language contribute significantly to our culture of discourse (*hē tōn logōn paideia*). Hence, they are right to think that all who have skill at speaking are students of Athens.

[297] Be careful to avoid becoming utterly ridiculous by condemning as something trifling this reputation that you have among the Greeks more than I have among you. You will clearly be convicting yourselves of the same injustice, [298] and you will have acted just as if the Spartans should attempt to punish those who practice military arts, or the Thessalians thought to punish those who practiced horsemanship.[97] You must guard against this so as not to make such a mistake about yourselves, or to make the speeches of the city's accusers more credible than those of its encomiasts.

[299] I think that you are not unaware that some of the Greeks are hostile to you, and that others are as fond of you as they can be and lay their hopes of salvation in you. The latter say that Athens is the only city (*polis*), that the others are villages (*kōmai*), and that Athens rightly should be called the capital (*astu*) of Greece because of its size and the resources we provide to others, and especially for the character of the inhabitants. [300] They say none are more gentle, more sociable, or better suited to someone who would spend his whole life here. People use such warm terms that they do not hesitate to declare that punishment by an Athenian man is more pleasant than favorable treatment through the savagery of others. Others dismiss this praise; they describe the bitterness and wickedness of the sykophants and accuse the whole city of being unsociable and cruel. [301] It is up to the jurors who are sensible to destroy those who are responsible for such words, because they heap a great shame on Athens, and to honor

---

[96] Cf. 4.50; on the historical consistency of the Attic language, see Herod. 1.57–58.

[97] Isocrates here invokes three cultural stereotypes—Athenians as intellectuals, Spartans as militarists, and Thessalians as equestrians—all of which serve to affirm the superiority of Athens for pursuing intellectual, over the physical, arts.

those who contribute some part to the praise it receives, even more than the athletes who win in the prize competitions. [302] These men acquire a much finer and more fitting reputation for the city than athletes.[98] We have many rivals in athletic competition, but in education, all would judge us winners. Even those with slight ability to reason should make clear that they honor men who excel in those activities for which Athens is highly regarded, and they are not jealous but agree with the other Greeks about them.

[303] None of these things ever concerned you, but you have failed to perceive your interests to such a degree that you prefer to listen to those who slander you than to those who praise you, and you think that those who cause many to hate Athens are more democratic than those who dispose their associates to think well of the city. [304] If you are sensible, you will stop this confusion. You will not, as you do now, either treat philosophy harshly or dismiss it, but you will accept that the cultivation of the soul is the best and most worthwhile activity. You will encourage young men with adequate wealth and leisure to pursue education and this kind of training. [305] You will value those who are willing to work hard and prepare themselves for service to the city. You will hate those who live dissolutely and think of nothing other than how they can extravagantly enjoy their inheritance, and you will regard them as traitors, both of Athens and of their ancestors' reputations. If they see you treating either of these groups in this manner, the youth will gradually despise easy living and will be willing to attend to themselves and to philosophy.

[306] Recall the beauty of the magnificent achievements of our city and our ancestors. Reflect on them yourselves and consider who the man was who drove out the tyrants, restored the people, and established the democracy, who his ancestors were, and what kind of education he received;[99] what sort of person defeated the barbarians at the battle of Marathon and gained glory from this feat for our city;[100] [307] and who after him freed the Greeks and led our forefathers to the leadership and power they obtained. After he understood the

---

[98] For similar comparisons of intellectuals with athletes, see, e.g., Xenophanes 2 and Plato, *Apology* 36d.

[99] Cleisthenes; see above, 232.

[100] Miltiades, who is not previously named.

natural advantages of Piraeus, he built a wall around the city with the Spartans objecting.[101] And after him, who filled the Acropolis with silver and gold and made private households teem with great prosperity and wealth?[102] [308] If you look at each of these individuals, you will find that they did not accomplish these things living like sykophants, or negligently, or like the multitude, but rather they excelled and were preeminent not only in birth and reputation but also in their ability to think and speak. In this way they became responsible for all these benefits.

[309] So it is only reasonable that with these examples in mind you should examine this case in the interests of the people, that in their private disputes, they may obtain justice and have their due share of other public privileges, and you should cherish, honor, and cultivate those who are superior by nature and education as well as those who desire to be such. You know that leadership in noble and important enterprises, the ability to save our city from danger, and the protection of democracy are in the hands of such men, not sykophants.

[310] Although many other arguments come into my mind, I don't know how to fit them in. I think that each of the points I am considering would by itself appear plausible, but to lay them all out together would be tedious for me and my audience. I am anxious that the length of what I have already said may have made you feel this way. [311] Our appetite for discourse is so insatiable that while we praise timeliness (*eukairia*) and say nothing equals it, when we think we have a point to make, we disregard moderation; little by little, we continue to add more until finally we abandon timeliness altogether. Still, although I say this and understand it, I want to continue to speak to you.

[312] I find it difficult to watch sykophancy getting better treatment than philosophy, the former accusing while the latter defends itself. Who among our forefathers would have foreseen this state of affairs, especially among you, who have a higher opinion of wisdom than others? [313] It was not like this with our ancestors: they admired

[101] Themistocles; see above, 233. For his construction of the long walls around Piraeus, see Thuc. 1.93.
[102] Pericles; see above, 234. Pericles moved the treasury of the Delian League from Delos to Athens; cf. Thuc. 2.13.

those who were sophists and envied their students but regarded sykophants as responsible for most evils. This is the greatest proof. They
considered Solon, the first citizen to be called a "sophist," worthy to
lead the city, and they made the laws harsher for sykophants than for
other criminals. [314] They tried the most serious crimes in just one
of the courts, but against these individuals, they admitted indictments
(*graphai*) before the Thesmothetae, public prosecutions (*eisangeliai*)
before the Council, and denunciations (*probolai*) in the Assembly, for
they thought that those who practice this profession [i.e., sykophancy]
surpass all other evils.[103] Others try to avoid detection when they do
evil, [315] but these display their savagery, inhumanity, and conten-
tiousness in front of everyone.

This is how they were viewed in the past; yet, far from punishing
them, you use them as prosecutors and legislators for others, although
you now have more reason than before to hate them. [316] Previously
they injured their fellow citizens only in everyday matters of local interest. But when Athens increased in power and gained control of an
empire, our ancestors became overconfident and grew jealous of the
power of those aristocrats (*kaloi kagathoi*) who had made the city
great; they came to desire wicked men, full of brashness, [317] thinking that their bold and contentious nature made them capable of preserving the democracy, but because of their base origins, they would
not be ambitious, or desire other forms of government.[104] As a result
of this change, what disaster has not befallen the city? What great evil
have men of this nature not accomplished through their words and
actions? [318] Did they not criticize those citizens who are most respected and best able to benefit the city for being oligarchical and
of imitating Spartan ways? Did they not persist until they compelled
their [victims] to become what they were accused of being? Did they
not abuse our allies and bring false accusations against them, depriving

---

[103] In this section Isocrates lists a series of legislative measures introduced by
the historical leaders of Athens to curb the activities of the sykophants. He emphasizes the seriousness with which the activities of the sykophants were *previously*
viewed.

[104] I.e., unlike traditional aristocratic leaders who might wish to establish an
oligarchical government.

the best citizens of their wealth and consequently inciting them to revolt from us and to desire friendship and an alliance with Sparta? [319] Thus we found ourselves in war. We sat by, watching some of our citizens killed in battle, others captured by the enemy, and others lacking the necessities of life, as well as the democracy twice destroyed, and the walls of the fatherland torn down. But the worst of all is that the whole city was in danger of being enslaved, and our enemies inhabited the Acropolis.[105]

[320] Although I am carried away by the force of my anger and I have lapsed into arguments and criticisms that could last days, I perceive that my waterclock is running out.[106] Thus I have omitted most of the calamities brought about by these men, and put aside many of the points still to be said about their sykophancies. I will now mention a few minor points and then shall conclude my case. [321] I note that when others in peril come to the end of their defense, they beg and plead and bring out their children and friends,[107] but I do not think anything of this kind is appropriate to a man of my age. Apart from holding this view, I would be embarrassed if I were saved through any means other than the arguments (*logoi*) I have uttered and written. I know I have employed them righteously and justly with regard to the city, our ancestors, and especially the gods. Thus if the gods are in fact concerned with human affairs, I don't think they will overlook anything that has happened to me. [322] For that reason, I do not fear anything you may do to me; instead, I am encouraged and have great

---

[105] The described calamities are the Peloponnesian War; the overthrow of the democracy by the oligarchy of the Four Hundred in 411 and then by the Thirty Tyrants in 404; the collapse of the long walls connecting Athens to Piraeus; and the Spartan occupation of the Acropolis.

[106] Legal cases could not last longer than a day, and litigants had to speak within the time constraints set by a waterclock. The amount of water granted to the speaker varied with the nature and value of the case; see Harrison 1971: 161–163, also 156. It was a commonplace for the speaker to acknowledge the constraints of time; see Aes. 2.126, 3.197; Dem. 43.8, 53.17.

[107] For the clichéd devices that orators use to gain the jury's sympathy, see Plato, *Apology* 34c (which this passage directly echoes); Aristoph., *Wasps* 568–574; Dem. 21.99 and 186–188; Arist., *Rhetoric* 1354a.

hopes of reaching the end of my life whenever it is best for me. I take it as a sign that I have lived my life until this day as is fitting for men who are righteous and dear to the gods.

[323] That is my view. I think that whatever you decide will be beneficial and advantageous for me.

May each of you vote as he pleases and wishes.[108]

APPENDIX: SECTIONS 222-224 FROM THE *LAURENTIANUS* CODEX

It is unfair to slander those who practice philosophy well because of undisciplined and wicked people. Even if some citizens are sykophants and evildoers, as my accuser is, it is not proper to think that everyone else is the same: each person must be judged separately. For this reason, I read my speeches to you and listed my students. I wished to show how different we are from others. You will find none of these things in our activities, speeches, exercises, or claims. My students associated with me for none of the same reasons as the others, for the latter seek to share in boasting, whereas my students seek to share in culture (*paideias*). In addition, you would see that those who cause trouble in all the Greek cities and seek individuals to deceive are justly hated, while my associates who come from every place are truthful and serious. I would gladly ask Lysimachus what he thinks about those who sail here from Sicily, Pontus, and other places to me to be educated and whether he thinks they make this journey because they are short of wicked people where they come from? But one might find a great abundance of people everywhere who wish to conspire in evil and wrongdoing.

---

[108] A final Platonic reference to *Apology* 35d5–8. And there the similarities with Socrates' end, for where Plato's philosopher receives the death penalty, Isocrates and his philosophy can only be victorious in light of the speech's fictional staging.

GLOSSARY

〰〰〰

Isocrates' vocabulary is of special interest because many of its terms became canonized in Aristotle's *Rhetoric,* a generation later. Care has been taken to translate these terms consistently, but since the English translations rarely convey the full range of meaning of the Greek, the reader may wish to consult specific passages in order to determine more accurately Isocrates' meaning.

antidosis: "exchange" is the legal process by which a citizen called to undertake a liturgy (see below) can propose that a wealthier individual either assume the liturgy in his place or else exchange properties with him. If the challenged citizen refuses both options, the case is then brought as a suit to decide between the two (*diadikasia*), and the jurors assign the liturgy to the one they judge to be richer.

aretē: "virtue," "human excellence," "morality" is the central human value, excellence in character. Soundness of mind (*sōphrosynē*) and a sense of justice (*dikaiosynē*) are also considered *aretai* (3.29, 3.43). For Isocrates, as for Plato, it was questionable whether *aretē* was really teachable (13.6, 20). In epideictic speeches, like 10 and 11, displaying the *aretē* of the person being praised is the primary object of the speech (10.12, 11.10). Cf. Arist., *Rhetoric* 1.3.3, 1.9.

doxa: "opinion," "conjecture"; sometimes "reputation" or "glory" (1.17, 2.7, 13.8). *Doxa* is often set in contrast to a fixed body of knowledge, *epistēmē,* which was prized by Plato and his followers, but Isocrates contrasts *doxa* favorably with *epistēmē* (10.5, 13.8, 15.184, 15.271). The establishment of a good *doxa* ("reputation") is among the highest goals Isocrates sets for himself and his students

(15.184); with it the public speaker hopes to gain the approval and support of his mass audience.

eidos: "form," as of a speech (13.17) or an argument (15.280; cf. 9.9). Isocrates distinguishes between an exhortation (*paraklēsis*) and an address (*parainesis*) (1.5) and between a speech of praise (*epainos*) and defense (*apologia*) (10.14–15, 11.5). He also recognizes a prosecution (*katēgoria*) as a distinct form (10.21) and refers to an *epideixis* ("display") (11.44, 15.55, 15.147). See also *idea*.

elenchos: "test" (2.52, 19.41). Isocrates refers to several processes or pieces of evidence that may serve as an *elenchos* of his position, like the torture (*basanos*) of a slave (17.12, 17.53), or a document (17.30). He also refers to a more technical use of the term, in its verbal form (*exelenchein*), as a refutation (3.7, 10.4).

enthymēma: "consideration"; the verb *enthymeisthai* = "consider," "bear in mind" (13.16, 15.17, 21.18). It sometimes seems to refer to thoughts that the listener must introduce, since they lie outside the obvious facts of the case but are relevant to them (9.10).

epieikeia: "fair-mindedness," "honesty"; it is often translated "equity" (1.38, 1.48, 15.212). It is a central value for Isocrates, to which his teaching contributes (11.1, 13.21).

hēgemonia: "hegemony" refers to Athens' political and cultural leadership among the Greek states; see esp. 15.293–294.

idea: "form" of thought or argument, a basic building block of argumentation (13.16). One or more *ideai* (10.15, 11.33) make up the *eidos* of a speech, which the speaker must perhaps match to *kairoi* (10.11).

kairos: "circumstance" (10.11, 15.184), "occasion" (1.32, 9.34, 13.13), "crisis" (1.25), or "opportunity" (2.33, 2.52, 3.19, 9.54–55).

leitourgia: translated "liturgy" (but not with the same sense as the English word). A form of taxation imposed on the wealthiest Athenians, obliging them to fund a choral production, a dramatic performance, or the maintenance of a trireme for a year. Litigants frequently attest their sense of civic responsibility by citing liturgies they had performed. Isocrates broadens the understanding of a liturgy to encompass any service, including the teaching of rhetoric, performed for the overall benefit of the community; see in particular 15.158, 224–226; also Lys. 21.19 for the idea that the best liturgy is good citizenship.

logos: "word," "argument," "speech" (1.4, 1.12, 10.12).

paideia, paideusis: "education." A slight distinction can be made between *paideusis*—the process of educating or training, in which Isocrates and other sophists engaged (3.57, 9.50, 11.1, 11.49)—and education as an ability (15.192) or quality of character, that is, being educated, which is called *paideia* (1.2, 1.33, 15.6, 15.189), although Isocrates is not entirely consistent. He promises that his *paideusis* will make his students more skillful at public speaking (13.13), but he does not promise to improve their character (13.21, 15.274).

parrhēsia: "frank speech." Isocrates invokes this mode of discourse frequently in his presentation as political adviser and teacher: cf. 2.3, 2.28, 5.72, 9.39, 11.1, 12.96, 15.43, *Epistle* 4.4–7 (where Isocrates' former pupil Diodotus is commended for his outspokenness), *Epistle* 9.12. "Frank speech" is also associated, however, with the discursive excesses of a dysfunctional democracy, characterizing the discourse of orators and comic poets; see 8.14.

philosophia: "philosophy." During the fourth century, the Platonic pursuit of abstract and precise knowledge, which has become the modern discipline of philosophy, was only one of many versions of "philosophy." Isocrates rejects Plato's version since it renders a man incapable of public service (12.26–30, 13.18, 15.184, 15.271; cf. Callicles' objections to philosophy at *Gorgias* 484c–485d); his own idea of philosophy combines politics and study (11.22) with, above all, skill at using language (what we might call rhetorical ability). This enables an individual to contribute to the betterment of his society (15.266, 15.271–275), which in turn brings him great reputation (1.3–4). Isocratean philosophy need not rely on education (13.14, 15.190) but may benefit from it (13.21).

pistis: "basis for argument" (3.8, 15.125), often translated "proof" (in the New Testament it comes to mean "faith"). The basis for argument or belief can be something concrete, such as an oath or pledge, but in rhetorical contexts it often refers to themes upon which an argument can be based (10.22, 11.37). Aristotle (*Rhetoric* 1.2.2, 1.15) formalized a system of *entechnoi* ("artistic") and *atechnoi* ("nonartistic") *pisteis* (see *technē,* below). The former include the logical aspects of the speech itself, the character of the speaker, and the emotional response of the hearers. The latter consist of laws, witness testimony, contracts, torture, and oaths, which were used primarily in forensic oratory.

pleonexia: "advantage" is often used by others to mean purely personal gain but for Isocrates is the broad range of advantages that come from public service and a virtuous life (3.1, 15.281–283).

prepon: "propriety," "appropriateness" (13.13). Isocrates does not elaborate on this term, but it seems to involve matching the right forms of argument (*ideai*) and considerations (*enthymēmata*) with the circumstances (*kairoi*) of the speech (13.16, 15.74).

rhētorikos: "rhetorical." The adjective denotes individuals who have the ability to speak in public and does not necessarily have negative connotations in the writings of Isocrates: see 3.8 and 15.256.

sēmeion: "sign," "indication" (10.12, 13.13). The word is often used in conjunction with *tekmērion* but with a weaker force (1.2, 1.13, 17.36, 18.15).

sophistēs: the word "sophist" often bears strongly negative connotations in the fourth century. For Isocrates, it designates the denizens of contemporary rhetorical culture who are responsible for the troublesome litigation that afflicts the Athenian upper class and who attack the true rhetorician (see, e.g., 12.5–6, 16–21). Their direct ancestors were the Presocratic philosophers, whom Isocrates calls the "older sophists" (15.268) and whom he accuses of confusing people through their ontological quibblings. But "sophist" has fluid connotations and references, and Isocrates also seeks to reclaim the noun so that it denotes a responsible political leader, exemplified by Solon (cf. 15.313–314).

technē: "art," "craft" (3.6), such as divination (19.6) or poetry (10.65). *Technai* (= *Technai logōn*) are *Arts,* handbooks of rhetorical precepts (13.19).

tekmērion: "evidence." Aristotle (*Rhetoric* 1.2.17–18) calls it a sure, or necessarily valid, sign (*sēmeion*), but Isocrates is less precise (17.31, 17.36, 18.14–15, 21.4).

tyrannos: literally "tyrant." Denotes a "monarch" or absolute ruler and may not always have negative resonances, especially when used before the fourth century; see Andrewes 1956: esp. 20–30. Isocrates' use of *tyrannos* in *To Nicocles* (2.4) may serve to evoke a nostalgic ideal of kingship.

BIBLIOGRAPHY

Andrewes, Antony, 1956: *The Greek Tyrants*. London.

Austin, Norman, 1994: *Helen of Troy and Her Shameless Phantom*. Ithaca, NY.

Benoit, W., 1991: "Isocrates and Plato on Rhetoric and Rhetoricians," *Rhetoric Society Quarterly* 21: 60–71.

Cahn, M., 1989: "Reading Rhetoric Rhetorically: Isocrates and the Marketing of Insight," *Rhetorica* 7: 121–144.

Christ, Matthew, 1998: *The Litigious Athenian*. Baltimore.

Cohen, Edward E., 1992: *Athenian Economy and Society: A Banking Perspective*. Princeton.

Cole, Thomas, 1991: *The Origins of Rhetoric in Ancient Greece*. Baltimore.

Cooper, John, 1985: "Plato, Isocrates and Cicero on the Independence of Oratory from Philosophy," in *Proceedings of the Boston Area Colloquium in Ancient Philosophy* I, ed. J. J. Cleary. New York and London: 77–96.

Davidson, J., 1990: "Isocrates against Imperialism: An Analysis of the De Pace," *Historia* 39: 20–36.

Davies, John K., 1971: *Athenian Propertied Families*. Oxford.

de Romilly, J., 1958: "Eunoia in Isocrates or the Political Importance of Creating Good Will," *Journal of Hellenic Studies* 78: 92–101.

Forster, Edward S., 1912: *Isocrates. Cyprian Orations: Evagoras, Ad Nicoclem, Nicocles aut Cyprii*. Oxford.

Foxhall, Lin, and Andrew D. E. Lewis, eds. 1996: *Greek Law in Its Political Setting: Justifications Not Justice*. Oxford.

Fuks, A., 1972: "Isokrates and the Social-Economic Situation in Greece," *Ancient Society* 3: 17–44.

Gabrielsen, V., 1987: "The *Antidosis* Procedure in Classical Athens," *Classica et Medievalia* 38: 7–38.

Gagarin, Michael, 1981: "The Thesmothetai and the Earliest Athenian Tyranny Law," *Transactions of the American Philological Association* III: 71–77.

Gagarin, Michael, and Paul Woodruff, 1995: *Early Greek Political Thought from Homer to the Sophists.* Cambridge.

Halliwell, S., 1990: "Traditional Greek Conceptions of Character," in *Characterization and Individuality in Greek Literature,* ed. C. Pelling. Oxford: 32–59.

Harris, William V., 1989: *Ancient Literacy.* Cambridge, MA.

Harrison, A. R. W., 1971: *The Law of Athens: Procedure.* Oxford.

Heilbrunn, G., 1975: "Isocrates on Rhetoric and Power," *Hermes* 103: 154–178.

Highet, Gilbert, 1949: *The Classical Tradition: Greek and Roman Influences on Western Literature.* New York.

Hignett, Charles, 1952: *A History of the Athenian Constitution to the End of the Fifth Century B.C.* Oxford.

Howland, R. L., 1937: "The Attack on Isocrates in the *Phaedrus,*" *Classical Quarterly* 31: 151–159.

Jaeger, Werner, 1938: *Demosthenes: The Origin and Growth of His Policy. Sather Classical Lectures,* vol. 13. Berkeley.

————, 1940: "The Date of Isocrates' *Areopagiticus* and the Athenian Opposition," *Athenian Studies Presented to William Scott Ferguson. Harvard Studies in Classical Philology,* Supp. vol. 1. Cambridge, MA: 409–450.

Jebb, Richard, 1876: *The Attic Orators,* 2 vols. London.

Johnson, R., 1959: "Isocrates' Methods of Teaching," *American Journal of Philology* 80: 25–36.

Kennedy, George A., trans., 1991: *Aristotle, "On Rhetoric": A Theory of Civic Discourse.* Oxford.

Knox, Bernard, 1968: "Silent Reading in Antiquity," *Greek, Roman, and Byzantine Studies* 9: 421–435.

Lattimore, Richmond, 1939: "The Wise Adviser in Herodotus," *Classical Philology* 34: 24–35.

Livingstone, Niall, 1998: "The Voice of Isocrates and the Dissemination of Cultural Power" in Too and Livingstone (1998): 263–281.

MacDowell, Douglas M., 1978: *The Law in Classical Athens.* London.

————, 1990: *Demosthenes, Against Meidias.* Oxford.

Marrou, Henri I., 1956: *A History of Education in Antiquity*, trans. G. Lamb. New York.

Martin, Richard P., 1984: "Hesiod, Odysseus, and the Instruction of Princes," *Transactions of the American Philological Association* 114: 29–48.

Misch, Georg, 1950: *A History of Autobiography in Antiquity* I, trans. E. W. Dickes. London: esp. part I, chapter II.

Momigliano, Arnaldo, 1971: *The Development of Greek Biography: Four Lectures.* Cambridge, MA.

Moysey, Robert A., 1987: "Isocrates and Chares: A Study in the Political Spectrum of Mid-Fourth Century Athens," *Ancient World* 15: 81–86.

Ober, Josiah, 1996: *The Athenian Revolution: Essays on Ancient Greek Democracy and Political Theory.* Princeton.

Papillon, Terry, 1995: "Isocrates' *techne* and Rhetorical Pedagogy," *Rhetoric Society Quarterly* 25: 149–163.

———, 1996a: "Isocrates on Gorgias and Helen: The Unity of the *Helen*," *Classical Journal* 91: 377–391.

———, 1996b: "Isocrates and the Use of Myth," *Hermathena* 161: 9–21.

———, 1997: "Mixed Unities in the *Antidosis* of Isocrates," *Rhetoric Society Quarterly* 27.4: 47–62.

Pomeroy, Sarah, 1975: *Goddesses, Whores, Wives and Slaves: Women in Classical Antiquity.* New York.

Poulakos, Takis, 1997: *Speaking for the Polis: Isocrates' Rhetorical Education.* Columbia, SC.

Roberts, Jennifer T., 1994: *Athens on Trial: The Antidemocratic Tradition in Western Thought.* Princeton.

Russell, D. A., 1979: "*De Imitatione*," in *Creative Imitation and Latin Literature*, eds. D. West and T. Woodman. Cambridge: 1–16.

Schiappa, Edward, 1990: "Did Plato Coin *Rhētorikē?*" *American Journal of Philology* 111: 457–470.

———, 1995: "Isocrates' *Philosophia* and Contemporary Pragmatism," in *Rhetoric, Sophistry, Pragmatism*, ed. Steven Mailloux. Cambridge: 33–60.

Shorey, Paul, 1909: "*Physis, Meletē, Epistēmē*," *Transactions of the American Philological Association* 40: 185–201.

Sinclair, R. K., 1988: *Democracy and Participation in Athens.* Cambridge.

Sykutris, J., 1976: "Isokrates' 'Euagoras'" in *Isokrates*, ed. Friedrich Seck. Darmstadt: 74–105; originally published in *Hermes* 62 (1927): 24–53.

Tatum, James, 1989: *Xenophon's Imperial Fiction: On the Education of Cyrus*. Princeton.

Thomas, Rosalind, 1989: *Oral Tradition and Written Record in Classical Athens*. Cambridge.

———, 1995: "Written in Stone? Liberty, Equality, Orality and the Codification of Law," *Bulletin of the Institute of Classical Studies* 40: 59–74; (= Foxhall and Lewis [1996]: 9–31).

Timmerman, David M., 1998: "Isocrates' Competing Conceptualization of Philosophy," *Philosophy and Rhetoric* 31: 145–159.

Too, Yun Lee, 1995: *The Rhetoric of Identity in Isocrates: Text, Power, Pedagogy*. Cambridge.

———, 1998: "Xenophon's *Cyropaedia*: Disfiguring the Pedagogical State," in Too and Livingstone (1998): 282–302.

Too, Yun Lee, and Niall Livingstone, eds., 1998: *Pedagogy and Power: Rhetorics of Classical Learning*. Cambridge.

Trevett, Jeremy C., 1992: *Apollodorus the Son of Pasion*. Oxford.

Usher, Stephen, 1990: *Isocrates Panegyricus and To Nicocles*. Warminster.

von Reden, Sitta, 1995: *Exchange in Ancient Greece*. London.

Wallace, Robert, 1985: *The Areopagos Council, to 307 B.C.* Baltimore.

———, 1986: "The Date of Isokrates' *Areopagitikos*," *Harvard Studies in Classical Philology* 90: 77–84.

Wells, C. Bradford, 1966: "Isocrates' View of History," in *The Classical Tradition: Literary and Historical Studies in Honor of Harry Caplan*, ed. Luitpold Wallach. Ithaca: 3–25.

Wilcox, Stanley, 1943: "Isocrates' *Genera* of Prose," *American Journal of Philology* 64: 427–431.

———, 1945: "Isocrates' Fellow-Rhetoricians," *American Journal of Philology* 66: 171–186.

Worp, K. A., and Rijksbaron, A., 1997: *The Kellis Isocrates Codex*. Dakhleh Oasis Project, Monograph 5. Oxford.

Zagagi, N., 1985: "Helen of Troy: Encomium and Apology," *Wiener Studien* 19: 63–88.

INDEX

Abas, 57
Abdemon, 145 n.20
accounting. *See euthyna*
Achilles, 43, 143 n.10, 144
Admetus, 58
Adonis, 45
Adrastus, 39
Aeacus, 143, 178
Aegeus, 36
Aegina, 112–113, 115
Aegospotami, battle of, 67, 109,
    187 n.17, 229 n.50
Aegyptus, 47
Aeolus, 51–52
Aeschylus, 240
Aethra, 36
Agamemnon, 17, 46, 49
Agenor, 52
Agesilaus, 139
Ajax, 144
Alcibiades, 18, 51, 67–79
Alcidamas, 64
Alcmene, 36, 45
Alcmeon, 73, 254
Alexander (Paris), 41–43
Alexander the Great, 3
Amathus, 139
Amazons, 199
Amphilochus, 98
Amphitryon, 45

Anaxagoras, 248, 253 n.83
Anchises, 45
Andocides, 69, 96
Androtion, 2
animals, 245
antidosis (exchange), 201, 202 n.1,
    206, 265
Antikles, 222
Antisthenes, 32
Anytus, 103
Aphareus, 2
Apollo, 58
Apollodorus, 49, 52, 80
apologia, 31, 35, 51, 266
apragmonestatoi, 247
apragmosynē, 206, 233
arbitration, 86, 97, 100–101
Archestratus, 92
Archidamus, 3
Archinus, 98
Areopagus, 138, 182–183, 191–195
Ares, 58
aretē, 20, 35, 36, 40, 45, 52, 63, 265
Argos, 68
Aristogeiton, 223 n.40
Aristophanes, 137
Aristotle, 15, 32, 33, 34, 35, 51, 62, 65,
    66, 105, 130, 133, 139 n.1, 140,
    186 n.14; *Rhetoric*, 1, 31, 51, 52, 133,
    267, 268, 265

Artabazus, 200 n.51
Artaxerxes, 139, 144 n.19
arts (*technai*), 47, 65, 171, 243, 268
astrology, 252–253
Astyages, 148 n.28
Athena, 41
Athenaeus, 62
Athens, 1–3, 5, 17, 18, 31, 32, 36, 49,
    61, 67–68, 74, 75, 80–81, 96, 112,
    128
atimia, 238 n.63
Atreus, 46

banking, 80–81, 82, 84, 91, 93, 94
barbarian, 43, 179, 184–185, 194, 199,
    200, 220, 258
basanos. See torture
basileus, 158 n.2
Belus, 52
Black Sea, 80, 82, 87, 90, 91, 92, 94
body, 21, 27, 124, 239, 244, 251
Busiris, 16, 17, 49–60
Byzantium, 182, 185 n.12, 217

Cadmus, 47
Callias, Treaty of, 200 n.49, 226 n.45
Callimachus, 96–110
Callippus, 222
Castor and Pollux, 36, 45, 46
centaurs, 143
Ceos, 116, 117
Cerberus, 38
Cercyon, 39
Chaeronea, 3, 5
Chalcideans, 226
Chares, 200 n.51, 229 n.51
Charicles, 68, 77
charis, 26, 105
Charmantides, 222
Chios, 182, 185 n.12, 217
chorēgia, 76, 89, 120, 194 n.36

Cicero, 1, 204
Cilicia, 152
Citium, 139
Cittus, 80–81, 84, 87–88, 93
Cleinias, 73–74
Cleisthenes, 73, 186, 204, 247–248,
    253, 260
Cleomander, 62
Cleon, 165, 194 n.37, 248 n.76
cleverness (*deinotēs*), 20
Clytemnestra, 49
Cnidus, battle of, 139, 153 n.36
comedy, 166
Conon, 137 n.1, 139, 150, 151, 185, 197
Corcyra, 225–226
Coroneia, 74
corruption of students, 221–222
Cos, 182, 185 n.12
Cratinus, 108
Crithotes, 225–226
Cronus, 58
Cycnus, 43
Cyprus, 19, 150, 152, 158
Cyrus, 147, 148

Damon, 248, 249 n.76
Danaë, 45, 57
Danaus, 47
Delian Confederacy, 184 n.6
Demeter, 37, 45, 69
democracy, 4, 5, 18, 40, 65, 76, 107,
    172–173, 210, 219, 260 n.99
Demonicus, 19, 20
Demosthenes, 1, 6, 80, 97
dēmotikoi, 196
diadikasia, 112, 265
dikaiosynē. See justice
Diodorus Siculus, 67
Diodotus, 267
Diomedes, 67
Dionysius (tyrant of Sicily), 2, 174

Dionysius of Halicarnassus, 1
display (*epideixis*), 59, 137, 216, 233
dokimasia, 74, 190 n.26, 191
doxa, 37, 41, 63, 203, 240, 254, 265–
266

Echo, 45
education (*paideia, paideusis*), 1, 3–
6, 15, 60, 64, 160, 180, 190, 207,
238–239, 241–246, 255, 257–258,
260–261, 264, 267
Egypt, 16–17, 49–50
eidos, 20, 61, 65, 266
eisangelia, 69
elenchos, 33, 266
Eleusinian Mysteries, 68, 69
Eleusis, 39
Eleven, the, 249
Empedocles, 253
encomium, 31, 138, 139–140
enthymeme, 61, 65, 214, 266, 268
Eos, 43, 45
epainos, 266
Epaphus, 52, 57
ephetai, 182
Ephialtes, 183
Ephorus, 2
epideictic, 16, 35, 59, 266. *See also*
display
epieikeia, 50, 66, 105, 190, 198, 233,
242, 245, 266
epistēmē, 32, 63, 240, 265
eranos, 37, 50
eunoia, 181, 231, 256
Eunomos, 222
Europa, 47
Eurydice, 51
Eurystheus, 38, 39
Eurythea, 38
euthyna, xviii, 188 n.20
Euthynus, 122–133

Evagoras, 3, 137 n.1, 139–156, 169,
175, 178
exetasis, 57

fees (for teaching), 62, 63, 137,
207 n.26, 245, 247, 249
Forty, the, 249
Four Hundred, the, 195 n.38,
263 n.105

Ganymede, 45
genealogy, 214
geometry, 252–253
Gorgias, 2, 6, 16, 17, 33, 234, 254
Great Panathenaia, 189 n.21
gymnasiarchiai, 76
gymnastics, 141, 192, 239, 240 n.64,
251, 253

Hades, 37, 38
Harmodius, 223 n.40
Heduto, 2
hēgemonia, 266
Helen, 16, 17, 31, 32, 35, 37–39, 41–
43, 45, 46
Heliastic Oath, 209 n.15
Hēlios, 38
Hephaestus, 58
Hera, 41
Heracles, 21, 29, 36–39, 49, 57, 143
Hermaphroditus, 45
Hermes, 58
Herodotus, 49, 169
Hesiod, 17, 157, 166
hiatus, 7
Hipparchus, 73
Hipparetē, 75
Hippias, 2, 73
Hippolaïdas, 81, 91
Hipponicus, 19–21, 75
Homer, 17, 29, 47, 157, 167

homoioi, 196 n.40
hybris, 70, 123–126
Hyperbolus, 77
Hyperides, 2, 224 n.43

Iasion, 45
idea, 34, 35, 57, 61, 65, 266, 268
image (*eikōn*), 165, 207
imitation (*mimēsis*), 140, 155, 181,
    200, 242
instruction of princes, 138 n.1
Ion, 253, 254 n.85
Iphicrates, 229
Iphigenia, 50
Isaeus, 2
Isocrates: language and style, 6–9;
    life, 1–3, 19, 20, 50
—works, 9–11; *Against the Sophists*,
    3, 6, 242; *Antidosis*, 4, 7; *Epistles*,
    2–3; *On the Peace*, 218; *Panathena-
    icus*, 5; *Panegyricus*, 216 n.32, 217,
    5; *To Nicocles*, 219; *To Philip*, 5

jury pay, 194
justice (*dikaiosynē*), 21, 27, 32, 44,
    62, 66, 74, 92, 94, 95, 99, 102,
    105, 106, 110, 122, 124, 125–127,
    132, 161, 170–171, 175, 177–178,
    191, 218, 225, 255, 265

kairos, 24, 35, 64, 65, 147, 151, 164,
    173, 179, 240, 266, 268
kalos kagathos, 178, 231, 245, 250, 255,
    262
katēgoria, 37, 51, 108, 125, 266

lawcourts, 1, 3
laws, 115, 122, 124, 127, 157–158, 161,
    171, 180, 182, 186, 190 n.23, 191,
    192, 220–221, 238, 251. *See also*
    nomos

lawsuit, 161, 213–214, 247
Leda, 36, 45
Leuctra, battle of, 185 n.9, 226
Libya, 17, 96, 128
liturgy (*lēitourgia*), 2, 76, 120, 180,
    188, 201, 233, 235, 266
Lochites, 123–126
logographer, 2, 15
logos/logoi, 1, 5, 8, 20, 60, 63, 138,
    141–142, 170, 202–204, 239–240,
    244, 247–248, 251–252, 255, 259,
    266
logos politikos, 11
Lysander, 77, 101, 109, 129, 150 n.30,
    197 n.42, 229
Lysianassa, 52
Lysias, 128
Lysimachus, 202, 208, 210, 224, 232,
    234, 236, 249, 252, 264
Lysitheides, 222

Macedonia, 5
Marathon, 260
Megacleides, 201
Megara, 36
Melissus, 33, 254
Melos, 117, 226
Memnon, 43
Menelaus, 43, 46
Menestheus, 229 n.51, 230
Menexenus, 80–81, 83–85, 87, 89,
    92, 94
metaphor, 142
Miltiades, 260 n.100
mimēsis. *See* imitation
moderation, 164, 177, 178, 191, 241,
    259. *See also* *sōphrosynē*
monarchy, 169, 172–174
mousikē, 141
myths, 153

Narcissus, 45
nature, 212 n.24, 241–242, 244, 246, 261
Nemesis, 45
Nicias, 122–133
Nicocles, 2, 3, 139–140, 154 n.39, 155–175, 213, 218, 219
Nicomachus, 100–101
Nicophemus, 150 n.29
nomos, 21 n.5. *See also* laws
nurture, 212 n.24

oath, 24, 96–97, 102, 104
Odysseus, 51
oligarchy, 4, 161, 172–174, 188, 195–196, 198, 203, 210
Orpheus, 51–52
Ovid, 49

paideia, paideusis. See education
panhellenism, 3, 5, 216
paragraphē, 96–97
parainesis, 20, 266
paraklēsis, 266
Parmenides, 33, 254
Paros, 117
Parrhasius, 206
parrhēsia, 50, 158–159, 163, 187, 267
Pasinus, 117
Pasion, 80–95
Pasiphaë, 38
Patrocles, 98–99
pederasty, 177 n.16
Peisistratus, 73
Peithō, 250
Peleus, 143–144
Peloponnesian War, 2, 263 n.105
Pelops, 48
Pericles, 4, 53, 74, 138, 194 n.37, 204, 206 n.6, 226, 233 n.56, 248
Persia, 5, 152 nn.34–35

Persian King, 151, 153, 176, 185, 200
Persian War, 184 n.6
Pharnabazus, 151 n.31
Phidias, 205
Philip (of Athens), 92
Philip of Macedon, 2, 3, 5
Philomelus, 83, 92, 222
Philon, 102
Philonides, 222
philosopher, 27, 31, 47, 171
philosophy (*philosophia*), 2, 3–6, 8, 15, 33, 50, 55, 56, 138, 142, 155–156, 164, 183, 192, 202–203, 207, 211, 215, 233, 236–240, 242, 244, 250, 253, 254, 256, 260, 264, 267
Philourgus, 109
Phocylides, 166
Phoenicia, 144
Phormio, 74
phronēsis, 54
Phrynondas, 109
physis, 21 n.5
Pindar, 58, 236, 237 n.61
Piraeus, 71, 78, 97, 105, 107, 109
Pirithoüs, 36, 37
pistis, 37, 58, 267
Pittheus, 36
Plathane, 2
Plato, 1, 8, 15, 17, 31, 32, 35, 49, 58, 62, 63, 65, 66, 96, 146 n.24, 183, 267
pleonexia, 170, 176, 196, 255–256, 267–268
Pnytagoras, 152
poet, 160
poetry, 157, 159, 166–167, 214
Polemaenetus, 114, 121
politeia patrios (ancestral democracy), 182, 186
politics, 1, 3–6
politikos, 149

Polycrates, 16, 34, 49, 50, 59, 60
polypragmosynē, 54
Polytion, 69
Pontus, 264
Poseidon, 36–38, 43, 52, 57
Potidaea, 225–226
poverty, 184, 195
prepon, 61, 64, 268
Presocratics, 203, 253 n.82
priesthood, 219
probability (*to eikos*), 256
Prodicus, 2
proeisphora, 201
promise, 220
Protagoras, 17, 33, 208 n.14,
    240 n.64, 257 n.91
proxenos, 237
Prytaneum, 223
Pseudo-Plutarch, 1, 9
Pyron, 86–87
Pythagoras, 56
Pythodorus, 80, 82, 89

religion, 22, 36
rhetoric, 1, 2, 4, 8, 15, 66, 202–204.
    See also philosophy
rhētorikos, 171, 252, 268
Rhinon, 98–99
Rhodes, 185, 217

Salamis, 139–140, 144 n.17, 154,
    184 n.6, 213
Salmacis, 45
Samos, 226
Sarpedon, 43
Satyrus, 80–84, 86–88, 93
scholē (leisure), 54
Sciron, 39
Second Athenian League, 3
sēmeion, 35, 268
Seriphos, 113

Sestus, 225–226
Sicily, 264
Siphnos, 115, 117, 120
slander, 223, 224 n.43, 234, 236
slaves, 84–86, 87, 94, 129
Social War, 182, 185, 224 n.42
Socrates, 4, 31, 32, 51, 60, 202,
    223 n.40, 254 n.87, 264 n.108
Soli, 139, 145 n.21
Solon, 4, 73, 138, 157, 183, 186, 202,
    204, 224 n.40, 247, 248, 253 n.82,
    262, 268
Sopaeus, 80, 82
sophist (*sophistēs*), 1, 2, 3, 4, 6, 16–
    17, 30, 34, 137, 158, 160, 202–204,
    233, 242–243, 245–246, 248, 253,
    262, 268
sōphrosynē, 21, 54, 63, 158, 175–176,
    191, 241, 255, 265
Sopolis, 113–114, 116–117, 120–121,
    122
soul, 21, 22, 23, 26, 27, 55, 63, 65,
    239, 241, 244, 251
Sparta, 5, 32, 46, 54, 67–68, 70–72,
    77, 81, 90, 104, 107, 110, 174,
    176 n.14, 184, 191–192 n.29, 197,
    198, 216, 220, 226
stasis, 73
statues, 155
Stesichorus, 46
Stoa Basileios, 191 n.29
Stratocles, 81, 83, 90
style, 6–7
sykophancy, sykophant, 18, 62, 91–
    92, 97, 130, 137, 202–203, 209,
    210 n.20, 218 n.36, 236, 238, 249,
    257, 261–262

Tantalus, 29
technē, 47, 63, 64, 65, 268. *See also*
    arts

tekmērion, 268
Telamon, 143, 144
Teucer, 144 n.17, 175
text, 9
Thebes, 5, 39, 47, 185
Themistocles, 4, 138, 204, 248, 261 n.101
Theodorus, 2
Theognis, 19, 166
Theophrastus, 62
Theopompus, 2
theōria (festival observance), 75
Theramenes, 2, 18
Theseus, 21, 31, 36–41
Thesmothetae, 249, 262
Thetis, 36, 43, 144
Thirty, the, 187 n.17, 195 n.38, 196, 197, 198, 263 n.105
Thrace, 185, 225
Thrasybulus, 103
Thrasyllus, 112–114, 121–122
Thrasylochus, 112–122
Three Thousand, the, 197 n.45
Thucydides, 75, 167 n.14, 170, 248 n.74
Thyestes, 46
Timodemos, 132
Timotheus, 2–3, 150 n.30, 183, 185 n.13, 202, 216 n.32, 224, 225–230
Tisias, 2, 67, 68, 77–79
Tissaphernes, 72

Tithonus, 43, 45
Torene, 225
torture, 84–86, 88, 94, 130, 266
tragedy, 167, 231
treaty, 103–104
trierarchy, 2, 76, 109, 201, 206
Troezen, 39, 117
Trojan War, 141
tyranny, 40, 73
tyrant (*tyrannos*), 147, 158 n.2, 159 n.3, 211, 218, 260, 268
Tyre, 152

Uranus, 58

Velleius Paterculus, 204

will, 115
wisdom, 254, 261
witnesses, 82, 84, 86, 89, 90, 91, 99, 100, 101, 108–109, 128, 130

Xenophanes, 58, 223 n.40
Xenophon, 49, 139, 183
Xenotimus, 94, 100
Xerxes, 184 n.6

Zeno, 33, 254
Zeus, 29, 36, 37, 41–43, 45, 53, 57, 143, 156, 175, 178
Zeuxis, 206

Lightning Source UK Ltd.
Milton Keynes UK
09 January 2010
148306UK00001B/106/P